West Asia

Civil Society, Democracy and State

West Asia

Civil Society, Democracy and State

Edited by

Sujata Ashwarya Cheema
Assistant Professor,
Centre for West Asian Studies,
Jamia Millia Islamia, New Delhi.

NEW NC CENTURY
New Century Publications
New Delhi, India

NEW CENTURY PUBLICATIONS
4800/24, Bharat Ram Road,
Ansari Road, Daryaganj,
New Delhi – 110 002 (India)

Tel.: 011-2324 7798, 4358 7398, 6539 6605
Fax: 011-4101 7798
E-mail: indiatax@vsnl.com • info@newcenturypublications.com
www.newcenturypublications.com

Editorial office:
LG–7, Aakarshan Bhawan,
4754-57/23, Ansari Road, Daryaganj,
New Delhi – 110 002

Tel.: 011-4356 0919

First Published: **July 2010**

ISBN: **978-81-7708-228-9**

Published by New Century Publications and printed at Salasar Imaging Systems, New Delhi.

Designs: Patch Creative Unit, New Delhi.

PRINTED IN INDIA

Contents

About the Book

Civil society constitutes a range of interest groups and political parties that occupy the space between the individual and the state. The notions of democracy and civil society are inextricably linked—democracy fosters the development of civil society as it allows freedom of association to the individuals. This space then links the individuals to the state. In the backdrop of wave of political liberalization sweeping through the region since the early 1990s, the debate on democratization in West Asia has been associated with the study of three crucial issues, namely whether civil society exists in the region? What are its strengths? What are its weaknesses and what the future holds for its existence? Evidence from the political processes of some countries of the region—such as Jordan, Turkey, and Gulf States—reveals that civil society has strengthened in the region in the recent past.

This book is an attempt to understand the notion of civil society and its relations with democracy and state in the context of West Asia.

Editor's Profile

Sujata Ashwarya Cheema is an Assistant Professor at the Centre for West Asian Studies, Jamia Millia Islamia, New Delhi. She did her M.A. in International Politics and M.Phil. and Ph.D. in West Asian Studies from Jawaharlal Nehru University (JNU), New Delhi. She taught briefly at the Indraprastha College for Women, University of Delhi

She was awarded Graduate Fellowship (2002-03) of the Government of Israel to conduct research at Hebrew University of Jerusalem, Israel. She was also the recipient of Hermes Post-Doctoral Fellowship (January-October, 2007) at Maison des Sciences de l'Homme (MSH), Paris. She was also awarded a visiting fellowship (2009) at the MSH under the Indo-French Social Scientist Exchange Programme. She was also associated with the Times of India and Hindustan Times as a journalist. Her areas of teaching and research interest include Israeli politics and foreign policy, Arab-Israeli conflicts, and politics in West Asia. She has published research papers in national and international journals of repute.

Contributors and Their Affiliations

M.S. Agwani	Formerly Professor and Vice-Chancellor, Jawaharlal Nehru University (JNU), New Delhi.
Anwar Alam	Professor and Director of the Centre for West Asian Studies, Jamia Millia Islamia, New Delhi.
A.K. Ramakrishnan	Professor, Centre for West Asian and African Studies, School of International Studies, Jawaharlal Nehru University (JNU), New Delhi.
A. K. Pasha	Professor and Director of Gulf Studies Programme, Centre for West Asian and African Studies, School of International Studies, Jawaharlal Nehru University (JNU), New Delhi.
Javed Ahmad Khan	Associate Professor, Centre for West Asian Studies, Jamia Millia Islamia, New Delhi.
Sameena Hameed	Assistant Professor, India Arab Cultural Centre, Jamia Millia Islamia, New Delhi.
Rushda Siddiqui	Research Fellow, Indian Council of World Affairs (ICWA), New Delhi.
M.H. Ilias	Associate Professor, India Arab Cultural Centre, Jamia Millia Islamia, New Delhi.
Shelly Johny	Ph.D. student, Centre for West Asian and African Studies, School of International Studies, Jawaharlal Nehru University (JNU), New Delhi.
Moinuddin Ahmed	M.Phil. student, Centre for West Asian Studies, Jamia Millia Islamia, New Delhi.
Mujib Alam	Assistant Professor, Academy for Third World Studies, Jamia Millia Islamia, New Delhi.
Shahid Jamal Ansari	Associate Professor, Centre for West Asian Studies, Jamia Millia Islamia, New Delhi.
Ishrat Aziz	Formerly, India's Ambassador to Tunisia, Saudi Arabia and the UAE. Presently, an independent writer and analyst.

Acknowledgements

I would like to thank all the contributors for taking their time off from their busy schedules to write for this book. I would like to express my special thanks to Professor Mujib Alam, my friend and colleague, for his encouragement and assistance while this book was under preparation. I extend my sincere thanks to Ms. Tazeen for her secretarial support. Thanks are also due to my daughter Brinda for bearing with my frequent absences and academic preoccupations with good humour and understanding. Finally, I place on record my deep appreciation for Mr. Sandeep Sury, Chief Executive, New Century Publications, New Delhi, for showing patience and extending co-operation at various stages of the completion of this work.

Introduction

Sujata Ashwarya Cheema

Civil Society is a term used to denote groups and organizations (non-state and non-governmental) that advocate the diverse interests of various sections of society. The existence of a civil society indicates that people are part and parcel of democratic governance, where liberty and the right to associate without fear or pressure, constitutes the foundational principles of social order. Individual is the fundamental category of the notion of civil society as it is the product of his free will and action. It is difficult, therefore, to imagine the existence of civil society in an authoritarian political order, where individual liberty is subordinated to the dictates of the regime. Democracy and civil society are linked in a relationship of mutuality. Liberty and democracy fosters the development of civil society and a vibrant civil society by aggregating and articulating the interests of people expands the democratic space. This space constitutes a vital link between the individual and the state. It is a conduit through which people communicate their aims and aspirations to the state. The state is then able to carry out informed distribution of values and resources. Civil society, by constantly debating issues in the process of interest articulation, maintains a vigilant eye on the actions of government, thus keeping a check on possible abuses of power.

The term acquired common currency in the early 1990s as a result of a series of global events, significant enough, to set the tone of international politics in the coming decades. First, the demise of authoritarian regimes of the Soviet-East European block in the late 1980s and the emergence of societies free to engage in associational activities without the fearing a clamp down provided impetus to the notion of civil society. Second, groups representing, advocating, and fulfilling citizens' interests became significant aspects of political and social life with the shrinking of state in the developing world as a result of the impact of globalization. Third, under the Washington consensus, donor agencies such as the World Bank and IMF channelled loans to debt-ridden countries through non-governmental organizations, in effect, bypassing inefficient and corrupt governments. This allowed the NGOs to become significant players in governance, thereby, strengthening people's participation in the development process. Moreover, withdrawal of people from electoral process in developed countries (evidence in the declining percentage of voter turnout in the US and Europe) and a prevailing sense of apathy among them rendered civil society an attractive notion. It had the potential to reengage people back into the political life by initiating debates on issues of common concern, thus fostering solidarity in the public sphere. [1]

With the emergence of a plethora of social movements on a global scale in the early 1990s, embodied in ecology movement, gay right movement, and various peace movements, among others, civil society emerged as a key terrain of affirmative action to construct 'an alternative social and world order.' [2] There is an increasing recognition that international organizations and national governments have to recognize the significance of civil society in the life of the citizens. The United Nations set up a high level panel on civil society 'with a view to identifying new and better ways to interact with non-governmental organizations and other civil society organizations; to identify ways of making it easier for civil society actors from developing countries to participate fully in United Nations activities; and to facilitate, manage and evaluate the relationships of the United Nations with civil society and to learn from experience gained in different parts of the system.' [3]

The Civil Dialogue initiated by the European Commission in the 1990s was a first attempt by the European Union to give the institutions of society and businesses a voice at the policymaking tables. [4] In the same spirit, a 2004 report of the WTO, advises nation-states on the best way to share sovereignty for mutual benefit and examines the impact of what authors call the 'global associational revolution'. They consider the rise and influence of civil society to be irreversible and advise the WTO on how best to engage with and negotiate with the non-state actors. [5] Civil society is here to stay with the notion being regularly acclaimed by scholars, political activists, and policy makers.

Civil Society, Democracy and State: Background

Philosophers have since the days of the Greek city-state tried to understand the pressing issues of their time relating to the nature of the state and society, powers and practices of the state and government, rights and duties of citizens, coexistence of individual and collective good, the expanse and limit of freedom, management of differences of capacity and opinions, and dispensation of justice. However, an endeavour to employ civil society as a framework to understand these issues emanates from an eminently modern conception of the individual, society and the state. Civil society is based upon the notion of individual rights and liberty: free individuals associate to regulate their lives in a manner compatible with their self-interests. The concept of civil society can be directly related to the rise of capitalism, which has individualism as its core principle. It is essentially, therefore, a modern concept. The Greeks, for example, would not have appreciated the concept because they did not have a notion of inalienable individual rights. They did not distinguish between state and society. State, for them, was an ethical entity, an end in itself as human beings could attain self-fulfilment and self-perfection only through the state. [6]

The theories of social contract which emerged to justify the emerging bourgeois society considered state to be an artificial creation, a product of a contract among free individuals. The state became necessary because human beings were incapable of living without the existence of a defined political authority. While English philosopher Thomas Hobbes (1588-1679) emphasized the need for an absolute power because this alone could save men from anarchy and chaos, John Locke (1632-1704), supported a limited state. Both held the essence of human nature could be gainfully understood in conditions of the 'state of nature', a logical abstraction from society. Hobbes asserted that human beings are motivated by self-interests. More often than not, the interest of one human being is contradictory with the interest of the other. All human beings are equal (the nature having made them so in the faculties of body and mind), such that, as Hobbes says, no one can claim for himself any benefit to which another may not pretend. [7] Therefore, the state of nature is a condition of war of all against all. In such as situation life is 'solitary, poor, nasty, brutish and short.' [8] Guided by the instinct of self-preservation, which illuminates their reason, individuals realize the need for a mechanism to protect themselves.

Each individual, hence, agrees to enter into a covenant with another, to give up one's natural liberty and sovereignty to a common power. Hobbes calls the multitude so united in a common power, state, or Leviathan. Hobbes does not distinguish between the state and society; the contract establishes both. It appears that Hobbes proposes two kinds of relationships: One, between the individuals and the sovereign, in which the former by their own free will submitted to the latter; and second among the individuals, wherein, under the watchful eyes of the Leviathan, are compelled for reasons of peace and security, to limit their natural rights in a way that would be compatible with the rights of others. The first arrangement denotes the state and the second represents the civil society. Hobbes' paradigm shows that the state is imperative for the sustenance of civil society. [9]

Another theorist of social contract, John Locke, put forward the concept of a limited state and a limited society. In Locke's view, individuals are both social and rational and therefore the state of nature is peaceful and orderly. It is governed by the law of nature. In the state of nature individuals possess the right of liberty, health and property. However, it was marked by uncertainties because the laws of nature were understood by the individuals in their own way and was therefore not definite. This threatened natural rights and regression of society into anarchy. It was out of this concern that people enter into a contract and constitute a common public authority. In *Two Treatises of Civil Government*, Locke sets forth the nature of government and the system of reciprocal obligations between government and individuals. [10]

Locke envisages two contracts. In the first, people place themselves under public authority to protect themselves from the inconveniences and shortcoming of the state of nature. This authority has the power to make laws and enforce them. And the second contract imposes limitations upon this authority; individuals never surrender their natural rights to the authority and thus the powers of the state are limited. It is limited also because it derives power from the people and because it holds power in trust for the people. Moreover, it is must operate within the bounds of civil and natural law. [11] According to Locke, social life existed prior to the birth of the state, as even without authority people lived in society in an orderly fashion. The notions of primacy of society in relation to the state, inalienable natural rights of individuals, and limits on state power gave shape to the liberal tradition in state- (civil) society relations.

Both Hobbes and Locke set forth an idea in which peaceful coexistence among individuals could be ensured through social covenants. They considered civil society as a realm governed by reason and guided by natural rights of the individual. However, they did not view civil society as a realm separate from the state. Rather they underlined coexistence of state and society. In their analysis of relation between state and society, Hobbes and Locke were influenced by the experiences of their times. They challenged the divine right theory of the state in their claim that human beings are capable of fashioning their political order.

The contract theorists were speaking for the emergent capitalism and the bourgeois class. Strongly influenced by the chaos during the Civil War in England, Hobbes built his philosophy of state and society on the founding principles of capitalism: self-interest of individuals and a state with unlimited legal sovereignty that would provide a framework of positive laws for the reconciliation of individual interest in their various associations in society. Before Hobbes, the fundamental question was: anarchy or order? Locke, on the other hand, grappled with struggle between the divine rights of the king and the political rights of the parliament in the context of the Glorious Revolution of 1648. This influenced Locke to propound a theory of a limited state, where free-market capitalism could flourish without interference. In making life, liberty, and property the inalienable rights of the individual, Locke laid the foundation of the 'possessive individual', of the capitalist society. [12] Individuals with their repertoire of natural rights would associate freely in capitalist relations of production in society, and the conflict, if any, resulting from such an association would be resolved by the law-adjudicating authority in the state.

The thinkers of Scottish Enlightenment were the first to explicitly link the notion of civil society with market economy. One of its leading exponents, Adam Ferguson, uses the term almost interchangeably with market society. In his influential text, *An Essay on the History of Civil Society*, Ferguson says that civil society emerges with market economy. In a market economy, production outside the household and for commercial use brings together individuals in a relationship of interdependence. This fosters the development of civil society, where individuals aggregate their energies for production, based on the assurance that private gains in the form of property would be safeguarded. [13]

Hegel, too, linked the rise of civil society with the development of capitalism. He held that civil society emerged to serve the interests of the market economy. In *The Philosophy of Right*, he distinguished between *burgerlichen gesellschaft* (civil society) and *der staat* (the political state). He defined the former as a set of social practices created by the capitalist economy that reflects the ethos of the market. It is a realm that offers opportunities for self-realization in ways in which earlier forms of society did not. Being a product of the market, civil society must also succumb to the same pitfalls as the market itself, which originate in self-interested action. [14] When inequalities created by self-interest and avariciousness 'affords a spectacle of extravagance and want as well as of the physical and ethical degeneration common to both' [15], civil society can no longer be viewed as part of man's moral end. That is why civil society must be controlled by the state in order to sustain moral order in society.

Agreeing that civil society is linked to the capitalist mode of production, Marx held it represents the interests of the bourgeoisie. Unlike Hegel, he eschewed from assigning a positive role to civil society. The state as superstructure also represented the interests of the bourgeois class. Therefore, it was incapable of playing the role of a mediator in conflicts that arise in civil society. [16] For, Marx both would wither away in the event of a socialist revolution, to give way to a just society. Departing from Marx, Gramsci did not consider civil society as a part of the socio-economic base of the state but a constituent of the superstructure. The state is not to be understood in the narrow sense of the government; instead, Gramsci divides it between 'political society', which is the arena of political institutions and legal constitutional control, and 'civil society', which is commonly seen as the 'private' or 'non-state' sphere, including the economy. The former is the realm of force and the latter of consent. He stresses, however, that the division is purely conceptual and that the two, in reality, often overlap. Gramsci views civil society as a site for problem solving and calls it a realm where ideological capital of the bourgeois state is produced and reproduced, which ensures the hegemony of capitalism. [17] Gramsci believes that the revolutionary party is the force that will allow the working class to develop organic intellectuals and an alternative hegemony within civil society. He believes the proletariat's historical task is to create a 'regulated society' and defines the 'withering away of the state' as the full development of civil society's ability to regulate itself. [18]

Gramsci's account informs much contemporary thinking on the New Left on Civil Society. Robert Cox, for example, views civil society as a surrogate for revolution. Depicting globalization of production and neo-liberal economic orthodoxy as benefiting the integrated class and encouraging 'exclusionary and covert politics', Cox views civil society as 'crucial battleground' [19] for citizens to regain control over public life and as potential agents for transformation of the state. Others like Jurgen Habermas, with due recognition of the pluralism that pervades modern society, view civil society as necessary to defend democracy against the threat posed by modern state bureaucracy, which seeks to encompass more and more of social life. Rather than posing a problem as in earlier Marxist account, civil society is now viewed as providing a solution. Civil Society is seen as vital to protect autonomous public opinion and integrity of the public sphere, the two pillars of democracy. [20]

Making a clear distinction among civil society, state and the economy, the New Left sees 'civil society as an important site for counter-hegemonic struggle and assigns it a key role in defending the society against the state and market and in formulating democratic will to influence the state.' The neo-liberals are influenced by the conception of associational life given by Alexis de Tocqueville (1805-1859). Tocqueville, who did not use the term civil society, 'crafted his conception of associations as performing several key functions: meeting unmet social needs in the context of weak central government;

intermediating between personal and local interests and the national common good, preventing tyranny of the majority; limiting state power; and preventing abuse by the state.' His civil society, 'operating in conditions of socio-economic equality and political freedom is composed of voluntary associations that cooperate for collective purposes. The interplay of the interests of these associations would guard against domination by a single interest and check the tyranny of the majority and other excesses of democracy.' Tocqueville conception of civil society is based on a limited state that 'would confine itself to the political sphere and guarantee the legal framework and other conditions (such as socio-economic equality) necessary for the effective functioning of civil society.' [21] The neo-liberal school views civil society and its institutions in instrumental terms vis-à-vis the state, influencing state policy and not as distinct site for governance and reform that is independent of the state.

Taking into account the history of the development of the concept the following ideas emerge about civil society. First, free-willed individuals are at the core of the notion of civil society. Second, it is a realm within the state, where associational life is based on the notion of common good instead of fragmented self-interests. And, third, civil society is also an arena which protects public opinion and guards the public sphere from interferences of the state, two vital functions for the promotion of democracy. How are these reflected in the organization and functioning of civil society in West Asia? How do they promote democracy and what linkage do they provide with the state.

Civil Society, Democracy and State in West Asia

The term civil society gained currency in the context of the promotion of democratization in West Asia in the post-Cold War era. Civil society as non-state groups functioning at the level of citizenry and acting as vehicles of specific aspirations is considered to increase prospects for democratization.

Democratization in West Asia, therefore, has become strongly linked with the study of whether civil society exists in the region, together with its strengths and weaknesses and its future prospects. A number of events there fuelled optimism regarding the existence of a vibrant civil society in West Asia. The Iranian revolution led by the merchant class, the rise of Islamist movement in the 1980s claiming to represent the people, and the declining oil prices with implications for weakening of state structure buoyed those expecting to see a flicker of democracy in a largely authoritarian region.

A number of writers of Orientalist disposition such as Bernard Lewis, Daniel Pipes, and Samuel Huntington reject the possibility of the existence of any kind of civil society in the Arab countries of the region. They contend that the absence of the notion of individual and individual rights make civil associations antithetical to the concept of collective *umma* present in Arab and Muslim societies. They further argue that Arab and Muslim societies are inherently despotic which precludes the possibility of having social and political institutions mediating between individual and the ruler. Others such as Augustus Richard Norton, Muhammad Muslih, Michael Hudson and Asad Abu Khalil believe that with economic liberalization and the consequent weakening the state, civic groups have grown into a thriving sector, placing a check on many regimes. [22] Civil associations serve as a means to mediate with the authoritarian governments for social justice and human rights, and provide a forum for mobilizing people towards alternative forms of negotiation and political action. Civil society, thus, harbingers indigenous paths to democratization and political pluralism in the region.

The issue of autonomy of civil associations is a crucial issue in an authoritarian political milieu. As the civil associations are dependent on the state to provide legislations and institutional mechanism to guarantee their autonomy, that fact that such legislations rarely exist in contemporary West Asia, accentuates their dependence and forces them into negotiations with state officials, to enforce an imprecise set of rules and regulations. In the context of such negotiations, neo-orientalists have pointed out that civil society produces authoritarianism not democracy, as the states in the region are unwilling to share power or show tolerance towards these groups. They 'assert that the proliferation of social movements will discourage any trend towards power sharing and greater tolerance in the region, if it does not breed civil war and anarchy'. [23] From a neo-orientalist perspective, therefore, the absence or presence of civil society cannot be linked indisputably to the unfolding of democracy in the region. Egypt, Jordan, Lebanon and Gaza Strip are cited as examples where the absence in the past or the contemporary growth of civil society in the present has not ushered democracy, at least not in its full form. On the other hand, many others point to the strong empirical evidence between the growth of civil society and the promotion of democratization, citing the examples of the countries mentioned above.

The argument linking civic activism and democracy is based on the assumption that associational life has the potential to defy authoritarian regimes, force liberal reforms, and trigger the process of democratic transition. Indeed, 'people power' would set off a 'ripple effect' that would be the key to democratization in West Asia. Development agencies such as the World Bank, the UNDP, the EC (the Barcelona Process) and the USAID, subscribe to the same belief that sustained opposition from below will generate regime shifts from above and have, therefore, consistently provided financial support to civil society groups. However, this optimism needs a reality-check, especially in the context of the survival tactics of authoritarian regimes that construct a facade of political liberalization, while in reality they remain as repressive as ever.

The emergence of autonomous associations in Arab West Asia can be traced as far back as the Ottoman Empire. They subsequently proliferated during the period of the Mandate and were disbanded by the authoritarian regimes that emerged during the inter-war and post-war period. It was only in the late 1980s, when economic crisis and unemployment resulted in widespread dissatisfaction with the state, that civil society started acquiring a more prominent role. Given West Asian regimes' incapacity to meet popular economic and political demands, associational activity virtually boomed. This is how a public space was carved, where the dissenting energies of activists 'drew citizens into political life to an unprecedented degree', and thus generated the development of a wide range of associations with their own bureaucratic structure and preoccupation to formulate policy alternatives. Today, most scholars affirm that 'both intermediate powers and autonomous social groups exist in West Asia' [24] performing a crucial role in many societies of the region. They are primarily engaged in providing essential services to the people, where the state has failed or it has been absent. Certain crucial questions must be asked at this juncture. How well organized and autonomous are these groups? How capable are they in counterbalancing the state power? How do they help in promoting political liberalization and democracy?

To answer the questions posed above, one must begin with the challenges of founding a viable civil and democratic government in West Asia. Anwar Alam in his paper interrogates the theoretical underpinnings of notion of civil society and of the framework it offers to assess the process of political reform in West Asia. He opines that the idea of civil society is a product of modern western value system and therefore its applicability in the West Asian context produces debates that stick to an examination of the compatibility or non-compatibility of Islam with modernity, thus producing an intellectual stalemate. On the other hand, the practitioners of civil society in West Asia move beyond the confines of this debate. They contend over the eventual utility of civil society: the Islamists use it jostle for a legal share of the public space, whereas independent activists and intellectuals employ it to expand the boundaries of individual liberty. Such a bargaining with the state, which creates an impression of democratization, more generally, turns out to be a critique of the state rather an endeavour to bring about structural transformation. In this context, the states in many countries of West Asia have the capacity – both peaceful and coercive – to deal with such oppositional pressures. They do so by expanding and contracting the democratic space at will depending upon the nature and intensity of the challenges they face.

A. K. Ramakrishnan highlights the fact that the debate on civil society in West Asia has been associated with the issues of democracy, political reforms and human rights, without reference to the social movements as agencies of transformation. The role of women's movements, human rights movements, and Islamist movements in opening up the political sphere needs to be recognized. Here the American and European intervention to promote civil society and democratization from above runs the risk of discrediting these indigenous voices, which have long struggled for democratic transformation of their societies. Although the state remains a determining factor with regard to civil society, the evolving nature of both the entities ensures that greater democratization remains at the heart of the changes produced as a result of their interaction.

The importance of democratization in ushering participatory and inclusive governance cannot be overstated. In the GCC countries, A.K. Pasha argues, the state is the vehicle of democratization. However, the space opened for political participation remains restricted as attempts at electoral reform and popular representation, leave much to be desired. Civil Society organizations are weak and lack bargaining power vis-à-vis the state. Although, Islamic forces pose a challenge and represent the desire of the people for greater power sharing, they run the risk of being co-opted into the faux 'talk' of democratic reforms, fears the author.

While civil society organizations may not been successful in liberalizing the political arena in West Asia, their influence in the market sector is worth a note. Javed Ahmed Khan asserts that in the newly liberalized investment climate in the Gulf, they are increasingly became effective agencies for promoting business across borders. In doing this, they provide effective checks on governments and enhance accountability and transparency. In the wake of the recent 'structural reforms' in most Arab countries, a new middle class is emerging gradually. A group of liberal technocrats, who are determined to establish clearer boundaries between the state and society and greater independence for social and economic institutions, are being increasingly heard among the political elites. This new assertiveness, indicating liberalized social and political environment, portends well for the growth of civil society in the region.

Indeed the progress and prospects of civil society depends upon the behaviour and aptitudes of individuals, maintains Sameena Hameed, in her paper which tries to find the economic roots and linkages of the civil society in West Asia. The economic space, which invariably forms an important part of an individual's social existence, imparts important training by virtue of the process of 'learning by doing'. Thus the character of economy inculcates such attributes of behaviour and aptitude such as, self reliance, entrepreneurship and self confidence that become vital inputs in the evolution of a vibrant civil society. The paper envisages a pluralistic and participatory civil society, with larger participation rather than been represented by few associations, for a self-sustained movement. It finds correlation between distribution of economic resources between the state and the society in West Asia and the potential of civil society, which can demand larger freedom and accountability. It infers that civil society is more assertive in relatively poorer states of Yemen, Lebanon, Palestinian territories, and Jordan because larger economic activities have given the training of cooperation and self-help.

It also takes into account the impact of presence of foreign labour and women associations on the bargaining power of civil society in West Asia.

Individual and state are at two end of the continuum of the debate on civil society. While notions of rights and freedoms, both at the individual and societal level, are constantly challenging the authoritarian and patriarchal states of West Asia, the envisaged change has been limited. The state has successfully managed to suppress any viable socio-political movement, says Rushda Siddiqui. First, the colonial legacy has cultivated a power equation between the state and its society, which guarantees the failure of political pluralism in the region; and secondly, the coercive state apparatus ensures that the sting of the opposition is dulled, quick and fast. The Islamists by virtue of their cultural roots in the society have given a tough ideological challenge to the Western idea of the nation-state accepted by the authoritarian rulers in the region. However, they have not been immune to suppression or cooptation by their governments.

Internet, in Saudi Arabia, has created a virtual public sphere where opinions and attitudes of ordinary people are being moulded. M.H. Ilias examines the impact of new forms of media, particularly internet and satellite television in providing news spaces for diverse and critical views on the contemporary life in the Arab Gulf. This development is very palpable in Saudi Arabia, where new means of communication have successfully replaced old social spaces like *souks, bazaars, majlis* and Arab streets, as major locales for the emerging public sphere. Of these, the popularity of Internet speaks specifically of the existence of a 'counterpublic' – different marginalized groups seek to present their counter-arguments – against the hegemonic versions of the state, religion, and patriarchal society. In Saudi Arabia, this newly emerged communicative space enables the opposition to articulate their experiences, critique illiberal politics, and contest hegemonic practices.

Civil society may be thriving in the virtual landscape of the Arab countries giving a feel of democratization of socio-political life, in real terms, however, their influence in the development of democratic institutions has been limited. The all-powerful regime ensures that democratic institutions, if any, do not perform to their optimum. In his paper, Shelly Johny explores this dilemma, while identifying the peculiarities of civil society movement in Jordan. Civil society in Jordan appeared in the aftermath of the economic reconstruction and consequent political reforms of the late 1980s. Tentative political initiatives such as the introduction of the parliament did not mean that civil society had the space to develop to its full potential. This was because these reforms were introduced in order to provide security to the regime destabilized by the unravelling of the rentier economy. Nevertheless, political movements like the Muslim Brotherhood have used the space provided by civil society to reach out to the wider public and create pockets of substantial influence.

Moinuddin Ahmed looks at the circumstances under which civil society groups have emerged in Israel and the role they have played in the peace building process in the context of Israel-Palestinian conflict. The paper discusses the functioning of civil society groups under the all-embracing influence of the military-security doctrine, especially when the demands and activities of these groups clash with the national interest and the security issues of the country. The paper emphasizes that despite enormous constraints, civil society groups are playing a significant mediatory role in conflict transformation.

Turkey is a unique case in West Asia, where civil society functions autonomously of the state, as compared to other countries in the region. Mujib Alam says that civil society groups have been steadily increasing in number in the country since the establishment of the Third Republic in the early 1980s. The expansion of the civil society is linked to economic development and democratic consolidation in the country. In

Turkey, the state has been a facilitator for the growth of the civil society, although its possible use and abuse by the former cannot be denied.

The condition of civil society in other countries of West Asia may not be as bleak as it may seem at the first instance, argues Shahid Jamal Ansari. In general, civil society in the GCC states has shown steady development, particularly in Bahrain and Kuwait. These two states top of the list not only in terms of the increasing number of civil society groups but also in terms of the strength of the relationship between these groups and the existing political systems. In other GCC states, changes vis-à-vis civil society are also manifest, for example, Saudi Arabia officially constituted a press association, in 2004, even though the state retained the power to appoint one-third of its members. Conversely, strains between civil society and state constantly recur. A number of civil society groups were dissolved in Saudi Arabia and Bahrain a few years ago. The women's issues have, significantly, come to the fore in these traditional countries as a result of group activism.

The emergence of an autonomous civil society with considerable bargaining power in its relations with the state may still be far off, but internal and external factors have created pressures for more consultative governance in the societies of the Gulf, West Asia and North Africa, opines Ishrat Aziz. Without a genuine interactive partnership between the people and the leadership, these states could meet near-collapse, trying to adequately cope with the internal economic and political problems and external diplomatic challenges. Without people's mandate, regimes lack full internal legitimacy and external credibility, thereby limiting their effectiveness in dealing with various issues. Resistance to change from the beneficiaries of the status quo can be expected, but the forces at work to expand democracy are too powerful to be blocked indefinitely, says Aziz. The understanding that 'change can be delayed but not prevented' is increasingly defining the West Asian social and political landscape in contemporary times.

Notes

1. See Neera Chandhoke, "What the hell is 'civil society'?" Available at http://www.opendemocracy.net/democracy-open_politics/article_2375.jsp (17 March 2005).
2. Robert Cox, "Civil Society at the turn of the Millennium: Prospects for an Alternative World Order", in Louise Amoore, *The Global Resistance Reader* (New York: Routledge, 2005), pp. 103-4.
3. In the note by the Secretary General of the United Nations on *Report of the Panel of Eminent Persons on United Nations–Civil Society Relations*, available at www.un-ngls.org/orf/Final%20report%20-20HLP.doc(11June2004).
4. "What is civil society?" Definition by the Centre for Civil Society, London School of Economics, available at http://www.lse.ac.uk/collections/CCS/what_is_civil_society.htm (1 March 2004).
5. "Transparency and Dialogue with Civil Society" in WTO Report entitled, *The future of the WTO: Addressing institutional challenges in the new millennium* (2004), available at http://www.wto.org/english/thewto_e/10anniv_e/future_wto_chap5_e.pdf.
6. See Eric W. Robinson (ed.), *Ancient Greek Democracy: Reading and Sources* (MA: Blackwell Publishing, 2003), pp. 175-6.
7. Thomas Hobbes, *Leviathan*, edited with an introduction and notes by J. C. A. Gaskin (Oxford: Oxford University Press, 1998), p. 82.
8. Ibid., p. 84.
9. Hobbes' *De Cive* in ibid., p. xviii
10. See John Simmons, "Locke's State of Nature", in Christopher W. Morris (ed.), *The social contract theorists: critical essays on Hobbes, Locke and Rousseau* (Critical Essays on the Classics) (Rowman & Littlefield Publishers Inc., 1999).
11. See Joshua Cohen, "Structure, Choice and Legitimacy: Locke's Theory of State", in ibid., Christopher Morris, 1999, p. 156.
12. See C.B. Macpherson, *The Political Theory of Possessive Individualism* (Oxford, Oxford University Press, 1962). Also see

James Tully, *An Approach to Political Philosophy: Locke in Contexts* (Cambridge: Cambridge University Press, 1993), p. 80.

13. Adam Ferguson, *A History on the History of Civil Society* (Philadelphia, 1989), Part IV, available at http://books.google.com/books?id=04uAAAAYAAJ&pg=PR3&dq=Adam+Ferguson&source=gbs_selected_pages&cad=3#v=onepage&q=&f=false.
14. See "Civil Society", in Hegel's Philosophy of Right, available at http://www.marxists.org/reference/archive/hegel/works/pr/prcivils.htm#PR182.
15. Hegel, quoted in op. cit., Chandhoke, 2005.
16. See Karl Marx, *Critique of Hegel's Philosophy of Right* (Cambridge University Press, 1970), available at http://www.marxists.org/archive/marx/works/1843/critique-hpr/index.htm.
17. Perry Anderson, "The antinomies of Antonio Gramsci" in James Martin, *Antonio Gramsci: Critical Assessments of Leading Political Philosophers*, (London: Routledge, 2002), p. 346.
18. See Walter L. Admason, "Gramsci and the Politics of Civil Society," *Praxis International*, Vol. 7, Nos. 3-4 (Winter 1987-88), p. 322.
19. Op. cit. Cox in Amoore, 2005.
20. Muthiah Alagappa (ed.), *Civil Society and Political Change in Asia: Expanding and Contracting Democratic Space* (Stanford: Stanford University Press, 2004), p. 29.
21. Ibid., p. 30.
22. Beverley Milton-Edward, *Contemporary Politics in the Middle East* (Cambridge: Polity/Blackwell Publishers, 2000), p. 156.
23. Yahya Sadowsky, "The new orientalism and democracy debate", in J. Beinin and J. Stork (eds.), *Political Islam: Essays from the Middle East Report* (London: I.B. Tauris, 1997), quoted in ibid., Milton-Edward, 157.
24. Yahya Sadowsky, "The New Orientalism and the Democracy Debate," *Middle East Report*, No. 14-21 (July-August 1993) quoted in Ali R. Abootalebi, "Middle East Economies: A Survey of Current Problems and Issues," *Meria Journal*, Volume 3, No. 3 (September 1999), available at http://meria.idc.ac.il/journal/1999/issue3/jv3n3a6.html.

1

Civil Society, Democracy and State in West Asia

M.S. Agwani

An elementary lesson no serious student of West Asia would take long to learn is that it is extremely hazardous to make key generalization about the entire region. It is mainly because of the region's vast range of diversities in terms of language, ethnicity, religion, culture and natural resources. Its three hundred million people broadly fall into two categories: Arabs and non-Arabs. The non-Arabs primarily consist of the Turks, Iranians, the Kurds and the Jews. Arabic Persian and Turkish are the principles languages, but Kurdish and Hebrew are also gaining importance. Again, West Asia is not a monolith when it comes to religion. Almost all major and minor sects of Islam, Christianity and Judaism are represented here.

Alongside diversities, the region has also been endowed with countless connectivities in social, economic, cultural and intellectual fields during long spells of history. It is this distinctive mix of connectivities and diversities that has imparted this land mass the characteristics of a region. One such connectivity is the traditional political culture which has evolved over long centuries after the advent of Islam and which has undergone varying degrees of transformation in different parts of the region over the last two hundred years.

Broadly Speaking, the three pillars of Islamic political culture were the doctrines of the *ummah*, the caliphate, and the *shari'ah*. The community of all believers in Islam regardless of their language, race or region constituted the *ummah*. The *ummah* came to have a political head who, after the death of the Prophet, was designated as the caliph. Both the *ummah* and caliph were required to observe the *shari'ah* or the religious law derived from the Quran and the Prophet's traditions.

Having said this, one has to add that in present day West Asia there is not a single state which conforms to this model. In place of *ummah* we find a set of nation-state based on territorial rather than religious loyalty and each unit comprising all people living within its territory regardless of religious, ethnic or linguistic affinities.

The institution of caliphate also had a chequered existence. After the fall of the Umayyids in the middle of the 8th century A.D. the caliphate split into two, with one based in Iraq and another in Spain. And later, with the decline of the Abbasids of Baghdad, it morphed into a national entity and lingered as such until the Ottoman sultans adopted the title of caliph in the 16th century. However, the Ottoman defeat in the First World War the Turkish nationalists led by Kamal Ataturk consolidated their power in mainland Turkey and declared it a republic. In 1924, The Turkish parliament resolved to abolish the caliphate, arguing it was incongruent with republicanism.

Over the years, the doctrine of caliphate has been replaced by the idea of popular sovereignty and several states in the region subscribe to the dictum sovereignty rests with the people.

Finally the *shari'ah* now accounts only for a fraction of the laws in force in most of the West Asian countries and applicable to personal matters such as marriage, divorce and inheritance. A much larger body of laws belongs to the category of *qanun* or man-made law.

The pace and degree of transformation from the traditional to rational-legal political culture has varied from state to state. But the very process of transformation had inevitably thrown open the perennial question of political life, namely how power is to be acquired, exercised and transferred as also the rules governing political opposition. This has sparked a great deal of intellectual churning and public discussion on these issues in the late 19th and 20th centuries especially in Turkey, Egypt and Iran and the debate still continues.

However apart from Turkey, the ideas thrown up by these debates did not percolate deeper down in the societies in other countries. Nor could the modernist political elites institutionalize the new concepts and values firmly in the emerging systems of governance. And this opened the way for military intervention in one country after another.

Thomas Hobbes, a 17th century British political thinker had compared politics to a game of cards with this difference that in politics when no trump is agreed upon in advance clubs become trumps. And this is how things happened in some West Asian countries bringing in its train, censorship, strangulation of civil society and authoritarian rule.

I am tempted to recall my first visit to Egypt in 1958 when I spent about three months in that charming land of the Nile inhabited by a people with irrepressible sense of humour. The Egyptian military regime's popularity at the time was on the upswing, thanks to its land reform which brought tangible relief to tens of thousands of peasants; nationalization of foreign-owned Suez Canal Company which gave a big boost to Egypt's national pride. And, above all, President Gamal Abdel Nasser's stirring call for Arab unity that had galvanized good number of people across the Arab world from Iraq in the east to the Atlantic coast of Morocco. Even so, the common man in Cairo felt the pinch of press censorship. And it found expression in that favourite medium of Egyptian civil society called the *nuktah* or a telling joke. The story goes that a person approaches a newspaper vendor and asks for his favourite *Al Akhbar* but is offered some other newspaper. When the customer protests the vendor takes out his pen, crosses out the title of the unwanted paper, and inscribes *Al-Akhbar* over it, saying "maa'lish, mafish fara'", which, in the Egyptian colloquial, meant "never mind, it makes no difference".

Two year later President Nasser was on a state visit to India, and Prime Minister Jawaharlal Nehru invited him to address the Indian parliament. At the end of the address, Nehru introduced him to the leader of the different parties represented in the parliament. While introducing the leader of the communist party of India to Nasser, Nehru added in a lighter vein "Mr. President, you put your communists in prison, here they sit in the parliament".

Fifteen years of authoritarian rule in Egypt had a debilitating impact on Egyptian policy and morale. In June 1967 catastrophe was due to many reasons, but as Nasser himself admitted in the course of a marathon meeting of the top leadership in August, the same year, a major reason was the 'closed' system the military rule had created. The minutes of the historic meeting were recorded by Abdel Magid Farid, Secretary-General of the president's office from 1962 until Nasser's death in 1970, and reproduced in his book *Nasser: The Final Years* (Ithaca, 1996).

In Iran too, the Shah's despotic rule lasting for a quarter century, following the overthrow of the democratically elected government headed by Mohammed Mosaddeq by the machinations of the American central Intelligence agency, wrought havoc on the nation's political life. With external help the Shah systematically decimated all his secular opponents. The mosque was then left as the only forum for secret political activity beyond the reach of the Savak, the Shah's otherwise omnipresent intelligence outfit. By the time the Shah's regime was toppled by a protracted protest movement, the exiled religious leader, Ayatullah Khomeini, who had crossed swords with the Shah in the early 1960 over the question of granting immunity to American military personnel from Iranian laws, became the obvious choice of leadership.

The dominance of the clergy in the Islamic republic of Iran is in no small measure the result of the distortions caused by the Shah's dictatorship. The change has nevertheless made it possible for the civil society in Iran to assert itself. The political culture in Iran today is not exactly democratic, but not outright undemocratic either. Under the present dispensation candidates for elections are to be vetted by the clergy, and this is patently undemocratic. At the same time, these are multiple candidates for most of the seats and elections are free and keenly contested. Moreover, civil society has succeeded in creating space for itself for discussion on public issues and for mobilization. No wonder a liberal of the calibre of Mohammad Khatami had two four-year terms as President of Iran.

Another case in point is Iraq, which has all along had tremendous potential for becoming the most prosperous country in the entire Arab world. It is endowed with a sizeable population, adequate land and water resources and plentiful oil. But almost forty years of one-man rule, which allowed no room for dissent, lead Iraq into a disastrous war with Iran, a no less ruinous military adventure in Kuwait and a crippling economic blockade culminating in American invasion and occupation. The upshot of all this today is a real threat to Iraq's territorial integrity and political survival.

Before concluding I should like to add a word on the overall status of civil society and democracy in the region. I suppose 'civil societies', representing public opinion and attitude towards system of governance, are common to all political clusters whether authoritarian or democratic. There is, however, a vital difference between the two. In an authoritarian culture, the civil society remains subdued and is prevented from influencing public policy. The domestic political culture, on the other hand, provides space for creative interaction between the state and its citizens, thereby lending vigour and vitality to both.

As to the future of the democracy in West Asia, I saw an emerging consensus in the region among all stakeholders at level of civil societies on the desirability institutionalization in the two principles of *accountability of rulers* and *public participation in governance*. Hence the talk of imposing democracy from the top or by an interested outsider is utterly irrelevant. Democracy is indeed in great demand in the region and public pressures for its realization are most likely to grow.

2

Civil Society and its Implications for Political Reforms in West Asia

Anwar Alam

Introduction

The modernist notion of civil society has its origin in the early modern European intellectual tradition. However it is resurfacing as a dominant intellectual discourse in late 20th century has a new context and thrust. The context is the process of globalization while the thrust is its linkage with prospect of democratization or democratic rule in post-colonial societies. It is presumed that the phenomenon of globalization with its focus on neo-liberal economics and communication revolution has inherent potential to unleash and strengthen the forces of civil society that in turns affect the democratic changes in post-colonial societies. The linkage between the two, which is the theme of seminar, draws its legitimacy from two sources: an understanding of development of representative democracy in Europe and other parts of the West and the transition from authoritarian rule to relatively democratic rule in the South (Russia, East European, Latin American and some parts of Asian and African countries) in recent times. The latter was considered as the success of resilience of civil society that somehow managed to survive under political authoritarian dispensations. By the mid-1990s, the western academic and policy-making consensus was that the emergence of a dynamic civil society represented the sine qua non of democracy. [1]

According to one report, civic resistance played a vital role in driving 50 out of 67 modern transitions from authoritarian rule. In other words the discursive field of civil society was articulated as a pre-condition for the development of democratic rule. [2]

However the 'third wave of democratization', to use Huntington's phrase [3], did not make much desirable impact in the Islamic/Muslim world, particularly in Muslim West Asia. The failure of western efforts—both material and ideological—in Muslim West Asia is dominantly theorized as a case of 'Arab exceptionalism' or 'absence of civil society in Muslim society' or 'the structural deficiency of Islam' that acts against the value of modernity. As a result the bulk of dominant theorizations or narratives related to the aspect of civil society and democracy in Muslim West Asia ends up either with providing 'reasons' for the survival of authoritarian regimes/rules in Arab world [4] or alternatively the efforts have been to demonstrate the continuous existence of 'Islamic civil society' by highlighting the autonomous role of *ulema, bazaris*, urban character of Muslim city, guilds etc. [5] Thus the dominant intellectual polemical debate has not moved beyond an examination of compatibility or non-compatibility of Islam with modernity. This intellectual stalemate in part arises from projection of a specific western modern value system as general-universal values to be emulated in the name of 'idea of progress' that acts as ideal benchmark to evaluate the course of social and political changes in non-western societies.

Given this predicament and challenges of constructing a viable civil and democratic rule in Muslim West Asia, this paper attempts to interrogate and examine the theoretical underpinnings of notion of civil society and its theoretical potentials to unleash the process of political reform in the region. The term 'political reform' is not used here in the wider context of democratization or democratic rule as the latter involves the wider issue of structural transformation of society. Rather the term has specific meaning: to denote the changes in institutional and behavioural component of the state and its associated institutions. Since the notion of civil society is historically conceived in terms of 'opposition' to state, hence it is easier to evaluate the impact of growth of civil society (as it is understood) upon the direction of changes, if there is any, within the state institutions from the point of view of governance.

An examination of the role of civil society in the wider field of development of democratic rule that includes the aspects of political reforms begets the following questions at the outset: (a) What is civil society? Does it carry similar meanings in different cultural context? Or its meanings and thrust carries a specific overtone depending upon the cultural, political and economic context? (b) Does the linkage between civil society and democracy hold any empirical validity as the case is generally made out from European experiences or recent experiences in the South? (c) In other words, was democratic rule in the West, particularly in Europe preceded by the development of civil society? (d) What is the connection between the European discourses of 'civil society' and its historical entry into the non-western political discourse? (e) What is nature and strength of civil society, if there is any, in Muslim West Asia?

Civil Society in Western Liberal Traditions

In the modern western social theory, the concept of civil society seems to have three main meanings. All three meanings are based on dichotomous or contrasts. It is defined through its opposition to 'natural society' or 'state of nature' in early modern contract theory (for instance Hobbes and Lock's use); 'against the state' in the entire liberal tradition and 'contrasted to community' (*Gemeinschaft)* in a theoretical tradition of modern sociology. The image of civil society as an arena against the 'absolutist state' came from Locke and Montesquieu. For Locke the crucial question was the rule of 'limited state' so as to protect 'life, liberty and property'. Hence in the Lockean treatment the state or government is conceived as one sphere (based on the demarcation of activity) which exists against the other sphere composed of various associations. It is this space of other associations which is collectively called 'civil society' in later stages of the liberal tradition, and it is this mass of association in civil society which keeps the state in check be keeping it within its limits.

On the other hand, Montesquieu saw the internal division of the powers of the agencies of the state as a major guarantee of citizen's freedom. Gradually with the expansion of colonization the imaginative structure of civil society consisting of 'nation-state', 'citizenship', 'individualism', 'capitalist economy', 'rule of law', 'voluntary association', 'civil and political freedom' and 'cultural secularism' was institutionalized in terms of 'idea of progress' as well as 'marker' of Occidental/Western civilization vis-à-vis non-Western Civilization. These features remained the normative yardstick to measure the development of civil society and democratic rule in non- western societies.

Notwithstanding these features, the notion of civil society varies in tone and thrust depending upon specific political, economic and cultural context. In general, the global appeal of civil society has increased partly due to crisis of the modernization model of development. The trajectory of modernity and modern form of governance has everywhere strengthened the regulatory power of state at the expense of people's life. Even the 'matured democracy' in the West suffers from 'crisis of governability' and exhibits a strong sense of authoritarianism. In many cases democracy could collapse into authoritarian regimes, which in their turn could decay and degenerate into a complete decline of political order. Fifty years of political history has demonstrated that democracy is not just a matter of constructing a legally preferable, rationally justifiable constitution; these constructions could collapse pitifully in the face of determined hostility from well organized modern social groups, like armies or state bureaucracy or from traditional minded communities. Current 'civil society' discussion arises out of a critical engagement with these problems.

In order to understand the political imagination of each particular use of the term 'civil society', one has to move beyond the undifferentiated use of 'the state' and the traditional juxtaposition of democracy/authoritarianism and then identify what exactly it criticizes in the functioning of state power in local, regional or national context. The slogan of civil society in essence is to mobilise forces in society against the repressive, ineffectual or unresponsive character of state. If the state is repressive and interferes with all aspects of social life, as was the case with communist rule in many parts of the South, intelligentsia, human right and civil right groups expected from 'civil society' to come out of its suffocating control. [6] If the state is overextended but ineffectual as the case in many of West Asian countries, civil society means a demand for the creation of other bodies in society which can provide essential services instead of faltering bureaucracies. [7]

If the state is unresponsive, and the democratic party system appears too disorderly like in India, civil society is a call for the regeneration of grassroots organizations of marginal and dispossessed groups, who can not usually make their aspirations break through the regular format of political parties. [8] In the West, disillusion with the given 'boundaries' of politics and with the restrictions of what are seen as the increasingly decrepit processes of party politics, has provoked interest in civil society as a means of rejuvenating public life. In the Third World Countries, the term broadly signifies democratization and democratic rule.

Civil Society and Democracy: How Tenable?

What comes out of these specific meanings of civil society in different contexts is that it is not necessarily connected with the idea of democracy or democratic rule, despite the popular perception we gather from reading of literature on civil society, particularly in the context of the South. It is difficult to demonstrate that Enlightenment thinkers in Europe constructed the theory of civil society or argued the necessity of civil society as pre-condition for building of a credible democracy. It was best thought of as something which exists distinct from or in opposition to the state, and which might be supposed to possess causal independence/autonomy from the state, irrespective of its form. Thus, in the Hobbesian imagination, civil society was meant to replace 'state of nature' or 'natural society' and if one follows Dakeshott's famous interpretation of Hobbes, state signifies 'civic association'. [9] Lock did not use term civil society while advancing the thesis of 'limited state'. Montesquieu did not advocate the construction of civil society to exercise control over state but prefers to divide the power of the state to achieve the goal of a liberal state.

Hegel, who is credited with articulating a theory of civil society that consists all association between family and state, ends up in eulogizing the 'modern state' as 'March of God On Earth'. During the entire career of European liberal political theory the concept of 'sovereignty' as 'the' attribute of 'modern state' was/is retained at the cost of autonomy of realm of the civil society. In Marxian tradition the notion of civil society, as developed by Antonio Gramsci did not receive much attention beyond ideological hegemony of the bourgeois class. More recently Habermas' theory on public sphere demonstrates how public sphere or civil society actually helps in carrying the agenda and discourse of the state and as such civil society and state have not historically existed in opposition to each other but rather worked in tandem with each other.

Thus the linkage between civil society and democracy does not have any basis in the classical political and sociological theory. It is only with the development of modernity as institutionalized European/Western discourse that made this linkage popular to privilege the European identity vis-à-vis others, particularly the Islamic Orient.

Further, practice of some kind of representative democracy—both durable and non-durable—has been part of many post-colonial societies including India, Israel, Iran, Palestine, Kuwait, Bangladesh, Pakistan, Jordan, Morocco, Egypt, Algeria, Bahrain and so on. However to link the democratic experiment within these countries with relative formation of civil society (as understood conventionally) will be a far fetched idea.

In fact societies of the Third World have had experience of modern institutions sitting thinly over their traditional structures for close to two centuries, with admitted variations, but do not show signs of either a firm conceptual grasp of these ideas, or of a natural preference for these over more traditional ones. This raises all the difficult questions of the transfer of political concepts, and the seemingly inevitable displacement or slide that accompanies cases of institutional graft. Thus, a necessary association between civil society and a specific political form of liberal democracy cannot be assumed. It may be well that a viable democratic political order is not possible in the absence of a civil society, but as the East Asian and other cases make clear, civil societies can live without liberal democracy.

In fact civil society presupposes a concept of 'politics': a conception which both specifies the territorial and constitutional scope of politics, and recognizes an arena or set or practices, which is subject to regular and punctual publicity and which provides a terrain upon which competing claims may be advanced and justified. That is, it presupposes a conception of politics that embodies a common sense of its purposes, a sense of what it is that individuals and groups are competing for, of why they have associated and agreed to compete and disagree. [10] This need not exclusively take the form of, say, participation in the electoral practices of representative democracy, premised on the expansion of a conception of the citizenry. It can involve different and 'informal' ways of entering and acting in the arena of politics.

Civil Society in Muslim West Asia: Historical Context

Thus, given a fact in the light of above analysis that the discourse of linkage between civil society and liberal democracy lacks a firm theoretical and empirical ground, what explains the popular connotation of civil society in terms of democratization and democratic rule in South including the Arab world? An answer to this question requires, in part, an exploration of historical context of colonial-encounter through which the notion of civil society trickled down among the indigenous elites of South or what is referred as Third World countries. The colonial intervention in these societies decisively changed the normative foundation and structure of political authority. With the arrival of European colonialism, the state became an undeniable, unavoidable part of the business of social living; and the institutional organizations of the modern state invites a discourse in terms of a state/ civil society distinction. However the astonishing power of the sovereign states of the modern West created an enormous impression on the nationalist elites. But this was to create difficulties for principles of civil society after independence.

Through the national movements, these elites laid claim to a right to mobilize all sections of society, and extended the state's influence over all spheres of social life. The post-colonial state soon assumed the mantle of 'growth', 'development' 'progress' and vehicle of constructing a 'modern civil order'. Therefore as long as the state managed to derive its legitimacy from development it carried the aspiration of civil society without allowing the latter to flourish on its own. Further during the Cold War period the western governments preferred the 'authoritarian political stability' of post colonial societies at the cost of growth of civil society in order to prevent these societies from falling into the Soviet led socialist/communist orbit.

The scenario of West Asia became more complicated—the ever expanding state, the rentier economy, oil, Israel, continuous existence of war like situation, Western interest—

combination of all these throttled the potential for growth of civil society in this region. It is only with the end of cold war period, declining oil prices throughout mid-1980s and 1990s, and declining capacity of states to 'deliver and perform' that the discourse of civil society in this region, particularly in Arab World, acquires a new life of its own. It is emerging as an 'arena for articulation of grievances' against the increasingly perceived failing state. Externally, the idea of civil society received a widespread support from the West which was missing during much of Cold War period for two reasons. First, the notion of civil society with its focus on human rights provides a new ground for 'legitimate intervention' (including by force) in the post-colonial societies in the context of post-Cold War era and globalization. Second, a civil society in tandem with the state is required to expand the sphere of economic liberalization/privatization and defeat the forces of Islamic fundamentalism.

Third, the decline of socialism/communism as countervailing forces offered many in the West a unique opportunity to implement their vision of the world based on 'euro-centred idea of progress'. As a result, the support of the West to the discourse on civil society increased manifold that resulted in the mushrooming of a plethora of civil society organisations (CSOs) in many parts of the world, particularly in the Arab world. To this extent, civil society discourses are not free of political underpinnings.

Observers have hence concluded that any sustained process of democratization in Arab world will require an effective civil society, a sphere in which civic leaders can pool their resources and direct their social forces to defy the state. Scholars have traced the genesis of autonomous associations from Ottoman rule; their expansion under European imperialism, and then rapid demobilization under postcolonial populism; and finally, the renaissance of civil society by the late 1980s, when macroeconomic decay, demographic youth booms, and cultural tumult combined to produce widespread frustration with the state. [11] This then defines the internal and external context of emergence of civil society discourses in post-colonial societies including Muslim West Asian societies.

Civil Society in Muslim West Asia

Having delineated the context of the emergence of the discourse of civil society let us turn now to reflect upon the specific nature of organization and discourse on civil society and their patterns of engagement with the state authorities in Muslim West Asian nations in order to assess the direction of political reforms, if there is any, in these countries.

Since the early 1990s, civil society assistance has constituted the linchpin of international democracy promotion efforts in MENA (Middle East and North Africa) countries. The United Nations Development Program portrays civil society as a vital pillar in sustaining human development and fostering transparent political governance; the World Bank and European Commission (EC) employ a broad portfolio of aid to support civil society, often bypassing governments and transferring funds directly to designated groups; and the US foundations such as the Ford Foundation and the National Endowment for Democracy run numerous grant competitions for Arab CSOs, (civil society organizations) rewarding them with liquid funds, training workshops, and exchange programmes. Direct American governmental assistance also reflects the same patterns.

Between 1991 and 2001, the US Agency for International Development (USAID) allocated US$ 150 million to projects classified as 'civil society strengthening', representing the lion's share of a US$ 250 million MENA democracy promotion budget during the same time span. [12] Since 2002, the State Department's Middle East Partnership Initiative has targeted Arab civil society through millions of dollars of direct financial assistance, as well as sponsorship of high-level conferences between leading CSOs and their state counterparts. [13] From the US's 'freedom agenda' to the EC's 'Barcelona process', and from the World Bank's goal of 'sustainable development' to the UNDP's target of 'good governance', the diverse strategies of pro-democratic Western actors converge on a single plank--supporting Arab civil society through diplomatic, financial, and moral support, in the hope that a crescendo of opposition from below can elicit momentous regime shifts from above.

In terms of both the total number of CSOs and their 'density' (quantity of organizations per 100,000 inhabitants), Egypt, Morocco, Algeria, Tunisia and the Palestinian territories enjoy the largest and most active civil societies, the oil-rich Gulf countries the most enervated, and the other Arab countries in between. [14] The total number of CSOs in every Arab country has increased during the 1990s. Bahrain and Yemen experienced a staggering 400 and 1000 percent enlargement, respectively; CSOs tripled in number in Lebanon and doubled in Saudi Arabia and Kuwait; and by 2002, the region boasted nearly 130,000 recognized civil society groups. [15] The number of non-governmental organizations (NGOs) across the region grew from 20,000 in the 1970s to 70,000 by the mid-1990s. [16] Egypt alone holds about 14,000, while Morocco, Lebanon, Jordan, Yemen, and Tunisia collectively possess 21,000 more. [17]

However the notwithstanding the development of organizations and forces related to sphere of civil society as mentioned above, the reality is that nearly two decades after scholars heralded its rejuvenation, civil society has not yielded any results in pushing Arab states towards democratic transitions by undermining the foundations of their authoritarian institutions. All that was achieved in the name of democratization was a few democratic initiatives in political sphere. Thus, in the context of Arab world, all that the various governments promised was *ta'addudiya*, which means enhancing political pluralism by relaxing media restrictions, legalizing new parties, respecting a broader view of human rights and institutionalizing the process of elections. Even in monarchical Morocco, King Muhammad VI infused national discourse in the late 1990s with pledges of multiparty competition and release of dissidents. Saudi Arabia also moved in similar direction in post-9/11 period by initiating the process of election at the local level.

The failure of civil society organization in Arab world to push the agenda of democratic and political reform partly results from theoretical understanding of the notion of civil society by its practioners in the Arab world. The first problem concerns the theoretical parameters of Arab civil society. The simplest of questions—what is Arab civil society, and what counts as a CSO in the context of Arab society—reflect conceptual disarray. Civil society has become 'a normative football' in Arab discourse; public officials use the term 'to promote their projects of mobilization and 'modernization;' Islamists use it to angle for a legal share of public space; and independent activists and intellectuals use it to expand the boundaries of individual liberty.' [18] Most Western political scientists and liberal Arab research institutes, such as the Ibn Khaldun Centre for Development Studies in Cairo, define civil society as 'the place where a mélange of groups, associations, clubs, guilds, syndicates, federations, unions, parties, and groups come together to provide a buffer between state and citizen.' [19]

Second, the civil society movements in Muslim West Asia are internally fractured between secular civil society organizations and Islamists civil society organizations. Since the thrust of discourse of civil society is one based on Gesellschaft principles and not of Gemeinschaft, it fails to mobilize the wider section of society and therefore carries little weight from the point of view of exerting pressures on the state for the purpose of political reforms. Further, the reservation and suspicion about Islamic organizations as civil society organizations puts external democracy promoters in an uncomfortable position: major donors refuse to throw their financial and diplomatic weight behind Islamists, despite the fact that many command ardent grassroots support, lead large and efficient organizations, and, in many Arab societies, represent the strongest opposition against the ruling elite—all ideal traits that few secular CSOs possess.

The third pertains to the issue of the nature and functioning of CSOs in Muslim West Asia. Individual CSOs have not mobilized a critical mass of supporters throughout society. For example, although NGOs can limit the depredations of authoritarian rule by publicizing abuses such as torture of political dissidents, they cannot directly challenge the state without popular support, which is limited since most are single-issue oriented. It is difficult to contend that civil society organizations—whether of secular or Islamic varieties—are clearly working with a political vision of constructing alternative democratic order against the existing political order. Most of these CSOs are either engaged in providing 'apolitical' services in the area such as education, health, housing, sanitation etc.: areas from where the government has gradually withdrawn or failed miserably due to many reasons or opposing/highlighting the repressive state actions in the domain of human rights.

Even if one assumes that CSOs are working with alternative democratic vision, their adherence to modern/western conception of civil society, as elaborated in the beginning of this paper, fails to capture the collective imagination/memory of society. This is because they do not take into consideration of specific cultural conception of institutions and values associated with civil society as mentioned in the paper. Even the Islamists' thrust of an alternative 'Islamic order' follows from the structure of modernity and hence does not offer a credible opposition to the existing authoritarian modern state. In addition to this, the CSOs's assumption that liberal democratic order ought to be a 'natural preference' of all human societies is a problematic proposition. Different cultures have different expectations from governing institutions. If one goes through some of the credible anthropological account of Arab culture one finds Arabs, like many post-colonial societies, have different perception/understanding of rule of law, nation-state, individualism, property, private/public dichotomy—things which are associated with the meaning of civil society vis-à-vis Western understanding of the same. They also have different expectations from the state that has been historically shaped irrespective of the form of governments. These broadly concern the 'domain of justice', particularly the sense of distributive justice.

Therefore, an informed discussion on civil society in non-Western society must take into three considerations. It must not be ignorant of their specific cultural intellectual histories, and must understand the theoretical concepts and ideas which structure each intellectual tradition. It must also be sensitive to the existing structures of practice relating to the use of and opposition to power specific to each society. For these reasons, no cross-sector coalition unites these groups, and different segments regard each other with suspicion. The lack of any overarching anti-regime slogan results in cycles of 'dissonant politics' rather than consensus over pathways to reform, resulting in the absence of any united constituency for democracy. With few regional or national networks encouraging cross-organizational cooperation, combined with growing ideological radicalization, Arab civil society appears to suffer from weak broad-based support and endemic fragmentation. [20]

Fourth, new strands of research have highlighted additional associations that do not categorize as either secular CSOs or Islamist movements, yet still carry political importance. These include tribal councils and intermediary social institutions, such as informal mutual-aid neighbourhood networks, which thrive in the urban quarters of Arab metropolises like Cairo and Algeries; marginalized legislative parties that function more like advocacy groups rather than electoral machines, since they have little chance of forming the government; organizations that straddle the line between state and society, such as reformist social foundations run by royalists in Morocco; longstanding cultural authorities predicated on traditional religious reputation, such as *ulama* scholars in nearly every Arab society. These entities embody unique forms of social mobilization distinct from the state, economy, and family, but they have few analogues in the Western perspective.

Fifth, almost all Arab regimes utilize systematic policies of legal constriction that defuse civic activism long before it becomes threatening. In most Arab states, all CSOs must register with Interior or Social Affairs Ministries, which use complicated 'Associations Laws' to regulate new organizations. To receive operating permits, civic groups must clear arduous security investigations and promise to refrain from activities of 'subversion' (*siba*). Moreover, state administrators exercise tight authority over existing groups; they may audit operating budgets, direct the internal intelligence services (*al-mukhabarat*) to infiltrate major associations, cancel board elections of unions and syndicates, impose arbitrary fines for mismanagement, ban financial contributions from blacklisted donors, and dissolve any group found to commit minor legal infractions. 'Emergency laws' in many parts of Arab world including Egypt, Sudan, Algeria, Tunisia and Morocco, provide an additional safety buffer, since they freeze legal protections of activists and enable governments to activate draconian laws to periodically flatten public discourse and cow the media into subservience.

Finally, the method co-optation dilutes opposition forces and drives the civic sector towards dependency on the state. For instance, Arab authoritarian regimes often establish shadow organizations mimicking the function of independent CSOs, but which actually serve as surveillance mechanisms that silence discord through patronage. In Syria, the hegemonic Ba'th Party has co-opted the emergent bourgeoisie by funding its own professional associations and civic councils, siphoning middle-class support away from the reformists. The Jordanian regime's General Union of Voluntary Societies serves as the umbrella organization for all national NGO interests, colluding with the Ministry of Social Development to regulate civic activity; but because its operates on volunteers from existing NGOs, it lures CSO leaders into corporatist participation with the state.

Some Arab governments also run their own human rights boards, designed to appease foreign critics while usurping resources from grassroots activists. During the 1990s, the Algerian state operated the National Observatory for Human Rights (Observatories National des Droits de l'Homme), which published regular reports and enjoyed cordial relations with European embassies but seldom criticized ongoing military abuses. More recently, in 2003, Egypt's ruling National Democratic Party established the 27-member National Council for Human Rights, with appointees including acclaimed lawyers and diplomats. Yet the advisory body has ignored notorious infractions, such as crackdowns on Islamists in Sinai and the Spring 2005 persecution of Mubarak's foe, Ayman Nour; for many Egyptians, the Council already faces a 'credibility deficit'.

Thus, the theoretical weakness of euro- centred notion of civil society vis-à-vis other societies, particularly in the Arab world, and the totality of regime's soft and hard tactics enables Arab autocratic elites to regulate civil society, manipulating the rules governing the public sphere. Yet over the past two decades, Arab regimes have turned this equation on its head: the durable state permits the civic sector to bloom, because it can manage the resulting opposition through a battery of legal and coercive controls. This demonstrates that Arab civil society has little meaning outside the context of the state, and in turn that state's relations with structural dynamics that affect its will and capacity to rule. Thus civil society (in terms of liberalizing measures) grew not because the state retreated, but because authoritarian incumbents deployed a new tactic of control--they could reassert power and slake dissension by granting concessions too mild to produce systemic change, but hefty enough to merit symbolic applause at home and abroad. In this calculated survival strategy, Arab autocrats promote reforms that encourage political competition and liberal opposition; but when civil discord becomes a viable threat, the state deliberalizes, retracting its indulgence and intensifying repression until anti-regime sentiment has abided. Such repeated oscillation between narrow pluralism and brutal suppression is a trap, which Daniel Brumberg calls 'controlled liberalization'. [21]

Thus what actually goes in terms of oppositional activities of the CSOs, though carries the impression of democratization is a critique of the functioning of the state in general or critique of a particular action of the state and not the total de-legitimization of the state system. The state in many countries of Muslim West Asia retains sufficient capacity—both peaceful and coercive—to deal with such oppositional pressures. In fact it is the state that retains the initiative to 'expand and contract the democratic sphere' depending upon the context. Examples from Egypt, Saudi Arabia, Kuwait, Jordan, Iran, Turkey, Morocco, Tunisia, and other Muslim countries in the region testify to this trend.

Notes

1. See, for instance, Victor Perez-Diaz, *The Return of Civil Society* (Cambridge: Harvard University Press, 1993); Gordon White, "Civil Society, Democratization, and Development," *Democratization*, Vol. 1, No.3 (1994), pp. 375-90; and Nancy Bermeo and Philip Nord, *Civil Society Before Democracy: Lessons From Nineteenth-Century Europe* (Oxford: Rowman & Littlefield, 2000)
2. Freedom House, *How Freedom is Won: From Civic Resistance to Durable Democracy*, Special Report, May 2005 http://www.freedomhouse.org/research/specreports/civictrans/index.htm
3. Samuel P. Huntington, *Third Wave: Democratization in the Late*

Twentieth Century (University of Oklahoma Press, 1992).

4. Raymond Hinnebusch, "Authoritarian Persistence, Democratization Theory and the Middle East: An Overview and Critique", in Frederic Volpi and Francesco Cavtorta (ed), *Democratization in the Muslim World* (Routledge: London and New York, 2007), pp. 1-33.
5. See, Tareq Ismael and Jacqueline Ismael, "Civil Society in the Arab World: Historical Traces, Contemporary Vestiges," *Arab Studies Quarterly*, Vol. 19, No. 1 (1997), pp. 77-87; Nawaf Salam, "Civil Society in the Arab World," *Occasional Publications*, No. 3 (Harvard Law School Islamic Legal Studies Program, 2002) and Masoud Kamali, *Multiple Modernities, Civil Society and Islam: The Case of Iran and Turkey*, and "Islam, Civil Society and Modernization", pp. 6-27.(Liverpool University Press, Liverpool,2006)
6. Geoferey Hawthorn, "The Promise of Civil Society in the South", in Sudipta Kaviraj and Sunil Khilani, *Civil Society: History and Possibilities* (Cambridge University Press, Foundation Books, New Delhi, 2001) pp. 269-287.
7. Sami Zubaida, "Civil Society, Community, and Democracy in the Middle East", in Sudipta Kaviraj and Sunil Khilani, *Civil Society: History and Possibilities* (Cambridge University Press, Foundation Books, New Delhi, 2001) pp. 232-250.
8. Rajni Kothari, *Rethinking Democracy* (Orient Longman, Delhi, 2005).
9. Michael Oakeshott, *Hobbes on Civil Associations* (Oxford: Blackwell, 1975).
10. Sunil Khilani, "The Development of Civil Society" in Sudipta Kaviraj and Sunil Khilani, *Civil Society: History and Possibilities* (Cambridge University Press, Foundation Books, New Delhi, 2001), p. 26.
11. Saad Eddin Ibrahim, "Civil Society and the Prospects of Democratization in the Arab World," in Norton (ed), *Civil Society in the Middle East*, Vol. 1 (Leiden: Brill, 1995), pp. 41-42.
12. Daniel Brumberg, Amy Hawthorne, Carothers, and Ottaway, "Democratic Mirage in the Middle East," in *Critical Mission*(Washington, D.C.: Carnegie Endowment for International Peace, 2004); and Hawthorne, "Is Civil Society the Answer?" in Carothers and Ottaway (eds), *Uncharted Journey:*

Promoting Democracy in the Middle East (Washington, D.C.: Carnegie Endowment for International Peace, 2005, quoted in Sean L. Yom, "Civil Society and Democratization in the Arab World", *Middle East Review of International Affairs*, Vol. 9, No. 4 (December 2005), p. 17.
13. Ibid, pp. 17-18.
14. Sean L. Yom, Civil Society and Democratization in the Arab World, *Middle East Review of International Affairs*, Vol. 9, No. 4 (December 2005) pp. 14-33 and p. 16.
15. Salim Nar, "Good Governance for Development in the Arab Countries: Arab Civil Societies and Public Governance Reform," Working Paper of the UNDP Dead Sea Conference, UNDP Programme on Governance in the Arab Region, Jordan, February 2005, p. 8.
16. Ibrahim, "Civil Society and the Prospects of Democratization in the Arab World," p. 39.
17. (International Institute for Democracy and Electoral Assistance, *Democracy in the Arab World* (Stockholm: IIDEA, 2000), p. 7. See also Julie Peteet, "The NGO Phenomenon in the Arab World," *Middle East Report*, No. 193 (1995), pp. 26-27.
18. Bellin, "Civil Society: Effective Tool of Analysis for Middle East Politics?" p. 510. In Sean L. Yom, Civil Society and Democratization in the Arab World, *Middle East Review of International Affairs*, Vol. 9, No. 4 (December 2005).
19. Augustus Richard Norton, "The Future of Civil Society in the Middle East," *Middle East Journal*, Vol. 47, No. 2 (1993), p. 211.
20. Sean L. Yom, Civil Society and Democratization in the Arab World, *Middle East Review of International Affairs,* Vol. 9, No. 4 (December 2005), p 19.
21. Daniel Brumberg, The Trap of Liberalized Autocracy: Democratization in the Arab World? *Journal of Democracy,* Vol. 13, No. 4 (2002), pp. 56-68.

3

Politics of Civil Society in West Asia

A.K. Ramakrishnan

Introduction

This chapter tries to locate civil society dynamics in West Asia by pointing out certain salient political concerns that need to be addressed in any civil society theorization and activism. The debates on civil society gained momentum in West Asia in the 1990s due to a number of developments within and beyond the region. Many observers like Ali M. Ansari point out that 'the immediate reason why scholars went in search of civil society and the green shoots of democracy was the onset of the Persian Gulf War of 1990-91 and the popular scepticism surrounding its motivation' [1] The nature of West Asian states, continuities and transformations of several of their characteristic features and their general crisis of modernization is one major template that will help us comprehend the growth and functions of civil society in the region. Authoritarianism, rentier nature of many states, waning of pan-Arab nationalism, the crisis of traditional political organizations, the marginalization of left ideology and the overall legitimacy crisis of a large chunk of states in West Asia have to be taken into account for meaningful understanding of civil society in that part of the world.

The quest for participation and the demand for political reforms have been at the heart of civil society imagination. Many facets of internal and international developments contributed not only for the evolution and growth of civil society in West Asia but also for creating newer constraints on their functioning. What is particularly worth emphasizing is the non-availability of a monolithic notion of civil society given the diverse experiences of civil society dynamics in various parts of the West Asian region.

Contestations over the Idea of Civil Society

There have been debates and discussions about the usefulness of a 'Western' concept like civil society to capture the socio-political ethos of West Asian societies. Saad Eddin Ibrahim points out that civil society as a concept is used and over used to such extents that 'there is a serious theoretical threat to its sharpness and utility. [2] The dichotomy that is imagined between the Western and the West Asian resulted in a range of responses regarding the relevance of the notion of civil society—from total skepticism to measured acceptance. The gamut of international, regional, and above all, national level political and economic changes in the last two decades dictated the employment of the civil society idea to political discussions within the West Asian region. While skeptics challenged it as an 'imported idea', international donor agencies and institutions promoted it with great zeal. Major global state actors found it useful to employ the civil society idea as instrument of what they called 'promotion of democracy' in West Asia.

At the same time, for innumerable intellectuals and activists from the region, civil society is found to be an ally in their call for political reform, freedom of expression and human rights. The embracing of the civil society discourse by such a significant section of the society in no way produced a monolithic conceptualization and deployment of the notion of civil society. There are intellectuals who invoke the civil society idea by stressing upon the difference between the ways it is imagined in the West and in West Asia, while there are others who point out the its universality because they find conceptions and practice of democracy, freedom and human rights equally relevant for the region as they are for the rest of the world.

For many in West Asia, civil society is an arena of

political struggle. While the state, in certain cases, utilizes civil society as an arena and source of its own legitimacy, the 'Arab movements of opposition and political dissent, resort to the...concept [of civil society] to entrench themselves against state oppression and authoritarianism'. [3] Civil society activism in the West Asian region took up diverse dimensions of political issues from human rights to struggle against patriarchal power. It is significant to note that when ninety-nine Syrian intellectuals issued their manifesto in 2000 from a civil society standpoint, the demands raised by them were overtly political. They demanded the end of the state of emergency and martial law that existed in Syria from 1963; freedom of expression, assembly and rule of law; and pardoning political prisoners. [4] Civil and political rights of citizens become primary in their concern. The demands were obviously directed towards the state.

Political Debates on Civil Society

Given such an organic linkage of civil society with politics, any apolitical definition of civil society becomes problematic. We have been fed with an idea of civil society as a realm of the function of non-governmental organizations, of markets and of what is called social capital. The contemporary phase of capitalist globalization with its neo-liberal vision promotes a version of civil society that is associated with the preponderance of non-state actors. The non-state sectors in a way are supposed to be replacing the government in as much levels of human activity as possible. This neo-liberal separation of the cultural, social and the economic from the political creates a notion of civil society that is devoid of human agency. The dominant World Bank paradigm of development has been embedded in such an idea of civil society that detaches itself from concerns of the political.

Civil society is traditionally conceptualized as an 'interface between the state and society'. It is viewed as "the sphere of activity outside the political and legal authority of the state where, ideally or theoretically, citizens band together in free association to promote and pursue non-profit objectives". [5] It has to be understood not only in relation to the state but also in relation to the family. Many think about it as a private realm in relation to the public realm of the state. It is, at the same time, a public realm in relation to the family. It is also taken to note the sphere of engagement of community.

Wayne Hudson finds that Western categorizations of civil society by mixing up innumerable socio-political attributes will not be very useful in the Asian context. 'Civil society cannot be assumed to be progressive, democratic, modernizing and egalitarian.' According to him: many contemporary writers seem to confuse civil society with arrangements which initiate, enable or protect democracy, including the rule of law, freedom of the press, speech, assembly and religion, the practice of publicity, civility..., the existence of a public-private distinction, institutional recognition of the public sphere, pluralism, civic participation and citizenship, even though some at least of these arrangements could be put in place without establishing civil society. [6]

Harik asks the question whether 'the growth of a flourishing "civil society" is a prerequisite for the installation of a democratic government or, alternatively, whether the development of a civil society and a democratic government may be pursued simultaneously'. [7] There has been circularity in the arguments relating to the linkage between civil society and democracy. Harik's own conclusion on this matter is as follows: 'A focus on civil society alone is thus not likely to do much for democratization in Arab societies. A more inclusive approach is far better, because the interdependence between governmental institutions and private, civil associations is quite strong. Moreover, the strengthening of civil society in Arab countries may well depend upon the rise of greater governmental effectiveness.' [8]

Michael Edwards, in his book *Civil Society* asserts that in spite of the criticisms of civil society in the contemporary milieu, it 'can provide a valuable framework for understanding and changing key elements of our world.' He notes further '[t]he civil society debate will never be closed, because the essence of civil society is collective action, negotiation and struggle'. [9]

Major thinkers of civil society talks about it in relation to, or as contrasted with state. Antonio Gramsci saw civil society as a domain where hegemony is active in contrast to the state wherein coercive force monopolized. The way the values of dominant classes engage itself in civil society so that legitimation of the interests of state and such classes are obtained is an important aspect of the operation of hegemony, the indirect manner in which power operate in a given society. What we need to take into consideration is that civil society is a site of power, hierarchy and differential entitlements. It is a place where citizenship is articulated. Rather, civil society is a sphere of clash of interests and power. The political space of civil society exhibits not only ideological operations but also, or more importantly, strategic positionalities. In other words, dominant classes as well as citizens engage in civil society by articulating their interests through different strategic means. In West Asia, the coercive power of the state is still a major aspect of political and social life. Such a power of the state permeates into all aspects of people's life.

The nature of civil society's political engagement is two-fold: one, it raises collective voices for reform and change in the working of the state; and two, it in diverse contexts of each society raises issues of everyday life and challenges local traditional authority in many ways. Therefore, macro-political engagement with respect to the state on the one hand and micro-political engagement with respect to the society on the other hand show the assertion of power of civil society, whether successfully or not. Civil society discussions enabled political analysts to look at non-conventional arenas of the play of power. Politics of state and politics of everyday life of citizens become entangled in multiple ways in civil society.

The idea of civil society is integrally linked with notions of identity and citizenship. The diverse and layered identities that contemporary societies enable citizens to possess have not been fully asserted in most West Asian cases as there are still arenas of citizenship that are not allowed to be legitimately expressed. The limitations imposed on the articulation of multiplicity of identities denote the severe constraints under which civil societies operate in West Asia.

Movements and Civil Society

While civil society debates in West Asia have been dealing a lot with issues of democracy, political reforms and human rights, the way most often such discussion are conducted assume a process without an agency. Any discussion of civil society without reference to social movements as agency of transformation is politically fruitless. Such mobilizations and movements that address power and politics both at the macro and micro levels of society are too understood not as non-governmental sector and organizations that pre-exist any change in civil society, but as active agency which shapes change and which are shaped by such changes.

Women's movements and the human rights movements in West Asia have struggled in very adverse political and socio-cultural conditions. They want an accountable state that cares for rights of women and the minorities, one that cares for fundamental freedoms. The patriarchal nature of societies and polity in the region made things worse for women. But there have been active women's movements in a majority of countries in West Asia and many of them have been successful in gaining citizenship rights to political participation in varying degrees in different countries and in obtaining personal law reforms and property rights in certain societies. In some cases, basic issues of freedom of movement etc. have to be fought for. The politics of women's movement addresses patriarchal power and authority at both macro and micro realms of each society. The human rights movements' struggle for civil and political rights and for overall democratic rights met with stiff challenge from the state in most cases. Both the women's' and human rights movements have been accused in several instances as those inspired by the West. In spite of the enormous challenges they face, such movements provided the inevitable human agency for change in civil society.

One factor that has affected civil society debates in West Asia in a big way is the role of Islam and Islamist movements in determining the character of civil society. While there has been a proliferation of Islamic activism in the region for the past several decades, they had a love-hate relationship with other movements for change. The nature of claims put on state and politics by Islamist movements and secular movements differ in many fundamental ways. But there have been occasions necessary for struggling against authoritarian state in a combined manner. Even though both form oppositional voices in most societies, their own coming together have been problematic due to the differences in the very imagination of change in the society and state. While Islamists have been envisaging a reinvention of state in Islamic terms of their definition, an inclusive democratic agenda becomes important for other movements.

The women's movement and the human rights movement have been functioning in a precarious atmosphere that is caught between the authoritarian states on the one hand and the Islamists on the other. Egyptian human rights activist Farag Foda, who was killed in front of the Egyptian Organization of Human Rights in the early 1990s, was just one example of how dangerous the predicament of caught between the two could be. Nawal al-Saadawi, the famous Egyptian feminist activist and writer, had to face the wrath of both the state and Islamist elements a number of times.

While many secular activists and intellectuals believe that the Islamists do not form part of an envisaged civil society, others think that civil society engagement will moderate them in such a way that they learn to ply according the rules of modern civil society. The reality is that the Islamists still are a strong contender for societal and political power in a large number of West Asian societies.

When we consider the requirement of a political analysis of civil society, the fact that recent movements in Egypt and Iran and elsewhere exhibited open political agenda needs to be recognized. The direct addressing of politics of state by civil society activism comes to a large extent from the overarching power the state wields in the daily lives of people. Such a reach of the state most often constraints the ability of societal actors to engage in pursuit of desirable changes in favour of more freedom and flexibility.

Vickie Langohr is of the opinion that a significant 'trend in many Arab liberalizing regimes over the past decade has been the rise of advocacy nongovernmental organizations to the position of primary opposition to authoritarianism against the almost complete marginalization of opposition parties.' [10] *Kifaya*, the Egyptian Movement for Change, launched in 2004 has been an overtly political movement emerging from Egyptian society. It was not a conventional political organization. It was not a single-issue movement but a broad-based one and, at the same time, it shared many aspects of a new social movement. [11] In the initial years of its activism, it raised great expectations, but doubts have been raised on its continued effectiveness in recent times. The *Kifaya* movement's contributions in the past have been of significant political saliency, which cannot be assessed only with the measure of its outcome, but with the kind of dynamism it gave to the oppositional voice. As a recent article in *Al-Ahram Weekly* stated:

[f]ollowing its inception Kifaya played an important role in stimulating political activism. Before it was formed public opposition was unheard of. The movement has served as a model for other opposition movements, which gathered beneath its umbrella, including University Teachers for Change, Youth for Change and Artists for Change. Kifaya,

which quickly became synonymous with street activism, inspired people from all walks of life to publicly express their objections to government policy. [12]

The *Kifaya* movement utilized the new communication technologies for mobilization. The Internet was widely used. Blogs became a significant arena of opinion sharing and networking. The wide canvas of its reach in itself became a problem later in its functioning. State repression, organizational differences and issues of managing relationship with Islamic groups, among other things, contributed to its downward move.

The civil society in Iran has been very active in spite of severe state intervention against a host of such activities. Such activism has been galvanized more recently for the protest against the Ahmadinejad government on the issue of fraudulent conduct of the presidential elections. This is part of the overall struggle for political and social reforms. At one level, the Khatami era was facilitated by civil society enthusiasm for change from the stifling political order towards more freedom for an unintrusive socio-cultural life. In turn, the Khatami administration provided certain leeway for the functioning of civil society groups. But the failure of Khatami leadership to effectively deliver on reform promises and the subsequent assumption of leadership by Ahmadinejad created a difficult period for civil society activism. But, most importantly, the civil society became more militant when the chances of positive top-down reform have drained out or when the state became more intrusive.

Fred Halliday has stressed on the diversity of Iranian society—diversity in terms of the differences between Islam and secularism, diversity of currents within Islam itself and diversity in the linguistic and regional levels—as a salient marker of contemporary debates in a globalizing Iran.

The debates in Iran today draw on this diversity and history, not least in the attempt to forge a political system that takes account of Iranian reality while, at the same time, moving forward to meet the expectations of the younger generation. The balances of pre-Islamic and Islamic, of lyrical poetry and austere theology, of clerical authority and individual judgment are all part of these debates. [13]

As Farhad Kazemi rightly pointed out, 'civil society remains a vital part of Iran's life in spite of the Islamic state's attempt to dominate', even though '[t]he state has succeeded in limiting, and at times severely restricting, the full operation of civil society in many critical areas.' [14]

External Intervention and Democracy

Regarding the Arab world, there have been doubts expressed about the state's willingness to create conditions for the growth of a viable civil society. Sheila Carapico believes that 'the only escape from the authoritarian cul-de-sac seems to be for states voluntarily to cede space to formal interest groups.' She, at the same time, argues that '[i]n many cases, it can only be imagined that foreign pressure in the form of either positive influence or negative sanctions could make this happen.' [15] There is need to critically look at the both state's voluntarism and the desirability of external arm twisting with regard to the forward movement of civil society in the Arab as well as non-Arab parts of West Asia.

The American agenda of spreading democracy in West Asia had a negative impact on the civil society's propensity to act in favour of democratization from within. The challenge that came from the George W. Bush era was not only of military intervention and war in the region, but also the 'threat' that 'we will democratize you'. Efforts at enhancing imperialist interests and promises of democracy from above could not be but viewed by the people of West Asia with scepticism. While there is long history of demands and struggles which people waged for democratic transformation of their societies, most of the time, by risking their lives, the American and the European challenge of democratization paled the internal efforts and in many cases discredited such voices. Civil society cannot be perceived merely as a market for import of such grand ideas of democracy. Democratization is a process that involves an array of struggles from within civil society.

State-Civil Society Dynamics

Augustus Richard Norton the following valid claim regarding West Asian state-civil society linkages:

Given the space and the opportunity to develop, we have ample evidence to show that civil societies in the Middle East have the potential to become more robust and to lend durability to experiments in accountable, open government. This is not meant to imply that civil society is a panacea for reform, or that civil society exists in the absence of the state. Indeed, some elements of contemporary civil society support the authoritarian state and its abusive exercise of power. Moreover, in the absence of state scrupulously enforcing the rule of law, a standard which few Middle Eastern states presently meet, even a mature civil society can easily collapse into incivility. It is nonsensical to think of civil society in the absence of the state, because the state and civil society are bound up in a dialectical relationship that fundamentally shapes political life. [16]

Many conventional understanding of state- civil society dichotomy in West Asia assumed both state and civil society as entities that has already taken definitive shape and form. It is true that many contours of both these entities have been evolving for a long period of time. But that does not mean that they have already taken full shape. Both state and civil society are dynamic entities that have, as noted above, a relationship of mutuality. What is, at the same time, to be remembered is that the West Asian states have a largely determining role with regard to civil society. In most societies of the region, the civil society is yet to reach a stage of development that has the ability to drastically alter the nature of their states. This overarching influence of West Asian states in civil society defies the theoretical claim of the autonomy of civil society from the state.

Notes

1. Ali M. Ansari, *Iran, Islam and Democracy: The Politics of Managing Change* (London: Chatham House, 2006), 2nd edn., p. 18.
2. Saad Eddin Ibrahim, "The Troubled Triangle: Populism, Islam, and Civil Society in the Arab World", *International Political Science Review*, Vol.19, No.4 (1998), p. 373.
3. Hamdy Abdel Rahman Hassan, "The State and Civil Society in Africa: A North African Perspective", *African Journal of Political Science and International Relations*, Vol. 3, No.2 (February 2009), p. 66.
4. For the text of the manifesto, see *http://www.meib.org/articles/0010_sdoc0927.htm*.
5. Tareq Y. Ismael, *Middle East Politics Today: Government and Civil Society* (Gainesville, Florida: University Press of Florida, 2001), pp. 59-60.
6. Wayne Hudson, "Problematizing European Theories of Civil Society", in David C. Schak and Wayne Hudson (eds.), *Civil Society in Asia* (Aldershot: Ashgate, 2003), pp. 14-15.
7. Iliya Harik, "Pluralism in the Arab World", in Nicholas S. Hopkins and Saad Eddin Ibrahim (eds.), *Arab Society: Class, Gender, Power, and Development* (Cairo: American University in Cairo Press, 2006), p.345.
8. Ibid., p. 348.
9. Michael Edwards, *Civil Society* (Cambridge: Polity Press, 2009), p. x.
10. Vickie Langohr, "Too Much Civil Society, Too Little Politics: Egypt and Liberalizing Arab Regimes", *Comparative Politics*, Vol. 36, No. 2, January 2004, p.181.
11. Manar Shourbagy, "The Egyptian Movement for Change - Kefaya: Redefining Politics in Egypt", *Public Culture*, Vol.19, No.1, (Winter 2007).
12. Mohamed El-Sayed, "Whereto Kifaya?", *Al-Ahram Weekly*, Issue No.965, 17-23 . September 2009, *http://weekly.ahram.org.eg/2009/965/eg9.htm*

13. Fred Halliday, "Foreword", in Ali Mohammadi (ed.), *Iran Encountering Globalization: problems and Prospects* (London: RoutledgeCurzon, 2003), pp. xiii-xiv.
14. Farhad Kazemi, "Civil Society and Iranian Politics", in Augustus Richard Norton (ed.), *Civil Society in the Middle East*, Vol.2 (Leiden: E.J. Brill, 1996), p.150.
15. Sheila Carapico, *Civil Society in Yemen: The Political Economy of Activism in Modern Arabia* (Cambridge: Cambridge University Press, 1998), p.8.
16. Augustus Richard Norton, "Preface", in op. cit., Norton, 1996, p. xv.

4

Struggle for Democracy and Civil Society in Gulf Cooperation Council (GCC) States

A.K. Pasha

As early as in the 1920s and 1930s, there were demands for representative assemblies in Kuwait, Dubai and Bahrain. The British, who controlled most of these areas, ruthlessly suppressed these demands and exiled most of the opposition leaders. The British did not even spare some of the tribal leaders/members of the ruling families who were sympathetic to the demands for political participation. Despite setbacks, some wealthy merchant families did take initiative in establishing consultative structures. The struggle for democracy and people's demand to replace autocracy with democratic structures is a relatively recent phenomenon in GCC States.

But it was only with the discovery of oil and the consequent huge oil revenues that led to great changes. Even though the new found wealth made the ruling families fairly independent of the merchant class [also nominally to an extent from the British], but it actually increased their dependence on outside powers especially Britain and the USA. Nevertheless, Kuwait became a pioneer in democratizing its political system soon after its independence in 1961, but the other Gulf Arab ruling families were slow in allowing political participation after their independence in early 1970s with the sole exception of Bahrain. The oil revenues enabled the ruling families to embark on rapid modernization of their tribal societies. Focus on infrastructure and on education led to the emergence of a middle class desirous of playing an active role in the democratic process. Thus, the process of political change has intensified due to a number of internal and external factors.

Some of the external factors were the overthrow of regional monarchies, Arab nationalism, reform movements and the oil embargo of 1973. In particular the 1979 Iranian Revolution and the 1990-91 Kuwait crisis led to mounting demands for political participation. This prompted the GCC rulers to initiate political reforms and promise democratization of their absolute monarchies. Even though this enthusiasm soon waned due to a number of factors but the "explosion of the questioning process" has spurred the incipient process of democratization and test the legitimacy of GCC regimes.

The presence of outside forces posed a major challenge to the legitimacy of some of the GCC rulers where the political process is a family enterprise and also exposed their fragility and their inner weakness despite their enormous wealth. The dependence of GCC rulers on outside help is mainly due to the present processes of governance in these states and to their linkages with the outside world especially the US and UK.

All the GCC political systems which are authoritarian in nature, place the state structures at a very advantageous position, while relegating public institutions to the periphery. Although a new beneficiary class of oligarchs has emerged but the old auxiliary tribal-sectarian force reinforces the new class. The new phenomenon of political tribalism is used to channel the oil wealth and privileges to establish control over the political system.

The ruling families with sources of wealth and power under their control prevent the rise of social and political forces independent of the state expressing the interests and ambitions of various groups of the population. Thus, the rise of political parties, NGO's and others aspects of civil society is prevented and so is the rise of social and political movements which are not loyal to them. Even the religious institutions are directly supervised and controlled by the rulers. Interestingly, right to vote and contest for women is allowed in most GCC States with Kuwait giving it only in 2005. But most scholars argue that mere elections will not lead quickly to democracy in any of the GCC States. As Daniel Brumberg says "gradualism whose small steps trace the sad contours of an unvirtuous circle which does not offer a real path forward". Several scholars have argued that monarchism facilities democratization in the Arab world: but these arguments tend to focus on the ability of rulers to create a system of mutual security that reduces the risks associated with steps in the direction of democracy. But there is also serious doubt regarding the idea that the future of GCC States is surely heading towards revolution due to declining legitimacy.

Along with tribal alliances now sectarian alliances and kinship and patronage are used with newer methods and technologies of control. Although traditional ways of political behaviour and social conduct still prevail but the ruling families have devised newer and more efficient methods to control and manage societies mainly with outside help. At the same time it must be emphasized that new social forces are in the making which will eventfully force the pace of democratization to be accelerated.

The GCC regimes instead of trying to anchor political development and stability in the concept of legitimacy, seek that anchor in western protection. Foreign protection, thus, becomes a substitute for legitimacy. The simple truth is that the GCC rulers unwillingly to share real power and opposed to genuine people's participation in the political system and having a narrow social base in order to retain power widely use coercion and repression against their own citizens. Any group or social force calling on these families to share power are thus opposed and repressed as for instance the Shias in Bahrain during the period 1975-2002. The technology of control means use of security and intelligence apparatus to perpetuate their family rule. This structure of the government is the most modern, efficient and perhaps most developed and widely used or abused. The technology of repression has been upgraded by leaps and bounds with severe implications for popular participation and human rights in all the GCC States. There is absolutely no doubt that the dependency syndrome with the US will continue to promote repressive policies and discourage political participation. Thus, democracy is a victim of a political process in which legitimacy and consensus politics are truly wanting. Under such circumstances dissent is seen as treason. The concept of loyal opposition is not even known in GCC politics. Suspicion, paranoia, fear of assassination which in turn leads to repression including torture and execution or exile of dissenters is fairly widespread.

There is need to actively encourage the process of political change and modernization because once the GCC regimes become truly democratic and responsive to popular demands, not only their legitimacy would be enhanced but more significantly their dependence on outside states especially the US would come down and this may lead to reduction in outside military and political intervention which has periodically undermined peace, security and stability in the Gulf region.

Genuine political reforms would give the politically oppressed people a stake in the running of the political system as also much needed political stability and smooth transition. The abundant oil resources could then be used to advance economic development so as to engage the Gulf people in the process of political and economic progress. Undoubtedly, the threat of religious extremism and terrorism from the region can be contained if this democratic process takes shape. Along with these steps towards democratic transformation, steps to resolve the Arab Israeli Conflict would also be debated and discussed at all forums thereby allowing Arab leaders to take initiatives for meaningful steps along with serious US-Israeli steps (which are very essential). Both these steps would reinforce the momentum for change and then one can look forward to greater peace, security and stability in future. In certain GCC States, Islamic parties/groups have gained seats in legislature or come to share power learning in the process how to be responsible and accountable.

It is far easier to control terrorism and religious extremism in liberal democratic systems which have high level of legitimacy and strong domestic control than the present political set up where the rulers want to remain in total control of all state affairs. The long over due change has now become inevitable but if it is not coming soon internal and regional violence may be directed against such autocratic regimes unwillingly or unable to initiate political reforms. Instability, religious extremism and terrorism could spill over in the neighbourhood as security and stability in the other regions are mutually interlinked through a number of factors.

Democratization, if successful and sustained can produce accountable, transparent participation, inclusive governance, instead of exclusive and repressive rule. But what the GCC leaders have opted for is not the immediate establishment of full-fledged liberal democracy, but a gradual process toward participation in the political and economic life and governance of the country in harmony with the Islamic religion and social acceptability. In other words, gradual and controlled democratization would involve participation at the grass-roots level. But what is important is that the benefits of democratization apart from developing a vibrant civic culture should be in the form of more equitable, accountable, transparent and good governance by all and for all.

Political liberalization which involves promotion of human rights and freedom is being gradually encouraged in the GCC states but political democratization which includes popular political participation and elite accountability needs political liberalization but the latter can take place without the former. It is interesting to note that genuine democratization enshrined and consolidated in both constitutional arrangements and political practices is rare. Democratization should involve an avenue for active participation in national decision making processes, further entrenchment of popular participation in the political process and public demands for fair, legitimate and representative governance which should strengthen democratic structures. Islamic forces like in the earlier case of Arab nationalists may in the long run be "co-opted" or enticed into democratic processes. Political and social mobilization coupled with the rise of Islamic groups all of which is induced by urbanization, literacy, media exposure and a young population has not kept pace with the required structures for political participation like parties, trade unions, voluntary associations and free elections. This has led to political paralysis or decay and has in fact been accelerating political activism and violence involving Islamic and other groups. Thus, democratization is still in its nascent stage in all the GCC states.

The Gulf region dominated by foreign powers who for long have erected hurdles for democratization which if it were to involve broadening and deepening of political participation, like popular sovereignty, electoral representation and civil liberties would constitute political democracy. To supplement this, growth in social and cultural democracy is equally essential for democratization to make progress.

But it is still not very clear whether the GCC rulers due to domestic, regional and global factors would match public aspirations for greater political participation in the political system. As the US has accumulated enormous leverage over the GCC rulers and many GCC citizens feel there is an excellent chance now at this critical juncture to bring genuine democracy in the GCC states. In any case, there are no clear signs of US pressure for greater democratization on most of the GCC states. Perhaps it fears the end of its own hegemony and influence in these states if genuine democracy is established through written constitutions, parties, parliaments, elections, free press so on because most people realize that the GCC rulers will be under pressure from their own people (mostly Islamic groups which are anti-American) not to follow such polices from which the US is the chief beneficiary like excess oil production, investing surplus oil funds in US banks or treasury bonds or purchasing arms and goods from the US among other issues.

Ever since the 1979 Islamic Revolution in Iran and the overthrow of the Shah which was a great set back, the US has been consistently working to regain its influence in Iran. First, it encouraged Iraq's Saddam Hussein to invade Iran in September 1980 and with the help of other Western states supported Iraq in its eight year war with Iran. The GCC states were also induced by the US to help Iraq to contain the Islamic Republic. The US dual containment strategy exhausted both the major Gulf States. Secondly, during the Iran-Iraq war, the US gradually increased its presence in the Gulf as also in some GCC states. The US already had its naval headquarters in Bahrain for its naval fleet in the Gulf. In order to protect Kuwaiti oil tankers during the end of the Iran-Iraq war, the US sent more and powerful ships to the Gulf. Oman had already allowed the US to use its Masriah island facilities.

The Iraqi invasion of Kuwait by Saddam Hussein in August 1990 and the subsequent US liberation of Kuwait in early 1991 had led to US presence in Kuwait. Also, since then US military presence increased in other GCC states as well. Now there are about 25,250 US forces in Kuwait. Due to the continued presence of US forces in Saudi Arabia even after the liberation of Kuwait, Osama Bin Laden and al-Qaida launched their opposition to US presence in the holy land. King Fahd and Crown Prince Abdullah quietly asked the US to withdraw its military forces from the Kingdom especially in the wake of bomb attacks on continued US military presence. Now there are reportedly only about 300 US instructors in Saudi Arabia. The US Central Command was also shifted from its base in Dhahran-Saudi Arabia to Doha in Qatar which has become the focus of US military activities in the Gulf area especially the No-fly zones in Iraq and attacks on Iraqi installations before

US invasion of Iraq.

The overthrow of the Qatar ruler in June 1995 facilitated US presence over there which now stands at 6,540 US troops. Now the US military activity in Iraq is coordinated from Qatar. Coupled with this, UN economic sanctions on Iraq since 1990 even after the liberation of Kuwait was aimed at regime change in Iraq. After 9/11, the Bush administration orchestrated the campaign against Saddam Hussein and finally through Kuwaiti territory invaded Iraq in March 2003. The US mainly invaded Iraq due to alleged possession of WMD's, to establish a democratic regime and prevent invasion of neighbours and to protect Shias and Kurds but more importantly due to oil as Alan Greenspan, the former Chairman of US Federal Reserve wrote in his book *The Age of Turbulence: Adventurer in a New World* (p.463). At the moment the US has about 1, 21,600 troops in Iraq and it intends to stay in the oil rich country for the foreseeable future. If Republican candidate John McCain wins the US Presidential 2008 elections, he wants USA to stay in occupied Iraq for another 100 years. Besides, the US has 1,300 troops in UAE, 3000 in Bahrain and about 300 in Oman. Since 2001 invasion of Afghanistan, the US is also present over there together with access to air bases in Central Asia (two) and Turkey. But the largest presence in the Gulf is by the US Navy formed in battle groups consisting of aircraft carriers, destroyers, gunship boats, submarines and logistic ships. This is in addition to air and naval power in the entire Gulf region. From this formidable presence the US has threatened military attacks on Iran over the Iranian nuclear program as also regime change if possible.

Many citizens, civil society groups, associations and other democratic groups in the GCC states want the US to speak for democracy in their states. They are convinced that democracy in all its forms and dimensions will come soon if the US acts quickly and decisively because the US has accumulated enormous leverage over the GCC rulers and many Arabs feel there is an excellent chance now at this critical juncture to bring genuine democracy in the GCC states. Although many in the GCC are convinced that the US wants to see democracy in their states, but they find fault with it because they suspect the attitude of the US is not to push things, but to wish that things will go in the direction of democracy. According to critics, "that is a mistake. Wishing is not enough". The US has to clearly and unambiguously say to the world and to the ruling families that democracy must be established seriously soon enough in the GCC states. But will the US do it when it has a poor record in the past? In other words: Whether the US has the will to see democracy take shape and flourish in the GCC states. Many in the US argue that further democratization would not be in the interest of the US at all. That the US is wary about democratization in the GCC states is obvious by two statements.

In March 1991, when National Security Adviser to Senior Bush, Mr. Brent Scowcroft, visited Riyadh, the Saudis complained that there was too much talk of democracy in Kuwait. "That's not why we fought the war", one US official said. And not long after on April 3, 1991, there appeared a story in *New York Times* that said, the US was "not pressing Kuwait on [political] reform". In addition, when Senior Bush was asked whether he was disappointed about the lack of democratization in Kuwait, he bluntly reported: "The war was not fought about democracy in Kuwait". In fact, during the Kuwait Gulf war, many felt the US conduct was not inspired by democratic considerations at all. In any case, there are no clear signs of US pressure for greater democratization on most of the GCC states. As seen earlier, it not only fears the end of its own hegemony and influence in these states if genuine democracy is established, but looks at this process negatively which might undermine its global superpower status as well.

Also, the reason for lack of democracy in GCC states cannot be wholly attributed to the self interest of the ruling family members. One opinion is that it should not overlook the fact that these are relatively nascent political systems and democratic structures need time to take roots. The Amirs, Sultans and Kings are apparently playing a crucial role in the nation building and state formation process during which power according to them has to be concentrated and centralized. The massive socio-economic changes [and hence dislocation] which are part of this process, in fact, discourage the rulers from widening their social base and prevent them from accommodating the political demands of the new social groups that are produced by the very same process. Since these rulers are viewed by opponents as instruments of western policy in the area, but they are also seen by most citizens as actively engaged in nation building process.

Thus, legitimacy is side stepped in favour of coercive power, itself dependent on an unequal relationship with the US. In all likelihood the much suspected link with the US will continue to promote repressive policies and discourage genuine political participation until at least abundant oil and its revenues are available. The GCC regimes with US support have become confident, bold and thus more repressive. They use security and intelligence apparatus to perpetuate their undemocratic rule. This structure of the state presided over by the Minister of Interior [invariably by a ruling family member] in most cases, is the most modern, efficient and perhaps highly developed and widely used or abused. The technology of repression has been upgraded by leaps and bounds with severe implications for popular participation and human rights. Thus, democracy is a victim of a political process in which legitimacy and consensus politics are truly wanting. Under such circumstances dissent is seen as unacceptable. The concept of a loyal opposition is not even known in GCC states. Suspicion, paranoia, fear of assassination and of being overthrown are leading to expulsion, assassination, repression, incarceration, including torture and in some cases execution of dissenters under fake trials. To a very large extent this sad state of affair is also due to the ongoing Arab-Israeli Conflict.

More and more people in the GCC now believe that their dependent rulers due to the authoritarian nature of the political system and also under US influence cannot do anything to relieve their humiliation and improve their lot in political terms. Hence the emergence of Islamic groups which employ violence and suicide bombings. Moreover the secular groups also largely follow this strategy under popular support. One writer says "suicide bombings take root because they free the desperate from the need to rely on governments. Rather than being sponsored by states, this form of violence challenges states." Al Qaeda and other religious groups may be ultimately contained but newer groups would emerge and may follow their methods. Lack of democracy and suppression of political opposition invariably drives people to join Islamic groups and repression alone cannot eliminate terrorism. "Any successful counter terrorism strategy must thus address both the opportunities available to militants and the level of their motivations".

Most outside states which interact with the GCC States believe [obviously the US and UK are not in this category] that they should actively encourage the process of political change and modernization because once the Arab [Gulf] regimes become democratic and responsive to popular demands, not only their legitimacy would be enhanced but more significantly their dependence on outside states especially the US would come down and this may lead to reduction in outside military and political intervention which has periodically undermined peace, security and stability in the region. Genuine political reforms would give the politically oppressed people a stake in the running of the political system as also much needed political stability and smooth transition. The abundant oil resources could then be used to advance economic development so as to engage the Arab people in the process of political and economic progress.

Undoubtedly the threat of religious extremism and terrorism from the region would be contained if this democratic process takes shape early. Prince Turki al Faisal, Saudi Ambassador to the US recently said Americans wanted reforms and change in Saudi society but noted: "we don't mind being criticized. There is a well-known saying in Arabic: Your true friend is one who tells you the truth rather than one who simply agrees with you. But it is the way in which Americans criticize, whether it is politicians or public figures or a thought leader that causes us concern. We often hear political rhetoric and bombast and not constructive commentary". He acknowledged that the Saudi leadership is very much conscious of bringing about reforms in the Kingdom in a gradual manner, "but we're not going to change just because you tell us to. Making dictums leads nowhere. Constructive comments, on the other hand, are more helpful".

Also most external powers with huge stakes in the GCC States quietly keep in touch with some of the civil groups advocating democratization in the GCC states. It is obvious that most GCC regimes are going through severe loss of sovereignty and some even threat of disintegration, civil war and identity crises. Outside support to religious minorities, ethnic groups and to members of former ruling families is becoming sharper in the Gulf region. Abundant oil revenues, underwriting huge welfare policies, give GCC rulers ample power and influence to keep political demands under check. Let us take the examples of Saudi Arabia, Oman and Bahrain. Saudi rulers since the establishment of their Kingdom by King Abdul Aziz in 1932 have been promising their people that they would introduce a representative assembly.

King Saud [1953-64] in his struggle for power with his younger brother Prince Faisal and to appease the "democratic princes" led by Prince Tallal promised several steps towards a democratic and constitutional government. But King Saud finally lost the throne due to the determined efforts of Faisal [1964-75] who succeeded the former in November 1964. Prince Tallal criticized Faisal and his conservative supporters for their opposition to the establishment of a "popularly-elected assembly" and said this group did not "grasp the inexorable developments which will undoubtedly impose themselves". He stressed that Saudi citizens had become disillusioned with one-man rule and emphasized the need to share power and include others in the process of governance through a National Assembly. He warned that those who were opposing the establishment of a Parliament were "opposing the tide of development and tide of history, and time was not on their side".

Prince Tallal also demanded a written constitution because that would enhance the image of the Kingdom rather than saying Quran its Constitution. Faisal not only due to the challenge posed by Prince Tallal and his supporters, but also due to the Yemen war [1962] promised the promulgation of a Basic Law for the government and that a Legislative Council would also become a part of the Basic Law. With no threat to his rule, King Faisal quickly put to rest the promises in this connection. King Khalid in the wake of the Iranian Revolution and subsequent take over of the Mecca mosque by Islamic opponents of the regime seriously broached the idea of creating a Consultative Council. In fact a building for the Parliament was built in Riyadh in 1980. Khomeini's challenge to the Saudi monarchy encouraged the middle class to call for reforms in the political system. The Iran-Iraq war further accentuated this process, as more and more Saudi intellectuals saw the need for democratization of the tribal system. Successive Saudi rulers with enormous oil wealth at their disposal felt little need to turn to other sectors of society to legitimize their rule. The Wahhabi Ulema, traditional ally of the Saudis have been used to enhance the legitimacy of the monarchy. But the Iranian revolution confirmed to many Sunni groups that they too could seize power or at least mount pressure for political reforms. The call for reforms was seen as a challenge by the Saudi rulers and such demands were discouraged and in fact put down rather harshly. King Fahd repeated the promise for political reforms in early 1980's and in order to contain Iran supported Iraq in the Gulf war. During the Kuwait crisis Fahd sought the help of US military forces.

The presence of outside military forces posed a serious challenge to the legitimacy of the Saudis and also exposed their fragility and their weakness. Successive coups and challenges to Saudi rule have only made the Saudi regime more authoritarian and oppressive. Unwilling to share power and opposed to peoples participation in the decision making and having a narrow social base, the Saudi rulers in order to retain power widely use coercion and repression to silence the citizens. Not only the Saudi ruling elites are opposed to greater public participation they are also not interested in distributing oil wealth more evenly and widely [and restricting House of Saud expenses].

In fact oil revenues are used to neutralize opposition and consolidate the ruling family. In the wake of the Kuwait crisis there are two instances to show the assertive nature of the Saudi middle class. In November 1990 Saudi women [about 200] in an exceedingly rare public demonstration, set out to drive their cars in clear defiance of the ban imposed by the authorities against women driving cars. This was the first public act of defiance by Saudi women against their country's strict conservative customs which severely limit the rights of women, to appear in public or mix with men. Saudi women, who must be veiled, are not free to move anywhere unless permitted by husbands or male relatives. As expected the police cracked down on the violators and women drivers were stopped and detained. The second instance arose on 12 April 1991 when several key Saudi figures including 43 intellectuals and businessmen sent an open letter to King Fahd urging him to initiate steps towards political reforms like establishing national and municipal councils, changes in the field of human rights, right to vote for women, judicial reforms, creation of representative rule making assembly, change to constitutional monarchy, creation of political parties, freedom of expression and of the press. Immediately the Saudi ulema came out with their own memorandum for Islamic reforms.

On May 18 1991 a group of about 500 religious scholars presented a petition to King Fahd which among other things demanded the following: Consultative Council, greater Islamisation, fundamental changes of the army and arms purchases, equitable distribution of resources, radical judicial reforms and opposition to pacts and treaties with the West. The petition was a historic turning point in the struggle for political change in Saudi Arabia. The petitions were followed by demonstrations and political disturbances and crackdown on religious dissidents. It is in this background of petitions from intellectuals, businessmen and clergy together with the assertiveness and restive behaviour of the latter which finally propelled King Fahd to announce on March, 1, 1992 steps towards democratization and sharing of power. He announced the 83 article Saudi Basic System which defines the structure of government, administration of Justice and the role of Majlis al Shura.

The Majlis as King Fahd said would be "a partnership between the base and the Summit". King Fahd's determination not to go beyond political participation, in the context of the petitioner appearing before the King, his Majlis was clear from his interview with the Kuwaiti newspaper *Al Siyasa*, on March 28, 1992, when he said that the "prevailing democratic system in the world", was not suitable for his country and the region and that Islam favoured "the consultative system and the openness" between the ruler and his subjects rather than the free elections which might be suitable for other states. King Fahd's efforts to create new institutional structures to deal with the rising problems were aimed at neutralizing potential threats to its authority rather than mobilizing support for their rule.

In the background of the political reforms announced yet another petition [September 1992] the fourth since the Kuwait crisis signed by 109 members was presented to King Fahd. This included leading academics and well known figures from the Kingdom's three main Islamic groups. The 45 page document known in the Kingdom as the *nasiha* or memorandum covers most areas of the country's political life, including foreign relations, monetary policies, social services and the high oil production rates. It was called an election manifesto. The document was especially critical of the House of Saud, accusing the ruling family of corruption in handling of state finances. The petitioners asked for an annual audit of government expenditure to check "embezzlement and corruption".

It also called for an end to the construction of royal palaces from public funds and the monopoly of land ownership by a "certain elite". More significantly, in the field of foreign relations, it called on the government to end its special relationship with the US and put more emphasis on relations with Islamic states. Aid should stop to those Muslim states which oppose the more revolutionary Islamic movements in the Arab world, it demanded. The major outcome had been the Majlis al Shura whose membership initially was 60 then 90 and now 120 along with the speaker. One major reason why political conflict was virtually absent in the Kingdom was the manner in which the Saudi Kings showered their subjects with money and so no political opposition was serious. But having promised repeatedly since 1928 by the Saudi rulers about a representative Parliament and having failed to develop any institutional support, the Saudi family is seen as directly responsible for the state of the economy and the inequities in the distribution of wealth and power. The Saudi citizens quite rightly hold the ruling family responsible for creating artificial and unjust differences in a society that believes it to be primarily egalitarian.

In Oman on 23 July 1970 the British engineered a coup which replaced Said bin Taimur by the present ruler Sultan Qaboos. The major task before Qaboos was the rebellion in Dhofar province which was finally suppressed on 11 December 1975 with the help of Iran, Jordan and Britain. Despite low level of literacy [30 percent] Qaboos was concerned with the implications of Iranian revolution. Despite Qaboos' stand that any attempt to create political structures in the absence of competent people and modernization is futile, he decided on November 3, 1981, to have the State Consultative Council [SCC]—a 45 member house with a Chairman. All the members were personally appointed by the Sultan to the SCC who could send opinions and recommendations to the Ruler. In 1983 SCC membership was expanded to 55. A new Majlis was established by November 25, 1991 with 59 members one each from the 59 Wilayats plus a Chairman. A list of three candidates indirectly selected from the Wilayat in which notables, local dignitaries and people of "valued opinion and experience" took part. The list was presented to the Sultan who would choose one member for each Wilayat from the list. The term of membership is three years. Elections were held to the second Majlis in 1994 where for the first time two women were elected for the Majlis. The number of members was increased to 80 in December 1994 and the term to three years. Meanwhile the Sultan promulgated on November 6, 1996 the Basic Statute of 81 articles covering-the state and the system of government, the principles guiding the state policy, the political, economic, social, and cultural and security principles. Elections for the third Majlis were held in October 1997 for the 82 seats from 59 Wilayats.

Women were for the first time allowed to vote and stand for election throughout the conservative Arab Gulf state. Two women were among 164 candidates who were elected. The Majlis can review, discuss and advise on all social, cultural, educational, economic draft laws, prepared by the Ministries before their enactment. It can also evaluate state development plans and can recommend amendments by a two–third vote. But it is barred from reviewing foreign and defence policy issues and cannot question ministers on these areas. Elections have been held since then regularly every three years for the Majlis. We must also keep in mind Oman's growing population especially the fact that 40 percent of the population is under 15 years of age. Despite announcements of new Omanisation targets and creation of job opportunities, unemployment figures are as high as 25 percent. Few private companies were willing to employ Omani nationals due to lack of skills. For instance South Asian expatriates in Oman were available for as little as 60 Omani Riyals (US$ 200) a month, whereas the minimum wage for an Omani Secondary School Graduate was closer to 200 Omani Riyals (US$ 650). This large young population and lack of job opportunities together with lack of genuine steps towards political participation (democratization) is leading to growing role from the Islamists and challenge to the existing political order.

It is in this backdrop one should view the 1994 challenge in which large number of Omani's were arrested many of whom were accused of forming an illegal Political Party procuring arms and conspiring with foreign fundamentalist groups to undermine state security and topple the regime. Defendants included people like the designated Ambassador to the US, Under Secretary at the Ministry of Commerce and Industry, businessmen, School Principals, engineers, entrepreneurs and merchants.

It is interesting to note that the pamphlets of the accused called for reforms on major foreign policy issues as well as radical changes in the economic policies. The second challenge came in late 2004 and early 2005 when Omani police arrested more than 300 suspects and seized arms. Apparently the popular Muscat Festival was the target. Bombings were also planned for Eid al Adha celebrations in Rustaq province, where Sultan Qaboos was to attend. It was reported that among those arrested were Professors at the Sultan Qaboos University and religious officials affiliated with the Theology College as well. Later it was reported that several lecturers, ministries of Health and education staff members, Petroleum Development Oman [PDO] engineers, ministry of religious affairs consultants and managers at the Diwan of the royal court and several military officials were also apprehended. Most were thought to be from the Nizwa region but no connection existed with Al-Qaeda. On May 2, 2005, the state security court delivered the final verdicts. Thirty men were convicted of plotting to "overthrow the regime by force of arms and replace it by an Imamate, by setting up a banned underground organization". It was reported that the Sultan commuted these judgments on June 9, 2005, just as he did for those convicted in the 1994 plot. It seems few hundred supporters of the group staged a peaceful march in Muscat a few days before sentences were announced, demanding full acquittal.

Soon after Bahrain's independence from the British on 14 August 1971, it came to have a written constitution which came into effect on December 6, 1973. Elections to the 30 member National Assembly [NA] took place on 7 December 1973. Unfortunately the Cabinet and the National Assembly could not cooperate on a number of issues including the refusal by all the members to ratify the draft State Security Decree and extension of the lease for US naval base which prompted the PM to publicly complain that the NA was obstructing the government from discharging its functions. The deadlock led to the suspension of the NA in August 1975. Subsequently the Amir enacted the law through an Amiri decree. The constitution was also suspended and some of the NA members were arrested.

The PM Sheikh Khalifah Salman ruled Bahrain through a tough policy using intimidation and repression, with violations of human rights and deportations being common. Bahrain is unique among the GCC states as majority of its citizens are Shia and the 1979 Iranian Revolution and the subsequent Iran-Iraq war certainly increased the level of mistrust with the Sunnis including the ruling Al Khalifahs. Concerns related to employment opportunities, corruption, treatment of opposition members and restoration of the NA became major issues during much of the period since 1975 up to the death of Amir Isa bin Salman in early 1999. The accession of his son Sheikh

Hamad led to improvement in the political situation. The new ruler soon released political detainees and held a referendum on 15 February 2001 to approve a National Charter. On 14 February 2002 Bahrain was made a constitutional Monarchy and the Amir became King. Soon he decided to hold municipal elections and in October 2002 elections to the 40 member Council of Deputies [Lower House] were held in which women also took part although no women were elected. The king opted for a bi cameral Parliament and the Upper Chamber known as Shura Council, has 40 members who are appointed by the King. It is purely an advisory body originally established in 1992. Interestingly if the two chambers disagreed the Lower house will not have precedence because if the lower house disagreed a joint sitting will take place in which two–thirds majority of both the houses can pass any legislation or any act.

The King can amend the constitution and pass laws by decree any time thereby curtailing the Parliament's powers. Some opposition groups boycotted the 2002 elections like the National Accord, Association of the Shias, National Democratic Action Society [secular]; National Democratic Rally and the Islamic Action Association. Elections were held for Lower House on November 25, 2006. One women candidate was already declared unopposed.

To conclude, democratization, if successful and sustained can produce accountable, transparent, participatory, inclusive governance, instead of exclusive and repressive rule. What the GCC leaders have opted for is not the immediate establishment of full-fledged liberal democracy, but a gradual process toward participation in the political and economic life and governance of the country, in harmony with Islam. In other words, gradual and controlled democratization should involve participation at the grass-roots level. Benefits of democratization apart from developing a vibrant civic culture should be in the form of more equitable, accountable, transparent and good governance by all and for all. Patterns of democratization [could be top-down vs. bottom up, or immediate vs. gradual]; costs and benefits; barriers to and support; internal and external factors; ties between Islam and Islamic groups and democratization. But genuine democratization enshrined and consolidated in both constitutional arrangements and political practices, is rare. Amin Saikal argues that some forms of popular representation and electoral legitimacy are far from sufficient to proclaim democratic governance and are often simply used to practice what is no more than concealed authoritarianism Democratization should involve an avenue for active participation in national decision–making processes, further entrenchment of popular participation in the political process and public demands for fair, legitimate and representative governance which should strengthen democratic structures. Islamic forces may in the long run be "co-opted" or enticed into democratic processes.

Due to colonialism and top-down political rule the democratization process is limited as it did not result in the creation of a broad-based civic culture and democratic political institutions and processes. Democratization usually takes a top-down approach, which is applied arbitrarily and is hostage to internal and regional forces. Political and social mobilization coupled with rise of Islamic groups all of which is induced by urbanization, literacy, media exposure and a young population has not kept pace with the required basic structures for political participation like parties, trade unions, voluntary associations and free elections. For all practical purposes, democratization is still in its very nascent stage in all the GCC states. Foreign powers are the hurdles for democratization which if it were to be removed would involve broadening and deepening of political participation, like popular sovereignty, electoral representation and civil liberties would constitute political democracy. To supplement this, growth in social and cultural democracy is equally essential for democratization to make genuine progress. But in the wake of the fall in oil revenues in the late 1980's and especially after the 1991 war over Kuwait, one noticed demands for political participation. Before the Iranian Revolution the prospects for democracy in GCC states were dim but the revolutionary changes in Iran prompted Gulf rulers to initiate modest political reforms and promise democratization of their absolute monarchies.

However, in the final analysis, despite mounting discontent and frustration, the GCC rulers have been able to quite adroitly maintain the political *status quo* with a judicious combination of cosmetic political changes [without however weakening their stranglehold over their power base], strong internal security structures and expanding military linkages with the US/ West.

References

Aarts, Paul, "Post-War Kuwait and the Process of Democratization: The Persistence of Political Tribalism", in Abbas Abdelkarim, ed. *Change and Development in the Gulf* (London: Macmillan, 1999): pp. 213-237.

— and Gred Nonneman, (eds. *Saudi Arabia in the Balance: Political Economy, Society and Foreign Affairs,* (London: Hurst & Co, 2005).

— *The Limits of Political Tribalism: Post-War Kuwait* [1995].

Abir, Mordechei, *Saudi Arabia: Government, Society and the Gulf Crisis* (London: 1993).

Abdo Baaklini, et al., *Legislative Politics in the Arab World: The Resurgence of Democratic Institutions,* [Boulder: Lynne Rienner, 1999].

Aburish, SK, *The Rise, Corruption and Coming Fall of the House of Saud* (London: 1994).

Ahmad, Talmiz, *Reform in the Arab World: External Influences and Regional Debates* (New Delhi: India Research Press, 2005).

Alexander Bligh, "The interplay between opposition activity in Saudi Arabia and recent trends in the Arab World", in Robert W. Stookey, ed., *The Arabian Peninsula: Zone of Ferment* (Stanford: 1984) pp.65-78.

Assiri, Abdul Reda, *The Government and Politics of Kuwait: Principles and Practices (*Kuwait: 1980).

Ansari, Shahid Jamal, *Political Modernization in the Gulf* (New

Delhi: Northern Book Centre, 1998).

Ayubi, Nazih N., *Over-Stating the Arab State: Politics and Society in the Middle East* (London: IB Tauris, 2006) pp.123-134; and 224-255; MS Doran, "The Saudi Paradox", *FA,* 83, 1. 2004, pp.35-51.

Augustus R Norton, Ed, *Civil Society in the Middle East*, Vols.1-2, (Leiden: EJ Brill, 1995-96).

Brynen, Rex, Bahgat Korany, Paul Noble, ed., *Political Liberalization and Democratization in the Arab world, Vol.1, Theoretical Perspectives*, (Boulder and London: Lynne Rienner. 1995) pp.3-60; 283-306.

Christopher Norris, *Uncritical Theory: Postmodernism, Intellectuals and the Gulf*, (Amherst: The University of Massachusetts Press, 1992).

Crystal, Jill, *Oil and Politics in the Gulf: Rulers and Merchants in Kuwait and Qatar* (Cambridge: CUP, 1990).

— *Kuwait: The Transformation of an Oil State* (Boulder: 1992); "Authoritarianism and its Adversaries in the Arab World", *World Politics*, Vol.46, January, 1994, pp.262-289.

David Graham and Mark Tessler, ed., *Democracy, War and Peace in the Middle East* (Indiana University Press, 1995).

Dale F. Eickelman, "Bin Laden, the Arab "Street", and the Middle East's Democracy Deficit", *Current History*, January 2002.

Daniel L. Byman and Jerrold d Green, "The enigma of Political stability in the Persian Gulf Monarchies", *Middle East Review of International Affairs*, Vol. 3, No.3, September 1999.

Daryl Champion, *The Paradoxical Kingdom: Saudi Arabia and the Momentum of Reform* (London: Hurst and Co, 2003).

Diamond, Larry, Marc F. Plattner and Daniel Brumburg ed., *Islam, Democracy in the Middle East,* (Baltimore and London: The Johns Hopkins University press, 2003) pp.76-90.

Ellen Lust Okar, *Structuring Conflict in the Arab World: Incumbents, Opponents and Institutions,* (Cambridge, UK: CUP, 2005).

— and Amaney Ahmad Jamal, "Rulers and Rules: Reassessing the influence of Regime type on electoral Law Formation", *Comparative Political Studies*, Vol. 35, No. 3, 2002, pp. 337-365.

Eleanor Doumato and Marsha p. Posusney, eds., *Women and Globalization in the Arab Middle East: Gender, Economy and Society;* (Boulder: Lynne Rienner, 2003).

Eric Rouleau, "Trouble in the Kingdom", *Foreign Affairs*, Vol. 81, no.4, July-August 2002.

Gulf Research Centre, Year Book, 2006-07 (Dubai).

Gwenn Okruhlik, "Networks of Dissent: Islamism and Reform in Saudi Arabia", *Current History,* January 2002.

G Dietl, G. Pant, AK Pasha and PC Jain Ed; *Contemporary Saudi Arabia and the Emerging Indo-Saudi Relations* (New Delhi: Manak Publications, 2007).

Gause III, F. Gregory, *Oil Monarchies: Domestic and Security Challenges in the Arab Gulf States* (New York: Council on Foreign Relations, 1994); Laith Kubba, "Arabs and Democracy: The Awakening of Civil Society", *Journal of Democracy*, Vol. 11, No. 3, July 2000, pp.84-90; Vickie Langohr, "An Exit from Arab Autocracy', *Journal of Democracy*, Vol. 13, No. 3, July 2002, pp.116-122.

HE Chehabi and Juan J. Linz, eds., *Sultanistic Regimes*, (Baltimore: Johns Hopkins University, 1998).

Hardy, Roger, *Arabia after the Storm: Internal Stability of Gulf Arab states* (London: RIIA, 1992).

Herb, Michael, *All in the Family: Absolutism, revolution and Democracy in the Middle Eastern Monarchies* (Albany: State University of New York Press, 1999).

Haya al Mughni, *Women in Kuwait: The Politics of Gender*, (London: Saqi, 2001).

Halliday, Fred, *Arabia without Sultans* (London: 1974).

— *Nation and Religion in the Middle East* (London: Saqi, 2000).

Hudson, Michael C., "State, Society and Legitimacy: An Essay on Arab Political Prospects in the 1990's", in Hisham Sharabi, ed., *The Next Arab Decade: Alternative Futures*, (Boulder: Westview, 1988) pp.22-27.

Marsha P. Posusney, "Behind the Ballot Box: Electoral Engineering in the Arab World", *Middle East Report*, 209, winter 1998 pp. 12-15;

— and MP Angrist, eds. *Authoritarianism in the Middle East: Regimes and Resistance* (Boulder: Lynne Rienner, 2005).

Mamoun Fandy, *Saudi Arabia and the Politics of Dissent* (New York: St. Martins Press, 1999).

MIT, *The Crisis of Governance in the Gulf: Legitimacy and Stability in a Dark Time*, CIS, 2006.

Mohammed al-Mutawa, ed., *Globalization and the Gulf* (London;

Routledge, 2006) pp.127-140.

M Steven Fish, "Islam and Authoritarianism", *World Politics*, Vol. 55, October 2004, pp.4-37; Barbara Geddes, "What do we know about Democratization after 20 years?" *Annual Review of Political Science*, Vol. 2, 1999, pp. 115-144; *Human Rights Watch*, "Opportunism in the face of tragedy: Repression in the name of anti-terrorism", New York, 2002;

Michael Ross L, "Does Oil hinder Democracy?" *World Politics*, Vol. 53, No. 3, 2001, pp. 325-361; Mohamed Talbi, Arabs and Democracy: a record of Failures", *Journal of Democracy*, 11, 3, July 2000, pp.58-68.

Madawi al Rasheed, "The Shia of Saudi Arabia: A Minority in Search of Cultural Authenticity", *British Journal of Middle Eastern Studies*, Vol. 25, No.1, 1998.

— *A History of Saudi Arabia* (London: CUP, 2002).

Naqeeb, Khaldoun Hasan el, *Society and State in the Gulf and Arab Peninsula: A Different Perspective,* (London: 1990); See also "Social Origins of the Authoritarian state in the Arab State", in Eric Davis and N Gavrielides, ed., *Statecraft in the Middle East* (Florida International University Press, 1991).

— "Globalization, Politics and Identity in the Arab World", in John W Fox and Nada Mourtada Sabbah.

Nimrod Raphaeli, "Demands for reforms in Saudi Arabia", *MES*, Vol. 41, No.4, July 2005; Anoushiravan Ehteshami, "Reform from Above: The Politics of Participation in oil Monarchies", *International Affairs*, Vol.79, No,1, 2003; Asad Abu Khalil, "Change and Democratization in the Arab World: The Role of Political Parties", *TWQ,* Vol. 18, No.1, 1997, pp.14-63; Lisa Anderson, "Arab Democracy: Dismal Prospects", *World Policy Journal,* Vol. 18, no.3, 2001, pp. 53-60.

Niblock, Tim, and E. Murphy, eds., *Economic and Political Liberalization in the Middle East,* (London: British Academic press, 1993).

Peter W. Wilson and Douglas F. Graham, *Saudi Arabia: The Coming Storm* (New York: ME Sharpe, 1994).

Peterson, JE, *The Arab Gulf States: Steps towards Political Participation* (New York: Prager, 1988).

Pasha, AK, *Aspects of Political Participation in the Gulf States*, (New Delhi: 1999).

— *Kuwait: Struggle for Survival* (New Delhi: Har Anand, 1995).

— "Effects of the Gulf war on Political formations in West Asia", *Détente*, Vol., ix, No. 6, March-June 1991, pp.1-5.

— "Recent Political Reforms in Saudi Arabia", *Journal of West Asian Studies*, (Aligarh) No. 9, 1993, pp.69-89.

— "Demography, Political Reforms and Opposition in GCC States", in G. Pant, ed., *The West Asian Political Economy: Demography, Democracy and Economic Reforms*, (New Delhi: Manak, 1994) pp.67-100.

— "The Struggle for Democracy and Political Change in the Post-War Gulf", in KR Singh ed., *Post-War Gulf: Implications for India*, (New Delhi: Lancers Books, 1993), pp.53-90.

— "Kuwait after Liberation: Stability or Turmoil", in AK Pasha, ed., *The Gulf in Turmoil: A Global Response*, (New Delhi: Lancers Books, 1992) pp.339-374.

— "The Struggle for Political Participation in Bahrain" and "Qatar: Independence to Dependence", in AK Pasha Ed., *India, Bahrain and Qatar: Political, Economic and Strategic Dimensions,* (Delhi: Gyan Sagar, 1999) pp. 1-9; 105-112.

— "Political Development in Oman", in AK Pasha Ed., *India and Oman: History, State, Economy and Foreign Policy* (Delhi: Gyan Sagar, 1999) pp.110-21.

— "Political System of Kuwait", in AK Pasha, Ed, *India and Kuwait: Strategic, Economic and Political Developments* (Delhi: Gyan Sagar, 1999) pp. 1-13.

— "Political Reforms in GCC States", *Sunday Mail* (New Delhi) December 20- 26, 1992, p. 1.

— "Power Struggle in Saudi Arabia", *Sunday Mail,* (Bombay) 10-16 January 1993.

— "Iraq and Political Conflict in Kuwait", *Détente*, Vol., X, No.1, July-August, 1991, pp.1-11 and 17.

— "Kuwait Today", *Link*, November 24, 1991, pp. 31-32.

— "GCC States Move Closer to West", *Sunday Mail*, 18-24 April 1993. p.11.

— 'Kuwait's Return to Democracy", *Sunday Mail*, November 29-December 5, 1992, p.10.

— "Kuwait after Elections: Democracy or Deluge?" *The Pioneer*, October 9, 1992.

— "Kuwait: Slow but Sure March to Democracy", *The Times of India*, February 25, 1993.

— "Security and Stability in West Asia and Gulf", in Alokesh Barua, ed., *Global Order: Recent Changes and Global Responses*, (New Delhi: Lancers Books, 1992), pp. 166-86.

— "Peace in the Gulf: GCC Perceptions", *Strategic Analysis*, Vol. XII, No.9, December 1988, pp.1025-1056.

— "The Kuwait Crisis: GCC Response", in AHH Abidi and KR Singh, ed., *The Gulf Crisis*, (New Delhi: Lancers Books, 1991) pp. 106-155.

— "Aspects of Political Participation in GCC States", and "The Role of Gulf States in the Arab-Israeli Peace Process", and "Iraq: Foreign Intervention and Regime Survival", in AK Pasha, Ed, *Contemporary Gulf: State, Society, Economy and Foreign Policy*, (New Delhi: Détente Publications, 1999).

— "Iraq and the GCC", *Third Concept* (New Delhi) November 1998, pp. 22-25.

— *India and the Islamic World* (New Delhi: Radiant Publishers, 1998) Co-edited with Riyaz Punjabi.

— *India and West Asia: Continuity and Change* (Delhi: Gyan Sager Publications, 1999).

— *Perspectives on India and the Gulf States* (New Delhi: Détente Publications, 1999); editor.

— *India, Iran and the GCC States: Political Strategy and Foreign Policy*, (New Delhi: Manas Publications: 2000); editor.

— *Iran, Iraq and the GCC States* (Delhi: Academic Excellence, 2009).

— "India and West Asia: Past and Future", in NS Sisodia and Ashok K Behuria, eds., *West Asia in Turmoil: Implications for Global Security*, (New Delhi: Academic Foundation, 2007) pp. 441-470.

— "India and the Gulf: An Overview", in Second *Netaji Subhas Commemorative Souvenir, INA Trust,* New Delhi, January 2008, pp.11-27.

— "India's Policy towards the Persian Gulf" in G. Kishore Babu, Ed, *India's Foreign Policy: Continuity and Change,* (Delhi: Academic Excellence, 2008) pp. 215-247. World Focus Series-Two.

— "India's West Asia Policy: Continuity and Change", *Strategic Analysis*, vol. XVI, no.6, September 1992, pp. 783-804.

— "Perspectives on Indo-Saudi Relations", *Asian Affairs*, Vol.1, No.12, September 1997, pp. 24-26.

— "India, Iran and the GCC States: Common Political and Strategic Concerns", *Encounter,* March, April 1998, pp. 66-74.

— "India and the GCC States: Challenges and Opportunities", *World Focus*, Vol. 24, No.2, (278) February 2003 pp. 9-15.

— "Why is the Islamic World Important for India? *Hard news*, Vol.1, Issue, 7, June 2004, pp. 56-57.

— "India and West Asia", *World Focus*, Vol. 25, October-December 2004, pp. 41-46.

— "India, Iran and its Regional Influence", *World Focus*, Vol. 26, No. 8, (308) August 2005, pp. 3-8.

— "The Iraq Crisis: An Overview", *World Focus*, Vol.25, No.1, January 2004, pp.3-6.

— "Iraq and its Future: An Overview", *World Focus*, Vol. 26, No.2 (302), February 2005, Issue on Iraq and its Future: Doubts and Fears, pp.3-6.

— "Iran and Iraq: Are they Becoming Friends?" *South Asia Politics*, Vol.4, No.5, September 2005, pp. 29-34.

— "Asian Security: Flash Points in the Gulf Region", *World Focus*, Vol. 26, Nos. 10-12, October-December, 2005, pp. 25-33.

— "India-Saudi Ties Ready for a new Dawn", *GCC-India Research Bulletin* (Dubai: UAE) Issue No.1, January 2006, pp. 6-7.

— "India-Oman: Emerging Security Partnership", *GCC-India Research Bulletin*, Issue no. 2, June 2006, pp. 10-11.

— "India and Persian Gulf: An Overview", *World Focus*, Issue on New Dynamics in Persian Gulf, Vol. XXVIII, No.2, (326), February, 2007, pp. 39-45.

— "Indian Perceptions on Persian Gulf", *World Focus*, Vol. XXVIII, Nos.11-12, Nov-Dec, 2007, pp.446-457.

— "Recent Developments in the Gulf Region: An Overview", *World Focus* issue on Persian Gulf, Vol. 39, no.2 (338). February 2008, pp. 43-47.

— "Indo-Saudi Arabian Summit is long over due", *The Pioneer*, 3, August, 1992.

— "50 Years of India's Ties with West Asia", *The Pioneer*, 19August 1997.

— "Relations to a New Dawn", *Arab News* (Jeddah), 26 January 2006. (With N Janardhan)

— "India-Saudi Ties", *Bahrain Tribune*, 20 January 2006. [With NJ]

Rashed Abu Namay, "The Recent Constitutional reforms in Saudi Arabia", *International and Comparative Law Quarterly*, Vol. 42, Part 2, April 1993, pp. 294-331.

R H Dekmejian, "Saudi Arabian Consultative Council", *MEJ,* Vol. 52, No. 2 , Spring 1998, pp. 204-218.

Rugh, William, "Emergence of a New middle Class in Saudi Arabia", *MEJ,* Vol.27, No.1, 1973.

Rumaihi, Mohammed, *Beyond Oil* (London: 1977).

— *Obstacles to Social and Economic Development in Contemporary Societies* (Kuwait: 1977).

Stephane Lacroix, "Between Islamists and Liberals: Saudi Arabia's New 'Islam-Liberal' Reformists", *MEJ*, Vol.58, No.3, Summer 2004.

Snider, Lewis, "Comparing the Strength of Nations: The Arab Gulf States and Political Change", *Comparative Politics*, Vol. 20, No. 4, 1988.

Stookey, Robert W., Ed, *The Arabian Peninsula: Contemporary Politics, Economics and International Relations*, (Stanford, CA: The Hoover Institution, 1984).

Simon Bromley, *Rethinking Middle East Polities*, (Cambridge: Polity Press, 1994) pp.119-154.

— "Autonomy, Necessity and the Small State: Ruling Kuwait in the 20th Century", *International Organization*, Vol. 45, No. 4, Autumn, 1991; Laurence Louer, "Bahrain's Fragile Political Reforms" *Arab Reform Bulletin*, Vol. 2, No. 1, 2004.

Salame, Ghassan Ed, *Democracy without Democrats: The Renewal of Politics in the Muslim World,* (New York: IB Taurus, 1994).

Singh, Gunmeen, *Lifting the Veil: Position of Women in GCC States*, (New Delhi: Samskriti, ORF, 2008).

Tetreault, Mary Ann, *Stories of Democracy: Politics and Society in Contemporary Kuwait* (New York: Columbia University Press, 2000).

— "Designer-Democracy in Kuwait", *Current History*, January 1997.

— "A State of Two Minds: State Cultures, Women and Politics in Kuwait" *IJMES*, Vol. 33, No. 2, 2001, pp. 203-220.

Tim Niblock, *Saudi Arabia: Power, Legitimacy and Survival* (London: Routledge, 2006).

Wenner, Manfred, "Saudi Arabia: Survival of Traditional Elites", in Frank Tachau, ed., *Political Elites and Political Development in the Middle East*, (New York: John Wiley, 1975).

5

Role of Civil Society Organizations in the Economic Integration of the Arab Gulf States

Javed Ahmad Khan

Introduction

The effectiveness of civil society in mediating between the individuals and state can hardly be disputed. In fact, the very idea of public communication is based on the existence of a vibrant civil society. The importance of civil society in the Arab world is underscored by the fact that it has the potential to engender democracy in an authoritarian political milieu. That is why in the contemporary Arab Gulf region, the idea of civil society has become increasingly important. The State officials in the region now use the term 'civil society' to promote their projects of mobilization and modernization. Even the Islamists use it to secure greater legal share of public space and independent activists and intellectuals use it to expand the boundaries of individual liberty.

However, another important dimension worth noting is the emerging civil society's role in the market sector or economic affairs where the significance of Arab world is gaining new momentum in recent years. In addition to their massive oil reserves, the diversification in a newly liberalized investment climate where the global players are entering for the various developmental activities in, make the region the centre of global economic activities. The central argument in this paper is that the civil society organizations are becoming new effective tools in promoting business climate, especially through their professional collaboration with other market and commercial agents across boundaries. One good example of this can be found in the Arab Gulf's economic integration with the developing countries primarily on the basis of economic rationality. In addition, these are being done under the region's privatization drive where the civil society is prominently visible.

The impact of this can also be seen on the Indo-Gulf economic and trade relations where the private participation through the individual organizations is now taking the lead. As a result, a more transparent business climate is beginning to emerge. With the civil society entering the market as significant players, the conflict of interests and rent-seeking attitudes of the policy makers are going down.

Thus, a general consensus is emerging that civil society organizations in the Gulf countries may provide checks on government power because they can help in better governance by enhancing accountability and transparency. In this context, civil society may include industry associations, trade unions, commercial associations, employers' associations, professional associations, media institutions, non-governmental organizations (NGOs), and officially recognized human rights organizations. Similarly, we can also see that the practitioners from the capital markets, banks, public and private sector representatives and other civil society groups have accepted the need to address corporate governance reforms as one of the crucial issues of civil society affecting economic growth and development. [1]

Economic Aspect of Civil Society in Arab World

In order to understand the significance of civil society in the Arab world, it would be worthwhile to know that prior to the advent of the political-economic restructuring of the 1980s, most West Asian countries were largely dominated by either nationalist-populist regimes (such as Egypt, Syria, Iraq and Turkey) or pro-Western rentier states (Iran and Arab Gulf states). Financed by oil or remittances, these largely authoritarian states pursued state-led development strategies. Income from oil offered rentier states the possibility of providing social services to many of their citizens. The ideologically driven populist states dispensed significant benefits in education, health, employment, housing, and in like areas. [2]

Even the region's economists now realize that for a peace full economic development in the Arab world, 'the institutions of civil society—parliament, political parties, trade unions, and interest groups—would play a more effective part in the management of social, political, and economic affairs given that a major justification for the dominant and intrusive state apparatus will be removed. Civil society in general represents the only credible commitment that these states can make as a guarantee against expropriation. [3]

In the Arab region, weakness in inclusiveness are reflected not only in differential business opportunities, with large or privileged firms being awarded contracts or favourable legislation, but also in rural dwellers having fewer public services, in gender inequalities, and in nepotism. Tribal affinity, patronage, or money may determine who has access to public services and who does not. Weaknesses in accountability are reflected in limited access to government information, limited freedom of the press, and restrictions on civil society. Constraints on civil society and non-governmental organization (NGOs), restrictions on the press, and other measures have constrained mobilization. [4] That is why some Arab countries do not have huge investments in joint ventures. There is also a lack of sufficient mechanisms to ease the flow of capital and facilitate funding of joint development projects. [5]

Keeping in view these drawbacks, Arab economists have begun to realize the need for a large civil society to drive the efforts at investment, trade, and economic diversification. The privatization drive has already shown the declining role of governments in some cases. More and more revenues are now utilized by the private sectors, where the civil society is also gaining a foothold. The deepening of civil society is affecting governance mechanism, thereby improving capacity and incentives. That is why, in contemporary times, the ruling family members of the Gulf monarchies are also taking up high-profile positions in civil society organizations, which had in the past been informally considered off limits. Posts in private business and state financial institutions, hitherto reserved for technocrats, are being increasingly filled by the relatives of the ruler. [6]

Arab World 2010 Report, which was released in May 2004 at the World Economic Forum, aimed to galvanize the predominantly young population from across the Arab world to face the challenges the region, namely growing populations, stagnating economies, and large unemployment. The 'Young Arab Leaders Community' envisaged by the Report includes business leaders, government officials, sports personalities, civil society leaders, journalists, musicians, artists and authors.

The importance of civil-political rights, civil society, and economic liberation are now considered as essential for the stability of a country in the international community. Gary Gambrill rightly says that 'economic liberalization usually necessitates some form of political liberalization for several reasons: economic liberalization demands greater political participation from the business community, which has a stake in increasing government accountability. Our contemporary concept of a civil society owes much to the tradition of reflection on social questions that began only with the growth of commercialism. The most cursory look at the concepts of property, tort law, or contracts shows that legal justice and commerce are intimately interconnected. Thus, free enterprise, it seems, is as important to democracy as democratic and civil law is to economic growth.' [7]

Arab Experiment

Civil Society in the Arab world is still in its rudimentary form if we compare it with the existing model in the West or with developing countries such as India where civil society organizations play a vital role in maintaining socio-economic stability. In the Arab world, till as late as the 1990s, civil organizations were mostly charitable organizations providing simply material assistance to needy people. Moreover, the non-Arab developing countries have diversified professional unions, labour unions, charitable societies, religious organizations, free clubs, cultural and technical associations, and neighborhood and area societies. In addition, they have advocacy groups of all kinds, such as, youth and women's organizations, and private-sector trade and industry associations. However, such organizations are yet to flourish in the Arab world.

It is, nevertheless, impossible to copy the development of civil society in the West or elsewhere onto the framework of the Arab world. This is because the historical evolution of civil society is different everywhere. For example, Arabs are generally connected to their rulers and regimes. There are tribal attachments which are hardly practiced in Western types of democratic institutions. Moreover, unlike the Western nations, Arab states are the only guarantor for the tribe. A pure western model of civil society may not be sustainable for Arab social and cultural environment. To understand civil society in the Arab world, we will have to turn to the moral community, and to the problems of accountability, trust and cooperation that all groups face. When we begin to examine how these problems could be overcome, we find tremendous variation in ideas about good government, virtue and responsibility. [8]

Since the human freedom is one of the pillars of civil society, it is rightly argued that preparing proper political and economic environment for establishing civil society must be the first priority for Arab states. However, with the recent economic and political reform initiatives in the Arab countries, a new middle class is emerging. A group of liberal technocrats with human rights awareness—who are determined to establish clearer boundaries between the state and society and greater independence for social and economic institutions—are being increasingly heard. Under such a new liberalized environment, the impact of rentier state on the formation of civil society is seen in negative terms. Revenue in a rentier economy gives state the power to weaken social groups by co-opting their key members. [9]

Religio-Cultural Factors

In recent years, people in Arab countries have been troubled by the 'elusive development' of their economies. Even the oil boom, reports suggest, has not been able to pull them out of economic stagnation. What is the reason behind this state of affairs? A response in the form of a 'return to the civil society institutions that were prevalent in the Arab region', has acquired currency. In yesteryears, economic infrastructure was built not by the state, but by civil society intuitions like the *awakaf* (charitable endowments). Islamists in the Arab world say that the economic recovery of the Muslim world will require free markets, just government, and a well-defined system of private property. In fact, when the colonial powers conquered the Muslim world, they dismantled the civil society institutions and turned their functions over to the state. The state was the only corporate entity they permitted here. [10] Interestingly, the civil society groups have been the main force behind the Islamist ideology. The Islamic movements and activists in West Asia and elsewhere have created both an alternative vision and complimentary non-governmental institutions in the form of schools, hospitals, and clinical society to legal, social and welfare services and professional associations. [11]

John Esposito has rightly pointed out that Islamists have often constituted both an ideological alternative and, on the ground, a state within the state. They have not only challenged but also currently responded to the failures and inadequacies of governments and elites by creating alternative non-governmental political, economic, and social welfare associations and institutions. Across the Arab world, such institutions have proliferated. Islamic bank is a shining example of an alternative institution. In fact, the current wave of Islamic banking was a non-governmental initiative, which later received acceptance of the respective governments. Islamic banks are not in business to make a profit; they are in the business for the good of the society as dictated in Shariah law. As such, they make investments for social purpose and give loans to the poor and needy without any charges. [12]

It is pertinent to ask here whether there are any religious or cultural inhibitions regarding civil society participation in the development of Arab Islamic countries. First and foremost, there are no inherent cultural or historical impediments inhibiting the populace from wanting a say in how their countries should be run. When permitted by governments, citizens form organizations to advance their interests. Some such organizations form around what are usually referred to in the West as 'traditional' bases—tribe and religion. Institutions emerging out of these bases have shown remarkable flexibility in adjusting to the circumstances of large bureaucratic states, modern technologies, and dramatically changed economies. Other civil society organizations have developed along more 'modern' functional lines. [13]

In fact, Islamic history provides examples of many non-state actors, institutions, and organizations that serve as intermediaries between the ruler/government and the people, between state and society. Religious endowments (*awqaf*) supported schools, universities, hostels, hospitals, and social welfare activities are examples. Civil society organizations have played an important role in the economic and social life of Muslim cities. Professional groups or guilds were organized around trade and commerce. Their activities included, 'regulating the production of goods, maintaining a professional code or civil society. Guilds often relied upon religion and religious rituals for rites of initiation and celebration and to legitimate their origins and activities, which was that of the market supervisor (*muhtasib*) who was responsible for the enforcement (*hisbah*) of public morals.' [14]

Drawing inspiration from the early Islamic period, the current upsurge in Islamic economic institutions can be seen as effective non-governmental institutions in the Arab Gulf, which carry on economic activities in accordance with the socio-cultural aspiration of the people of the region. In the oil rich Gulf States, Islamic organizations and associations have become part and parcel of the mainstream institutional forces in civil society. They have attracted members from the middle and lower middle classes (businessmen, bureaucrats, doctors, engineers, lawyers, journalists) and revenues from non-governmental domestic sources. [15]

However, the Arab world's present economic and political slow down cannot be fully attributed to the low profile of their civil society. Even the *Arab Human Development Report* (2005) has said that no Arab country, with a few exceptions, is now without a parliament or a cabinet or a local council where people, especially women can participate in an enabling manner. Moreover, progress towards political reform continues to be erratic and the gap between reality and the aspirations of the vital forces in the Arab countries continues to widen as a result of both the slowness of reform and the invigoration of civil society. [16] The state-civil society relations in the Arab world can be assessed from the fact that calls for political reform have come individuals and groupings within society which have no formal links with those in power. [17]

However, in the economic reform era, Arab regimes have started responding to the crisis by transferring economic functions to the private sector and education and welfare to the civil society. Hence, the role of civil society is increasingly becoming more important. As the state retreats, civil society advances, although it does not always occupy all the vacated ground. Voluntary associations bring in doctors, lawyers, journalists, and other professionals, whose growing wealth and sophistication, enable them to act independently. [18]

The effects of economic modernization and the expansion of civil society should not be underestimated. The impact of this freedom can be seen in the financial market of the region where the Arab investors make a choice to place their surplus funds in and out of the region in the form of private equity. [19] Here, the ordinary citizens are participating in economic activities through the privatization drive. One can see that in the Gulf region encouragement for free enterprises is gathering steam. Thus, the economic functions once performed by government agencies are now being fully or partially delegated to citizens and corporations, making for a more self-regulated civil society.

Another vital aspect worth watching is the mix of religio-cultural aspect in the organizational network of economic activities. For example, the Islamic financial institutions, the world Halal Forum, and the World Zakah Forum are new developments in this area and have been established not only to strengthen the charity works in and outside the region but also to establish alternative economic schemes based on cultural values. Observers say that while Islamic societies have adapted to modern marketing practices, they have yet to achieve an organic balance between consumerism and the Islamic values that bind these society together. In Arab Islamic societies, however, there exists a serious challenges and tension caused by the prevalent economic forces attempting to dominate the cultural and religious components of these societies. Others claim that 'Islamic society' would purify society, promote cultural progress, and provide universal justice. Islamization, they maintain, is the sole remedy for the ills afflicting contemporary Muslim nations. Many believe that an Islamic society, unlike a 'civil society', would be based on narrow religious ideology and would, by definition, concentrate too much power in the bands of the ulama and their associates. Such a religious administration, they claim, would be inherently authoritarian. Thus, rather than providing a solution for the problems of the modern world, Islamic administration would pose a dangerous threat to the civil liberty of Muslims [20]

Civil Society and Scope of Economic Reforms in the Arab World

Are Arab leaders reluctant to implement reform following the recent economic boom? There is a growing acceptance among prominent Arab leaders that only a comprehensive economic reform will enable the region to broaden its sources of growth and propel its development agenda forward. But what should be the priorities of the leaders as they embark on a process of reform? According to the Arab World Competitiveness Report, the region is at a crossroads and far-reaching reforms are required, including diversification and greater participation by the private sector. In this context, the civil society in Arab countries has much higher expectations today with regard to governments and their ability to deliver services and to be competent in macroeconomic management. What should top the Arab economic reform agenda? Although the leaders in the region are becoming more cognizant of the urgency for reform, the question is how can the private sector and civil society maintain pressure on governments to take into account the needs of the region's youth? It is generally accepted that the private sector and civil society must work in partnership with governments to plan for the long term. This has an economic rationale: if the transition from public sector- to private sector-driven development is to take place, there will have to be major improvements in the investment climate and better governance throughout the region.

Now, if the Arab countries were to become more attractive to FDI, one major attention should be paid to the creation or improvement of adequate market institutions, that would facilitate the influx of new technologies, increase access to international markets, and create desperately needed new employment opportunities. Moreover, the goal of combating corruption is yet to become a priority on the agenda of Arab governments. But all this can only be accomplished when the relationship between citizens and the state is strengthened through popular participation in decision-making, the establishment of alliances between governments and legislative bodies on the one hand and the private sector and civil society organizations on the other, ensuring the independence of public institutions, and embarking on a balanced development plan.

Promoting Indo-Arab Economic Relations

In this age of economic integration, when Arab regimes are searching business partners around the globe and that too, on the basis of economies of scale and competitiveness, the expansion of autonomous civil society institutions can serve as the basis for more participatory commercial activities. A number of Gulf regimes, recognizing the civil society have taken steps toward opening up their political and economic system. The goal of such steps should not be democracy in and of itself, but stable political evolution toward more participatory polities.

How far is this relevant in today's India-Arab economic and business partnership? To begin with Arab region has not been successful in integrating with the world economy, and private investment has not responded adequately here. One of the reasons among many others is that the civil society – comprising large sections of public sector employees, unions, civil society, media opinion leaders, and private enterprises – remains deeply wedded to the security and benefits of the old order. Since the oil-rich Gulf countries have a more complicated task in shifting from state-dominated and protectionist economic systems to open market systems, there is need for strong consensus and support from the private investment community, civil society, and others that reforms are urgent and needed. [21]

The current Indo-Gulf economic relation now hinges more on the civil society's role in promoting the economic interests of the two regions. The economic reforms initiatives in both the regions, especially since early 1990s, have given much more space to civil society groups, to be able to play an effective role. At present, both inside and outside Gulf region, international organizations, business groups, and civil society organizations are engaged in financing network as a private sector driven initiative. They encourage the involvement of business representatives of civil society in discussions with the respective governments on the improvement of the investment environment, including the issue of responsible business conduct. It is rightly seen that 'the investment reform agenda in the West Asian region should be flexible to accommodate each country's requirements.' Proposed reforms should be accompanied by a dialogue with business and civil society and the 'participating countries should adopt the policy of encouragement of established business and civil society representatives to act as advocates of investment policy reform.' [22]

Conclusion

Despite the existence of civil society in the Arab world, its activities in the public arena is limited as compared to other developing countries. However, in view of the on-going political and economic reform initiatives by the Gulf States, civil society organizations are increasingly gaining a foothold in the region and are progressively playing important roles in the integration of the Arab economies with other regions of the world, especially Asia. Their current engagement with both the public and private sectors is a positive development at a time when the Gulf regimes are in the process of economic liberalization. Civil society can be more effective in the expansion of financial and entrepreneurial activities. Additionally, the Islamist groups in the Gulf region through various religious and cultural institutions are also contributing to the revitalization of civil society and enhancing the political liberalization. Moreover, civil society organizations under the religio-cultural banners have also consistently raised their voice against the pro-West policies of the Arab states, which have proved to be ineffective in the economic development of the region.

Notes

1. Saed Karajah, "Civil Society in the Arab World: The Missing Concept", *The International Journal of Not-for Profit Law*, Vol. 9, Issue 2 (April 2007), pp. 25-26.
2. Asef Bayat, 'Activism And Social Development In The Middle East', *International Journal of Middle East Studies*, Vol. 34, Issue 2 (May 2002), p. 187.
3. Stanley Fischer, Dani Rodrik, Elias H. Tuma, *The Economic of Middle East Peace: Views from the Region* (Cambridge: MIT Press, 1993), p. 29.
4. Mustapha Kamel Nabli, *Breaking the Barriers to Higher Economic Growth: Better Governance and Deeper Reforms in the Middle East and North Africa* (Washington D.C.: World Bank Publications, 2008), p. 96.
5. Samir Ghawi, 'Need for building new economic model in Arab World', *Jordan Times*, September 7, 1998.
6. Mustapha Kamel Nabli, *Breaking the Barriers to Higher Economic Growth: Better Governance and Deeper Reforms in the Middle East and North Africa* (Washigton D.C.: World Bank Publications, 2008), p. 22.
7. Nicholas Capaldi, *Business and Religion: A Clash of Civilizations?* (Salem, M.A.: M & M Scrivener Press, 2005), p. 359.
8. C. M. Hann, Elizabeth Dunn, *Civil Society: Challenging Western Models* (London: Routledge, 1996), p.19.
9. Augustus Richard Norton (ed.), *Civil Society in the Middle East*, Volume 2 (Leiden: E.J. Brill, 2001), p. 260.
10. Imam Dean Ahmad, "Islam, Commerce and Business Ethicivil society', in op. cit., Capaldi, 2005, p. 9.
11. Op. cit., Norton, 2001, p.6.
12. John L. Esposito, François Burgat, *Modernising Islam: Religion in the Public Sphere in the Middle East and Europe* (London: C. Hurst & Co. Publishers, 2003), p. 6.

13. F. Gregory Gause, *Oil Monarchies: Domestic and Security Challenges in the Arab Gulf States* (New York: Council on Foreign Relations, 1994), p.74.
14. See Rodney Wilson, *The History of Islamic Economic*s (Leiden: E.J. Brill, 2008), chapters 1-4.
15. Munawar Iqbal, 'International Islamic Financial Institutions", M. Kabir Hassan and Mervyn K. Lewis (eds.), *Handbook of Islamic Banking* (Northampton, MA: Edward Elgar, 2007), pp. 361-383.
16. United Nations Development Programme, Arab Fund for Economic and Social Development, *The Arab Human Development Report 2005: Towards the Rise of Women in the Arab* World (Palo Alto: Stanford University Press, 2007), p. 51.
17. Tim Niblock, *Saudi Arabia: Power, Legitimacy and Survival* (London: Routledge, 2006), p. 90.
18. Emmanuel Sivan, 'Constraints & Opportunities in the Arab World', *Journal of Democracy*, Vol.8, No. 2 (Spring/Summer 1997), p. 104.
19. Harik, Iliya F. 'Pluralism in the Arab World', *Journal of Democracy* Volume 5, Number 3, July 1994, pp. 43-56.
20. Masoud Kavoossi, *The Globalization of Business and the Middle East* (Santa Barbara, CA: Greenwood, 2000), p. 33.
21. Dipak Das Gupta, Mustapha K. Nabli, *Trade, Investment, and Development in the Middle East and North Africa: Engaging with the World* (Washington D.C.: World Bank Publications, 2003), pp. 22 & 142.
22. *Private Sector Development in the Middle East and North Africa Making Reforms Succeed: Moving Forward with the MENA Investment Policy Agenda* (Paris: OECD Publishing, 2008), p. 27.

6

Civil Society in West Asia: Progress and Prospects

Sameena Hameed

Human society has invariably progressed from rudimentary state to a civilized one. In this process, the competence for striving for a desirable form of society extended from that of tribal heads to state and finally to the civil society. The dimensions of civil society have been subjected to different conception. During Cicero's time in Rome 'civilis societas' referred to the state as well as to the conditions in a civilized political community, determined by its legal systems, and citizens' participation in the multifaceted 'civil' life. While Locke's civil society essentially existed outside state domain. But if we consider civil society to be a network of voluntary associations that are independent of the state, then it carries with it the Ciceronean element of 'civilis societas' and the Lockean prerequisite of independence from some superior authority.

Civil society if conceived as the network of interactions and exchanges among individuals voluntary associating for the assertion of larger public interest, is both pluralistic and participatory. Pluralistic and participatory civil society is desirable for two reasons. First, it creates an inclusive civil society, which can create avenues for larger participation rather than been represented few associations. In this way, it is also self propelling. Second, broad based participation guards against the fear of co-option of civil society by State and international financial bodies like WTO. The dangers of co-option of civil society by the State and international funding agencies have often been speculated in the discussions of its role in establishing democratic traditions. [1]

Certain factors tend to accelerate or stall the process of formation and activism of civil society. This paper seeks examine the potential and prospects of the civil society in West Asia from the economic perspective. Though, the civil society in Asia has not developed solely on the articulation of interest of any economic group as was the case in Europe. But, the character of economy inculcates such attributes of behaviour and aptitude that become vital integrants in the formation of a vibrant civil society. These attributes are self reliance, entrepreneurship and self confidence. It was with the centrality of weaving charkha, that Gandhi was able to launch a strong civil movement. Gandhi used to says, 'always the *charkha* around which all activities revolve.' and claimed that weaving charkha was an alternative way to swaraj. [2] Even though, Tagore, in his article 'The Call of Truth' and 'The Cult of the Charkha' was especially averse to Gandhi's claim that if everyone turned the charkha for half an hour a day, India could get Swaraj in a year's time. [3] But it was not the material output of charkha, which activated the non-violent civil movements, but the essential attributes of initiative, self-reliance and self-confidence that came out of the process of 'learning by doing'. [4] These behavioural attributes have played a vital role in social mobilisation and civil assertion.

The economic structures which have given space to initiative and enterprise, even in their rudimentary stages as the tribal ones have created strange parallels in terms of competence for civil assertion. The tribal people in Uttarakhand during the Chipko movement was asserting for the same cause and at the same time when the famous United Nations Conference on Human Environment at Stockholms had the comity of nations discussing the same issues. [5]

The characteristics of the economies in West Asian countries give important clues about the progress and potential of the civil society. The civil society organizations have been performing vital role in facilitating essential services in many countries in the region and are therefore proliferating. But, that aspect of civil society that asserts itself for concessions from the state follows some distinct pattern. This pattern is to a large extent has been determined by their economies. More vibrant and vocal civil society is seen to have strong correlation with the distribution of economic resources between the State and the society. The rise of civil society necessitates a certain level of socioeconomic development but, more important, it requires a balanced development.

The unbalanced distribution of resources between the state and the society in oil rich rentier economies of west Asia has weaken the potential of civil society, which can assert for larger freedom and accountability. Table 6.1 shows some socio-economic attributes of the West Asian economies.

Table 6.1: Select Socio-economic Indicators in West Asia

Country	Unemployment 2007	Inflation 2007
Saudi Arabia	13	4.1
Iran	11	18.4
UAE	2.7	11.1
Kuwait	0.7	5.5
Bahrain	15	3.4
Jordan	17	5.4
Lebanon	18	4.1
Yemen	30	12.7

Sources: Statistical Economic and Social Research and Training Centre (SESRIC), *OIC Member Countries Economic Performance and Human Development 2000*-2007 online web: URL www.sesric.org/imgs/news/Image/Econ-HumDevelop2000-07.pdf

The oil rich economies have undiversified economic structures. Hence, employment opportunities have been highly restricted. Table 6.1 shows most of the oil rich countries have high unemployment rates. The unemployment rates among nationals especially among youths are much higher. Besides, large government control over the enterprises has made the available employment opportunities at the discretion of the government. The state retained control through large bureaucracy and public sector. The state used economy as a tool to perpetuate patron client relationship eventually consolidating their hold in the society. [6] Most of the urban middle class has been absorbed in state bureaucracy and public sector enterprises. The private sector has been small in most of these economies. Moreover, they have been largely employing foreign labour because they cannot match the salaries being given to the nationals in the public sector. Only 2 percent of the UAE national are employed in the private sector.

Civil society in monarchic regimes of West Asia, in order to become more vocal and effective should be able to sustain livelihood outside state patronage. The occupation of men determines their freedom of choice, opinion, as well as confidence with which they could fight for desirable state of social existence. The undiversified rentier economies of the oil rich nations have provided low employment opportunities to the people on one hand and huge oil rent to the State on the other. Rich rentier States have brought under its influence powerful families, elites and military and bureaucratic sub-classes through the distribution of oil rent through different channels.

Besides, this state of dependence is enhanced due to high inflation in some of economies like Iran, UAE and Kuwait as seen in Table 6.1. These rentier economies have low absorptive capacity for the huge oil revenues causing high inflation. Inflation hurts the common people by lowering their purchasing power. High inflation and unemployment have resulted in larger deprivations than that reflected by official poverty rates. Poverty rates as understood as access to minimum calories intake is low in these economies. But the wider concept of poverty as enunciated by United Nations Development Programme and inspired by Amartya Sen is 'the denial of opportunities and choices'. The incidence of such deprivations turns out to be much larger. It has a weakening effect on individual capabilities which in the face of a strong and wealthy State has a cumulative impact on the potentials of assertion if civil society.

The poor has been dependent on state social security compensations to have tolerable standards of life. The poor classes have been influenced through wide social security payments and subsidies. The state has provided huge subsidies ranging from food grains and other essential edibles, medicines, energy, water etc. The extent of government influence in terms of employment generation and social security payments is seen in Table 6.2. The government expenditure is significantly high in Saudi Arabia, Iran and Kuwait. The share of wages and salaries in total government expenditure is as high as 53 percent in Iran. The share of subsidies and current transfer is about 24 percent in Kuwait. Therefore, the emergence and growth of independent groups and associations has been slow. The middle class, which has been spear heading civil society activities in Europe and other countries, has been conspicuously absent. The potential of civil society, which can assert for larger freedom and accountability, is weak in the undiversified economies where private participation has been low.

Bahrain functions the least as a rentier state among the GCC countries and its per capita oil revenue is the lowest. [7] Within the group of oil rich states, Bahrain relatively more diversified and opportunities for private participation are larger. Larger opportunities of people participation have facilitated a more assertive civil society. In the year 2002, political associations and civic organisations launched a widespread movement and rejected the constitutional amendments and called for more rapid political reforms. In April 2005, over thirty political and civic organisations signed a statement rejecting an anti-terrorism bill, which was perceived to be restrictive for public and personal freedom of opinion, expression and political action.

Table 6.2: Government Expenditure on Wages and Salaries and Social Security (percent)

Country	Government Expenditures as % of GDP 2004	Government Expenditures	
		Wages and Salaries as % of total Expenditure (2000)	Subsidies and current transfers as % of total Expenditure (2000)
Saudi Arabia	31.7	43.4	4
Iran	27	52	10.3
UAE	6.3	35	18
Kuwait	39.4	35	24
Jordan	38.3	45	8
Syria	33.4	34.5	16

Source: Hossein Askari, *Middle East Oil Exporters: What Happened to Economic Development?* (Cheltenham, UK: Edward Elgar Publications, 2006).

In relatively poor states of Jordan, Lebanon, Yemen and Syria in the region, the distribution of resources between the state and the society is less inequitable. Besides, the state does not have ample resources to support the vast sections of poor through elaborate social security programmes. Except in Jordan, many segments of society have been abandoned to their own fate. Thus, the society has been trained in the culture of self help. The result was a perceptible proliferation of licensed activist associations. In 2000, there were about 250 independent associations in Lebanon. There has been mushrooming of service Non Governmental Organisations (NGOs), professional associations, Mutual Help societies, providing vital services and assisting in capacity building in Yemen and Jordan. This has been more visible in Palestine, which has been a stateless society. [8] Therefore, vindicating the proposition of 'Learning by doing', some of the more effective civil society assertion has also come from these states.

In Syria, different opposition groups united to issue the Damascus Declaration, which demanded the ruling party to adopt more concrete changes to the constitution for the conduct of presidential referenda and the alternation of political power. In Lebanon, following the assassination of the former Prime Minister, Rafiq al-Hariri, a mass movement took place that included the political parties and civil society organizations. Since then, a large number of Lebanese have been struggling for modernisation of state and social institutions to give the citizens due voice and representation in political and civic life. In Jordan, professional unions led a protest campaign against a new restrictive bill on professional associations, which required these groups to obtain prior permission from the Ministry of the Interior to hold public meetings and confine their discussion to 'professional issues'.

Though, there has been proliferation of many NGOs and professional associations in West Asian countries, yet one of the most vibrant and assertive elements of civil society, the labour unions are weak. The overwhelming presence of foreign workers in these countries has also inhibited the native labourers to organize themselves into labour unions and federations. Table 6.3 shows the percentage of foreign labour in the total labour force in some of the countries in West Asia.

Table 6.3: Foreign labour as percent of Total Labour Force in West Asia (2000)

Country	Foreign labour % of labour force
Kuwait	81.3
Oman	64.3
Qatar	81.6
Saudi Arabia	56
UAE	90

Source: "Economic and Social Commission for West Asia" (ESCWA), *Demographic and Related Datasheet* (2000).

The percentage of foreign labour in the labour force is 90 percent in UAE and above 80 percent in Qatar and Kuwait. The labour market conditions in the oil rich countries have passed on the benefits of employment to foreign workers as some of them are opening up their economies to private investment. The skills of the domestic labours and their wage expectations have forced the private investors to recruit foreign labour as in the case of UAE.

Only in Jordan labour groups have made limited strides in establishing itself as a national political force. The government has taken many proactive steps to labour market reforms and has regulated the work conditions of labour as per the international conventions. But, organized labour in the other states is yet to emerge in most of the West Asian countries. Even the foreign labour unions are relatively more organized and active in poorer states of Yemen and Jordan than in the Gulf States. The potential of their civil association could also be understood in the same framework of powers of State vis-à-vis the society emanating from the distribution of resources between them. Their bargaining power vs. the state is weaker in the oil rich economies of UAE, Saudi Arabia and Kuwait than in the relativity poor states of Jordan, Yemen, Syria and Lebanon.

Another aspect of civil society in West Asia is that women organizations have been dynamic elements both in the oil rich and poor states. Women have been acquiring capabilities through education. Most data show that equality between the two sexes in higher education has been achieved in Bahrain, Jordan, Kuwait, Lebanon, occupied Palestinian territory, Oman, Qatar, UAE, Saudi Arabia . The number of women registered in higher education is much larger than that of men for most of the countries in West Asia as seen in Table 6.4. In all the countries except Yemen, the girls' enrolment rates as a percentage of boys' enrolment rates in tertiary education were more than 100 percent. In Qatar and Kuwait, they were above 250 percent in the year 2002-03.

Table 6.4: Girls' Enrolment Rate as a Percentage of Boys' Enrolment Rates in Tertiary Education (%) in West Asia during 2002/2003

Country	In Percentage
Bahrain	180
UAE	250
Qatar	270
Saudi Arabia	147
Yemen	60
Jordan	110
Lebanon	120
Oman	160
Kuwait	255
Palestine	100

Source: *UNDP Arab Human Development Report* (2005), p.79.

But female economic participation rate in the Arab region has been one of the lowest in the world. For women aged more than 15 years, female economic participation rate has been about 33.3 percent as against 55.6 percent of the world. Women economic participation in Jordan is as low as 14 percent. Women organizations have been actively asserting themselves for larger opportunities of economic participation owing to their equal capabilities in the oil rich states. In poorer states, it has been feminization of poverty and distress that have activated their struggle.

Since decades, women have been forming civil society associations for their cause. The Iraqi Women's Union was established in 1945. The Lebanese Women's Council came into being in 1943, while the Association of Lebanese Women and the Committee of Lebanese Women's Rights existed since 1947. Their achievements have been significant when one considers the social and cultural drags on these societies. The women organizations have organised national campaigns to change discriminating laws against women. The Jordanian penal code related to 'honour crimes' is an example worth quoting. Jordan has also raised the legal age for marriage to eighteen years for both spouses and granted women the right to obtain a passport without their husbands' permission.

In political sphere, they have secured women's quotas in legislative bodies in Jordan, the occupied Palestinian territory, Iraq and Syria. Lebanon was among the first states in the region to give women right to vote and stand for parliamentary elections. After nearly forty years of struggle, Kuwaiti women gained complete political rights in 2005. Women now participate in the governments in all the countries of the region. Even in the conservative society of Saudi Arabia, the percentage of women in administration (31 per cent) is the highest among the Arab states. [9] Norah Al-Fayez became the first female Deputy Minister for Women's Education in Saudi Arabia.

The share of women in business and wealth has also increased. In Saudi Arabia, estimates of the number of women owned businesses range between 20,000 and 40,000. The number of female directors of bank branches and financial institutions providing services for women has also increased. The Kuwaiti Finance House in Bahrain opened the first bank branch for women. The branch, which offers Islamic banking services, has a women auditing coordinator. Starting from a low base the Arab region witnessed highest rate of growth in female economic participation of about 19 per cent against the world average of 3 per cent. [10]

The relative success of the women organizations and their vibrancy in both the petroleum rich and poor economies was mainly because of three reasons. First, the women's movements were affected by the common consciousness of their empowerment, which embraced most women, regardless of their class. Second, they could secure demands from the government because they were struggling for progressive interpretations of Islam and did not pose a threat to the regimes. The Arab women authors generally did not relay a specific political message in their writings. [11] Their common conscious of empowerment not only facilitated social mobilization cutting across different classes within the states of West Asia but also across wider Arab region. Therefore, their efforts in West Asian states got a major boost in Pan Arab women framework.

Third, women movements and associations have been well energised by the wealth of literature, which they produced. Literature serves to mobilize public opinion on issues of larger public interest. It imparts growth and vibrancy to the civil society. Women have been prolific writers, publishing books, journals and producing films in these countries. The lively press in Iran represented an organized women movement. They included *Zanan* (Women), *Zan-e-Rouz* (Today's Women), *Hoghough-e Zanan* (Women's Right) among many others. In Kuwait, the writings in 'Women's Corner' initiated and framed a public discourse on traditional practices of female seclusion. [12] The first Arab Women Book Fair in Cairo in 1995 was organized by *Noor*, a publishing house run by women. These literatures played a crucial role in mobilization of social opinion around issues of women emancipation and empowerment. Figures 6.1 and 6.2 show the survey result showing opinion of people on women participation and empowerment in Jordan and Lebanon.

Figure 6.1: Public Opinion on Women's Equal Rights to Own Assets

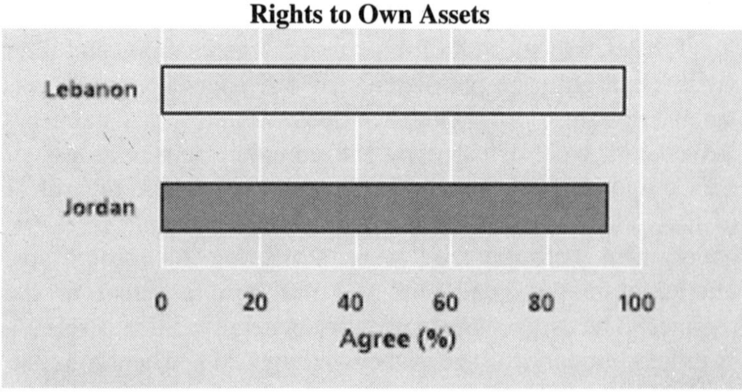

Figure 6.2: Public Opinion on Women's Right to Own Economic Ventures

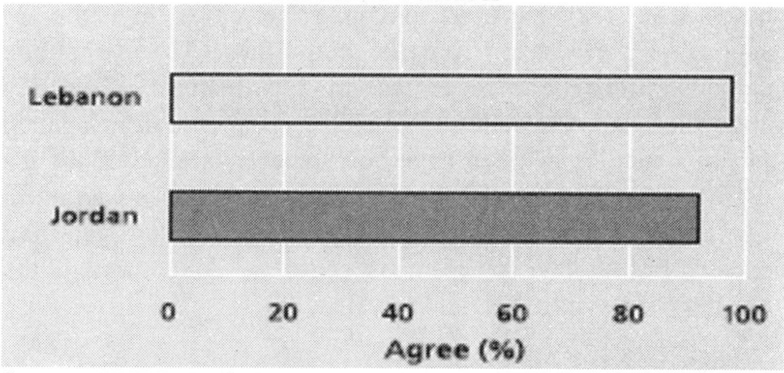

Source: *UNDP Arab Human Development Report 2005*, (2007), p. 90.

The figures show the positive outlook of people in these countries towards women economic participation and empowerment. About 90 percent of people surveyed in Jordan agreed that women should have equal rights to own assets and to own economic ventures. The same opinion was reflected by about 95 percent of the people in Lebanon. According to the field survey conducted for Arab Human Development Report 2005 other Arab countries of Egypt and Morocco have similar affirmative public opinion. Thus, women organizations have been contributing to the civil society through their literary efforts. All these made women organization and associations vibrant components of civil society.

Though, recently some instances of civil assertion have also been witnessed in the oil rich rentier states. In January 2005, a group of Islamists in Kuwait announced the formation of the Umma Party as the state's first publicly proclaimed political party. It attempted to affirm the right to form political parties which, according to it, is guaranteed by the Kuwaiti constitution but banned by the Government. The virtual space in the internet is providing new forums of civil associations. The beginning of the internet era has given civil society the possibility to create and defend alternative spaces for intellectual and political discourse, outside the realm of the regime-controlled established media. Iran and Saudi Arabia have seen the spurt of blogging activities in spite of suppressive measures from the authorities. Massive public demonstrations, unprecedented in the history of tightly controlled oil rich states of Kuwait, Qatar and Iran against Israeli atrocities in Gaza have been recently seen. But for the civil society to exert sustained pressure to extract meaningful liberties, a redistribution of resources between the state and society has to take place. This could be done through the efforts of diversification and privatization.

Conclusions

Pluralistic and participatory civil society creates avenues for larger participation rather than been represented by few associations and is thus, self propelling. The development of an assertive civil society is a function of the distribution of economic resources between the State and the society. The unbalanced distribution of resources between the state and the society in oil rich rentier economies of West Asia has weaken the potential of civil society, which can demand larger freedom and accountability. Civil society is more assertive in relatively poorer states of Yemen, Lebanon, Palestinian territories, Jordan as larger economic activities have given the training of cooperation and self help. Therefore, civil society would gain vibrancy with in a more diversified economy. Large presence of foreign labour has inhibited the formation of labour unions, which has in turn affected the bargaining power of civil society in West Asia.

Women associations have been vibrant elements of civil society in both the petroleum rich and poor states of the region. They have been able to extract important concessions from the State, which were otherwise not probable in conservative societies. Their common conscious of empowerment not only facilitated social mobilization cutting across different classes within the states of West Asia but also across wider Arab region. Their civil associations were energized by prolific literary movements, which have created favourable public opinion. Recently, some instances of civil assertion have been witnessed even in oil rich rentier states. The virtual space in the internet is providing them new forms of social mobilization and associations. But, the civil society can exert sustained pressure on the state if a redistribution of resources between the state and society takes place through diversification and privatization of the economy.

Notes

1. Elstub, Stephen, Towards a Deliberative and Associational Democracy(Edinburgh: Edinburgh University Press, 2008), p. 9.
2. Suren Morarji, "The Politics of the Indian Bourgeoisie" Workers' InternationalNews, Vol. 6, No. 5 (February-March 1946), pp.146-152.
3. The Tagore-Gandhi Controversy Revisited", Indian PhilosophicalQuarterly, Vol. XIX, No. 3 (July 1992), pp. 167-186.
4. Arrow, Kenneth J., "The Economic Implications of Learning by Doing", Review of Economic Studies, Vol. 29, No. 3 (1962), pp. 155-173.
5. See Bahuguna, Sunderlal, "Peoples Response to Ecological Crisis in the Hill Areas", in Bandyopadhyay, J. (ed.) India Environment Crisis and ResponseDehradun: Natraj Publications, 1985).
6. Mehran Kamrava, The Modern Middle East: A Political History since the First World War (London: University of California Press, 2005), p. 272.
7. Winckler, Onn, Arab Political Demography: Population Growth And Natalist Policies (Brighton: Sussex Academic Press, 2005), p.112.
8. Brynen, Rex, A Very Political Economy: Peace Building and Foreign Aid in the West Bank and Gaza, (Washington, D.C.: US Institute of Peace Press, 2000), p. 49.
9. United Nations Development Programme and Arab Fund for Economic and Social Development, The Arab Human Development Report 2005: Towards the Rise of Women in the Arab World (New York: Stanford University Press, 2007), p. 89.

10. Ibid., p. 8.
11. Badawi, Muhammed M., Modern Arabic Literature (New York: Cambridge University Press, 1992), p. 460.
12. Sakr, Naomi, Women and Media in the Middle East: Power through Self-Expression (London: I.B. Tauris, 2004), p.127.

7

Islamists, Democracy and State: Challenge of Change in West Asia

Rushda Siddiqui

There is a crisis of democracy in West Asia and North Africa. The region seems defiant to the very concept of having a participatory form of government. It seems that they are resistant not only to the idea of being democratic, but to the ideas of civil rights, human rights, liberalism and development itself. The resistance to the change in the direction of liberalism is most vocal from the Islamists of various hues in the region. Their attempts, as the world at large would understand it, is to take the society backwards in time, and keep the society in a regressive mode, dominated by a patriarchal- feudal mindset. The third wave of democratization that swept across the world, from 1975-1996, according to Samuel Huntington, failed to reach West Asia and North Africa.

This in brief, would summarise the arguments put forward by most western scholars, Marxists or neo-cons. Scholars over the years have evaluated variables that have been responsible for the failure of the region to accept democracy and political pluralism as an alternative. Reasons attributed to the failure of democracy to establish itself in the region range from the flaws within the socio-political and economic structures, to Muslims being resistant to the idea of change. Most importantly, there is a tendency to generalize the region as one and seek one solution to fit all problems. In the long run, this tendency to understand the region through limited prisms creates practical problems for the existing socio-political systems in the region. As the region gets more and more enmeshed within the global socio-economic systems, the perceptions of the region set by powers of the time has far reaching implications on the equations that the region shares with the rest of the world.

Scholars have long debated on proposed reasons for the relative absence of liberal democracy in the region. The reasons have been diverse ranging from the long history of imperial rule by the Ottomans and the subsequent European colonization and the contemporary political and military intervention by the United States. All imperial forces have been accused of supporting authoritarian regimes, repressing nascent socio-political movements and practicing a social discrimination against the natives. For the colonizers, the repression was needed to simplify the business environment, while enriching the governing elite and the companies of the imperial countries. As a result, the British are credited with creating bureaucracies and educational systems that would create a new set of elites who would be pliant to their needs. Similarly, the French have been accused of destroying the existing feudal patterns of governance and replacing them with their own structures. In brief, the pattern of colonial domination may vary, but the aim of colonization remained the same, i.e., of creating structures of governance that would render the colony dependent on the mother-colony, even after the colonizers had left.

The link between the colonizers and the rise of the socio-political movements in the region too are strong. The British are a classic example to demonstrate this point. They have left a legacy of parliamentary democracy in the countries they colonized. Even when the polities did not evolve into being classic parliamentary democracies, the political elites were a class created by the British and subscribed to the ideologies and political thought of the British.

Other explanations for the lack of democracy in the region include the problem of rentier states, which experience the theorized resource curse. Rentierism, is seen as the basic reason why the governments in the region are successful in retaining power and not facing a dissent. The rentier economies are alleged to bribe opposition by investing in social welfare, and subsequently get away with limited to no accountability. The only form of political representation that is needed in these states is to negotiate for more social welfare.

The scholars working on socio-political developments in West Asia and North Africa, have been broadly classified either as culturalist or economists. The culturalists look to socio-political history, culture, and socio-cultural frameworks for explaining the absence of democracy in the region. The variables hindering the growth of a democratic movement according to them lies in the history of the region that includes the rise and growth of Islam as a political movement, the Arab culture, the ideological differences between the Islamists and the secularists, the differences between the Muslims and other religions in the region, among others. The culturalists tend to understand the society as either being inherently factious or essentially binding. Variables like ethnicity or religion would be either binding factors as could be seen in the pan-Arab or pan-Islamic movements, or they would be inherently fissiparous movements that would lead to the collapse of any of the unifying movements.

Some culturalists have argued that democracy is incompatible with the religion of Islam, and as the adherents of the religion return to the religion for guidance the clashes between the 'Islamists' (as the fundamentalists are called) and the concepts of secularism, democracy, liberalism, and tolerance for other religions. Every few years a new ideologue re-defines and advocates his own views on religion as it should be practiced, state and society as they should conduct themselves and the nature of interaction between Muslims and the rest of the world. This has led to a cyclical loop of action and reaction between the Muslims in the region, and the rest of the world.

The second category of scholars, or the economists use the fundamental parameter of economic failure to assess change in the region. They argue that the lack of economic development in the region is leading to a socio-political crisis, which governments are suppressing with the assistance of their coercive apparatus. In the cause and effect rationale, they tend to ague that the economic crisis is caused by the failure of the governments to honestly implement a socialist experiment, or be a completely capitalist economy. The emphasis in a development process should be on an equitable re-distribution of the economic wealth. The effect, subsequently, is the rise in support from the urban middle classes for religion based political movements. These movements can take the form of being either radical or violently opposed to the governments, or they can be regular civil society movements that bridge the gap between the social demands from the state and the state's management of these demands.

The economists work on the premise that the economy is the central catalytic factor for change, which remain unaffected by other social-political or military developments in the region. Even when the external variables are studied, they are contextualized as being part of the state failure to respond to social demand. The role of the state remains the most important variable in the logic of the economists, as the state is the single largest owner of access to capital and natural resources available within the state. For the economists, again, the primary duty of the state is to earn and distribute its earnings as social welfare.

The problem with the explanations, whether cultural or economic, lies in the fact that they tend to view the religio-political movements as purely social movements expressing either political or economic discontent. Their parameters get limited, in the attempt to simplifying and explain a complex phenomenon. The difficulty arises in accepting that all parameters, however incomplete and with whatever limitations they may exist, may be true. If colonization by the Europeans is a cause, and poverty, dependency on the mother country even after independence is an effect of the cause, so is the inability of the societies to evolve from feudal economic, social and political structures. If the psyche of the Muslims does not allow them to be democratic, neither does the psyche of the Europeans accept the fact that the region would have its own valid reasons for trusting the Western concept of democracy.

An enforcement of abstract ideologies, like liberalism or neo-colonialism, cannot be quantified, however, what can be quantified are the events that acted as catalysts for change. In West Asia and North Africa, these would include European colonialism and the rise of Islamists as a political force, the creation of Israel, the Arab-Israeli Wars till the signing of the Camp David Agreements in 1978 and the acceptance of the failures of the pan-Arab and pan-Islamist movements, the Iranian Revolution and the subsequent US decision to establish military bases in Saudi Arabia and the Persian Gulf, the food riots in the region in 1988, the 1991 elections of Algeria, the occupation of Kuwait by Iraq and the liberation of Kuwait by the US troops, the 1994 elections in Algeria and Egypt, the elections in Palestine and the Israeli assault on Lebanon and Palestine in 2006 and 2008-2009. The resistance to democracy or the failure of political pluralism and social multi-culturalism to succeed in the region takes on special connotations, particularly after 9/11. With the rise of economic liberalism in the 1990s, and the shifting of regional dynamics in West Asia, after the 1991 US military intervention, there has been a shift in the state-society equations in the region in a major way.

This paper contends that the power balance between the states and their societies were in a flux since the end of the Second World War. The cold war, the experimentation of the local polities with socialism as a socio-political and economic system, and its subsequent failure led to a loss of legitimacy of the existing power elites. In the various polities across the region, the external powers played a special role in establishing a skewed power relation between the states and their societies. With the failure of the political liberalism to take shape, mostly as a result of external intervention, the region has started displaying characteristics of being centralized in bureaucracy, and using the coercive apparatus to retain power. The state is fast taking on the role of being its society's representative. The elites in power are the key for defining the social thought.

The power balance between the states and their societies were in a flux since the end of the Second World War. It is working on the premise that there is no single variable that can explain the failure of political pluralism to succeed in the region. The main argument of this paper is that, the failure of democracy in the region cannot be attributed to a single variable. All variables have combined to change the character of the polities in the region to ensure that democracy as a process remains limited to holding elections for administrative functioning. The process of state formation in the region is changing to ensure that the concept of nation state replaces any other form of state system in the region. In the process of this change, the state as successfully managed to suppress the only viable socio-political movement in their countries. They have done this by physically suppressing the movements or by co-opting them and overtaking their basic ideology. If we want to attribute the failure of democracy in the region, it would have to be due to the failure of Islamists to emerge as an alternative, be it at a local nation state level, or as a regional force.

The causes will need to include history, peculiarities of social formations and the differences in the patterns of evolution of state formations. The variables of change will need to include both internal and external variables. Failures in the socialist experimentation of economics in the post-colonial era are as much responsible for socio-political discontent in the region, as the presence of US forces in Saudi Arabia. The Islamists in the region are as responsible for destabilizing the region as the Zionists and the neo-cons. In brief, all variables will need to be understood as being inter-linked and inter-dependent.

There are two popular reasons for the incompatibility between democracy and the polities of the region, and though they seem unrelated, they are very strongly interlinked. The first is the colonial legacy of the region that has led to the rise of a power equation between the state and its society, which guarantees the failure of political pluralism in the region. The Western intervention in the region, from the time of European colonization, has been responsible for the society to distrust the west more than ape it as a model.

The second reason is the religio-political force of the Islamists. Islamists can broadly be defined as the political leadership in the region that is provided by Muslim fundamentalists. None of the Islamists have a solution to the chaotic power equations between the political elite and the societies under consideration. They do not offer a consistent ideology, or even a coherent leadership. Yet they represent the only face of opposition that western ideologies and concept witness in the region. What we need to understand is that Islamists are not a homogeneous lot of politicians. Anyone who turns back to the Quran or the works of any of the interpreters of it, or anyone who looks to the pre-European era for inspiration, is an Islamist.

The failure of the Islamists will have to be understood at both nation-state level and at the level of regional dynamics. In their attempts to retain their identity as nation states, local governments are using every means from suppression to co-option to take over as representative of their society, from the Islamists. It was a process set in motion by the European colonizers, and is continued by the local governments.

Variables of Change

In the process of state formation in the region, colonization was the first factor that impacted change. It created a political elite to govern, it created the state of Israel as a state whose identity was to emanate from religion to ensure social instability within the region. It created the system of centralized administration, a system to facilitate the economic integration of the colony into the global capitalist system even after the colonizers left, and most importantly, it set into motion forces that would ensure that the region would not only remain divided as nation-states, but would adhere to the concept for the future.

Emitting from the colonial legacy is a process of centralization of social, political, economic and coercive authority in the institution of the government. The governments are gradually changing their character from being representatives for the society to being representatives of the society. They are no longer seeking legitimacy from the society they govern. Their sources of legitimacy are external. In the various polities across the region, the external powers played a special role in establishing a skewed power relation between the states and their societies. With the failure of the political liberalism to take shape, mostly as a result of external intervention, the region has started displaying characteristics of being centralized in bureaucracy, and using the coercive apparatus to retain power. The state is fast taking on the role of being its society's representative. The elites in power are the key for defining the social thought.

Even when dealing with the issue of Islamists, or those Muslims who are looking to religion for political guidance, it is important to understand that the aims, objectives and political identity of the Islamists was given to them by the Europeans during their processes of social colonization. The Europeans were specific in targeting religion and to either discredit it in their effort to socially colonize or patronize it.

The importance of the process of colonization in the fact that it set into motion that the process of social and state transformation in the region. From being feudal polities, or segmentary states, the polities were now set into motion to be nation-states as the West understood it. Boundary lines were drawn, administration was centralized and socio-political systems were re-cast into identifiable patterns that would blend with the European patterns. Once in charge the Europeans lost no time in arguing that the culture they had colonized needed to be civilized. The civilizing mission resulted in disparaging the local cultures, customs, beliefs and value systems. The colonizers worked to replace it with the superior Western value systems. The colonial rule was marked by the hostility of the colonizers towards Islam and the accompanying legal and social value systems. They did not recognize the economic, criminal or civil laws of the colonies and at the very beginning worked towards acquiring immunity from the local laws. It became the basis for enforcing a separate set of laws, which discriminated between the Europeans and the local populations.

For the colonized people, religion provided the most important and influential pivotal point around which the disgruntled masses could be mobilized. In response to the European onslaught on the traditions and culture, the mosques and religious institutions had become the focus of religio-social reaction of the masses. They provided the masses with a framework within which to comprehend and analyze the colonial policies, strategies and practices. The reaction of the Islamists was to either look inwards for reforming the practice of the religion, or to vehemently oppose everything Western and demand the establishment of an Islamic state after the ouster of the colonizers.

Whether the colonization was direct or indirect, the attempt was to suppress the religion and culture of the colony. One of the moves to foster a domestic reaction to the local religion was to create a local middle class, which was urban, maybe partly educated in the West, affluent and aware of the power of the West. The division created in society by creating this class, and offsetting them against the local Arab-educated, stigmatized as backward and reactionary class, was permanent and the class conflict only accentuated with time.

"Invariably, the colonial mechanism was a centralized bureaucracy in alliance with wealthy merchants, large land owners and tribal sheikhs (chiefs), and linked the economies of the occupied countries to their own. To realize the linkage, the European powers monopolized foreign trade as well as the supply and management of public utilities. They also tied the local currencies and foreign trade earnings to their central banking system." [1]

The social reaction and the role of the social forces, under the colonial regimes, represented the reaction to the exploitative nature of the colonial policies. As the economy got more integrated into the larger global economy, it created economic, political and social structures which replicated the west. However, it also created a social and economic imbalance between the urban and the rural, the modern and the traditional, and the Westernized and the oriental and backward. The social forces reacting to the rural-urban, and the rich and poor divide were very different in nature, with only anti-imperialism being the common goal.

Democracy in West Asia and North Africa

The debates about the democracy, Islam and West Asia have special overtones. There are three variables that form the basis of change in West Asia and North Africa. The first is economy, which would mean all forms of economic changes in the region. It would encompass changes faced by the economies, be they rentier or non-rentier. The changes induced due to globalization of the economy, the changes set in due to the structural reforms, or due to the economic problems that resulted from the Arab-Israeli conflicts, are among some of the many indicators about how economic changes are influencing the patterns of change in the region.

The second factor is the US foreign policy in the region. Prior to the end of the cold war, the foreign policy of the USSR and the role of the United Nations did make a significant impact on the regional dynamics. The European role in shaping the regional dynamics remained the most important variable of change till the Arab-Israeli war of 1973.

During the war, the shift in the balance of power from Egypt to Saudi Arabia and the other oil economies first came to the fore. With the rise demand of oil, and the increased role in the Persian Gulf oil in the global economy, the shift in strategic power also took place. The most effective weapon, the region found, was in the blockade of regional oil supply to the global energy market. The global economic crisis caused as a result pushed the US in the forefront of West Asian and North African politics. The US was forced to re-structure its foreign policy and its Middle East policy to ensure that it did not have to undergo the economic crisis again. The Camp David accord, by which the front runner of the pan-Arab and pan-Islamic movements was bought over and compelled to acknowledge Israel as an ally was the biggest change that the US foreign policy was able to affect in the region.

The third variable for change in the region is religion. Different sets of historians have tried to trace the roots of conflicts between the three Semitic religions to various points in history. Some like Bernard Lewis have traced it to the origins of Islam, and claim that it was the rise and spread of Islam that led to intolerance and ethnic conflict in the region. It led to the crusades with the Christians and the opposition to the Jewish homeland in Israel after WWII. Another set of historians attribute it to the colonial legacy of divide and rule.

Halim Barakat, in his various works has pointed out that the British idea of creating Israel by displacing Palestinians was the first step in creating regional chaos based on religion. By creating an exclusive state, whose identity came from religion, the British had created roots for further fissiparous forces to divide the region in due course of time. This author too would like to re-emphasize that the rise of a political force in the region, that finds its ideology in the re-interpretation of Islam as a religion, has more to do with the colonial policies of the Europeans in the region that they practiced from the 1800s, than due to the mosaic nature of the society or the inherent fundamentalism within Islam as a religion. The author would like to posit that the rise of Islam as a political, and later economic ideology in the region, is the result of the colonial policies of the Europeans, who did not allow for any form of political or economic vents during their rule. The only channel of any social, political or economic opposition to the European rule that was possible, was through the clergy or the mosques.

With the end of the cold war, and particularly after 9/11, the changes in the regional dynamics can be attributed to two variables:

1. The external variable of the US foreign policy and its decision to integrate the concept of Democracy Promotion within its policy.
2. The domestic variable of centralization of political, economic, social authority in the hands of the political elite.

The complexity of the state-society equations that is responsible for the stagnancy in political and economic development in West Asia and North Africa. West Asian polities have evolved mechanisms to effectively balance political power, whereby the elites in power and the religio-political opposition. The polities have evolved to level that are neither classic democracies, nor classic dictatorships and neither are they complete theocracies. There is a level of stability that these polities have achieved that allow for them to maintain a level of status quo in the socio-political and economic equilibrium.

US Foreign Policy

The issue of Democracy as a solution in the region gained new impetus after 9/11. Prior to 9/11 the demand from the region was for political liberalism, multiculturalism and adoption of liberalism as an option to the authoritarian regimes in the region.

As an ongoing response to the terrorist attacks of September 11, 2001, and a justification for the U.S. invasion of Iraq, the Bush Administration has made the promotion of democracy in the Middle East a national security priority, stating that greater political freedom can undercut the forces of Islamic radicalism and indoctrination. The Bush Administration has made the promotion of democracy in the Middle East a national security priority, stating that greater political freedom can undercut the forces of Islamic radicalism and indoctrination. As U.S. democracy promotion policies have moved forward, policy makers have confronted a significant dilemma: how to respond to challenges posed by political Islamist movements (i.e. parties and political organizations that promote social and political reform in accordance with Islamic religious principles that may lead them to oppose U.S. foreign policy). [2]

As Gregory Gause III put it that in the aftermath of the Iraq War of 2003, when it became clear that the major public justification for the war—Saddam Hussein's possession of weapons of mass destruction—had no basis in fact, the George W. Bush Administration quickly emphasized a new public justification for the war. Post-Saddam Iraq would become a democratic beacon in the Middle East, leading to more open politics throughout the region. It is very tempting to assume that this change of message is simply public relations, an insincere effort to sell a policy to both American public opinion and to the world. Undoubtedly, at least in the public presentation element, there is some truth to this assumption. However, it would be a mistake to see the American "democratization" initiative in the Middle East as merely a cover for other, more traditional great power motivations. [3]

Gause goes on to debate the intentions of Bush when the latter tried to shift the reasons for wanting to start a democracy or a freedom campaign. They have shifted from democracy being a solution to terrorism, or democracy in the region as being important for the safety and security of its most important strategic ally, Israel.

However, Washington sees that the implementation of real democratic change in the Arab world could immediately work against a whole range of important American interests. What has emerged from this tension is an uncertain balance in Bush Administration efforts on the political reform question: a real commitment at the diplomatic level and a number of "on-the-ground" programs aimed at regional reform, but a willingness to "define democracy down" so that friendly states can meet Bush Administration reform targets without risking real democratic political change. [4]

According to Gause, the American foreign policy and its democracy promotion campaign in the region, is bound to contradict itself. On the one hand it would disturb the balance of power equations between states and their societies, and on the other it would allow for Israel's most important opponent, the Islamists to come to power. Access to state resources by Muslims who identify with religion to give them an identity is the most important challenge that Israel has to face.

Similarly, the works of John Rudey, Rodney Wilson and others clearly show that the political class that serves as the ruling government across the region has strong ties to the West. It is a class that was created by the Europeans that is at the helm of political, economic and political change in the region today. It is this class of cultivated and educated in western values that acts as a representative of the West in their countries. They portray themselves as the force that seeks to modernize their country and take it to the path of Western capitalist or socialist development. With independence, the elites managed to stay in power by coercing a change in the political aspirations of its society. Their source of legitimacy is more external than internal.

Scholars like John Esposito, point out that modernization for the Muslim world has not been a matter of making simple choices between Mecca and mechanization, static tradition and dynamic change, and secular leaders or intellectuals and ulama (the traditional religious elite). Countries as dissimilar as Afghanistan, Egypt, the Gulf states, Iran, Pakistan, Saudi Arabia, and Turkey demonstrate the complexity and divers nature of Muslim experience and experimentation, various patterns of modernization, and differing interpretations and implementations of Islam. The advent of alternative Islamic activist elite reflects new realities in the Muslim world. [5]

To understand the reasons the region has been defiant to the concept of democracy, two possible approaches can be adopted. The first would be to adopt the standard Western approach of looking at the mosaic of society, and deal with individual society's failure to adopt to the concept of democracy. It would lead to a blame game, whereby the blame could lie with the dogmatism of the Islamists, or the flaws within the religion, or the socio-political imbalance caused by the sectarian differences of society, or the class conflict between the governing elite and the marginalized masses. As Halim Barakat puts it, the literature on social diversity and cleavages in Arab society and the Middle East as a whole suffers from several fallacies, two of which are most pertinent here. One is the tendency, particularly among the Orientalists, to speak of the mosaic nature of Arab society and of the existence of a unified mentality, or one Arab mind, without any awareness of the contradiction between these two abstractions. The other is the emphasis either on communal cleavages or on class conflicts, with the result that one becomes explanatory while the other is ignored. [6]

As this paper is working on the hypothesis that it is the process of transformation of state formations that is the primary cause for the failure of democracy in the region, it would like to propose a study of the change within the framework of state responses. Keeping the various types of polities in the region in mind, we need to divide the existing polities in West Asia and North Africa into five broad categories, based on the political and economic practices of each nation-state in the region. Within each polity, one can look into the history and socio-political development to understand the linkage between Islamists, the Westerners and the concept of democracy.

1. The feudal polities that would include monarchies and emirates. These are states where the political, economic and political power is cantered in the institution of the feudal hierarchy (UAE, Saudi Arabia, Jordan, etc.);
2. One party or military backed regimes. These polities would include governments, military officers who have taken over as heads of state and have not relinquished power ever since;
3. Religion based states, or states whose religion shapes their identity. The uniqueness of these states lies in the fact that they are not theocracies in the classical sense of the term, neither are they secular, nor are they democratic, and most importantly, they are not dictatorships or feudal hierarchical polities. These would include the two states of Israel and Iran.;
4. Democratic polities. Though all states in the region claim to follow a form of democratic process, by definition there is only one government that practices democracy closest to its classical meaning. Lebanon, follows a confessional democracy, a political system that is supposed to provide political representation to all the sections of its society; and
5. The occupied states of Iraq and Palestine.

Though these are very broad categorizations, and the polities of the region can not be rigidly classified as one or the other. Common catalysts of change, external variables, socio-cultural commonalities, are some of the factors that for long have been responsible for the broad brush with which the society, polity and economy of the entire West Asia and North Africa has been understood. The focus needs to be on the similarities of religion, cultural heritage, and the history of conflicts between the three Abrahmaic religions.

With the creation of Israel, and the gradual shift in focus on the role of religion in shaping identities, the re-defining of socio-political relations too has come to the fore. 9/11 popularized the myths. All Arabs came to be understood as

Muslims, ignoring the nearly 15 million who are not. All Muslims were understood to be anti-Western, Israel hating radicals, and the term Islamists gained ground. All Islamists again were suspected to be terrorists, who were targeting non-fundamentalist Muslim governments along with secular and liberal governments. More interestingly, the religion of Islam was split beyond the existing sectarian divide of Shia and Sunni Islam. With the launch of the war on terror, President Bush sanctified the abstract divisions of the religion into being radical Islam, political Islam, *jihadi* Islam, moderate Islam, Wahabbi Islam among other classifications.

As this paper is working on the hypothesis that it is the process of transformation of state formations that is the primary cause for the failure of democracy in the region, it would like to propose a study of the change within the framework of state responses. Keeping the various types of polities in the region in mind, we need to divide the existing polities in West Asia and North Africa into five broad categories, based on the political and economic practices of each nation-state in the region. Within each polity, one can look into the history and socio-political development to understand the linkage between Islamists, the Westerners and the concept of democracy.

1. The feudal polities that would include monarchies and emirates. These are states where the political, economic and political power is cantered in the institution of the feudal hierarchy (UAE, Saudi Arabia, Jordan, etc.);
2. One party or military backed regimes. These polities would include governments, military officers who have taken over as heads of state and have not relinquished power ever since;
3. Religion based states, or states whose religion shapes their identity. The uniqueness of these states lies in the fact that they are not theocracies in the classical sense of the term, neither are they secular, nor are they democratic, and most importantly, they are not dictatorships or feudal

hierarchical polities. These would include the two states of Israel and Iran.;

4. Democratic polities. Though all states in the region claim to follow a form of democratic process, by definition there is only one government that practices democracy closest to its classical meaning. Lebanon, follows a confessional democracy, a political system that is supposed to provide political representation to all the sections of its society; and
5. The occupied states of Iraq and Palestine.

Though these are very broad categorizations, and the polities of the region can not be rigidly classified as one or the other. Common catalysts of change, external variables, socio-cultural commonalities, are some of the factors that for long have been responsible for the broad brush with which the society, polity and economy of the entire West Asia and North Africa has been understood. The focus needs to be on the similarities of religion, cultural heritage, and the history of conflicts between the three Abrahmaic religions.

With the creation of Israel, and the gradual shift in focus on the role of religion in shaping identities, the re-defining of socio-political relations too has come to the fore. 9/11 popularized the myths. All Arabs came to be understood as Muslims, ignoring the nearly 15 million who are not. All Muslims were understood to be anti-Western, Israel hating radicals, and the term Islamists gained ground. All Islamists again were suspected to be terrorists, who were targeting non-fundamentalist Muslim governments along with secular and liberal governments.

More interestingly, the religion of Islam was split beyond the existing sectarian divide of Shia and Sunni Islam. With the launch of the war on terror, President Bush sanctified the abstract divisions of the religion into being radical Islam, political Islam, *jihadi* Islam, moderate Islam, Wahabbi Islam among other classifications.

State Responses to Islamists

Islamists have also been classified as fundamentalists, who have been using the imagery of the golden era gone by and the promise of justice and prosperity in the future if they are able to establish an Islamic state. Abdel Azim Ramadan explains, that fundamentalists are people who wish to renew Islam, by purifying it of spurious beliefs, return to the essentials and reconcile Islam with the requirements of the modern age, to consider Islam as an appropriate instrument for government, and to believe in the capacity of Islam to bring progress rather than rely on Western secular political structures and laws. [7]

What has brought the political Islamists into focus is the state repression of the political Islamic movements and the extreme violence perpetrated in the name of religion by both the state and the Islamists. The period from the mid 1980s to the mid-1990s is extremely important in the history of political Islam. This was the period when the crystallization of the Islamist movements took place in the form of organized parties. From Algeria, to Iraq, due to strong state repression the radicals, even though they had been declared illegal and had lost considerable support bases, had managed to gain certain credibility.

The state has tried to deal with the political opposition by either crushing it or by co-opting it. Under the policy of co-option the state has been incorporating the changes being made by the political religionists like closing offices for Friday prayers, or closing the eating joints during the month of Ramadhan, etc.. Though they have incorporated the agendas on a partial basis, the governments have cracked down on the leaders of the movements that demanded the changes. This way it works towards fragmenting the opposition posed by political Islamist.

The state is capable of co-opting as well as repressing the religio-political movement. It has the power to manipulate the movement to its side or co-opt the ideas of the movement while suppressing the concept of political unrest.

Whatever Islamist political intentions may be, however, the ability of the government to co-opt, as well as repress is enormous. As they (the young fundamentalist movements) move from the arena of religiously inspired protest and reform to political engagement, they may be vulnerable to manipulation by secular political veterans. In this light the dramatic rise of political Islam in Algeria seems accounted for more by the failure, and subsequent face saving manoeuvres, of wizened secular political hands than by a popular Islamic movement, which in its organizational structural and political mechanisms, has been underdeveloped. [8]

A fallout of the tool of repression by the government is increasing the long-term position and credibility of the movement as an opposition group and justified its demands. In the case of post-coup Algeria, when the regime sought the persecution and liquidation of a group, the Islamic movement broke down into smaller but more cohesive–and generally more radical--splinter groups. [9]

The process of repression and co-option however, has not totally been able to eliminate the potential of socio-religious forces being a political force. As the government failed to deliver its promise of prosperity and political liberalism, the politicization of religion started asserting itself in more subtle ways. There was a marked increase in the attendance in religious services, rise in the observance of traditional social customs, like the veiling of women, or the growing of beards by men. All these came to symbolize a sort of protest against the ruling code of Westernisation, secularism, modernity and the general direction in which the government was leading the country.

Also, knowing their limitations, most governments and religious opposition parties work together to retain the equilibrium. The relationship between the government and the Islamic opposition has been symbiotic. Even in states where the confrontation between the government and Islamists is sharp, there are ways in which a political co-option takes place. The more popular reason for this might be the might of the state apparatus, but the other important reason for the Islamists to cooperate in the process, is their realization of the thinness of their mass base. [10] Lacking a broad-base of support but hoping to achieve one and inevitable joined in a high-stakes competitions with other Muslim groups, the fundamentalists frequently change tactics. [11] This is most commonly seen in the manner in which they work out political alliances to contest elections.

By the 1990s, the process of cooption had found takers even among the Islamists in the region. The constant conflict with the state, with its large repressive machinery had split the Islamic movements into two. Either the members had turned radical and taken to arms to establish their utopian Islamic state, or they had contracted with the other opposition parties in the state and decided to infiltrate the governing administrative ranks and become a part of the system. The separation of the movements, on the basis of their bases and activities, their memberships and support funding are used to differentiate a group of activists are the problem makers, and those who can be accepted into the mainstream. The differentiation provides proof that the larger sections of the Muslims are not anti-West or radical fundamentalists; rather it is the moderate political Islamic movements which are popular and need to be encouraged to get the majority of the population to come into mainstream politics.

The accommodation of the Islamists within the political system has been very tenuous. It was a very uneasy truce between the ruling regime and the moderate Islamists who wanted to be part of the system to change the system. Both tried to upstage each other in some manner or the other. If the government declared the Muslim Brotherhood and other Islamist parties to be illegal, they would contest election in collaboration with the other parties and prove that they are also a political force to be reckoned with. All Islamist parties in the region differed from their governments on different issues as and when they came up. Whether it was the question of truce with Israel or the question of interest on bank deposits, the Islamists always had an objection, supported by the religious texts. [12] The governments on the other hand, never missed an opportunity to condemn them as dogmatic, non-progressive misleaders of youth and suppressers o women's rights. The government constantly tightened its surveillance and control over the activities of the political religious groups. Under the label of threat to internal and external security the ministries dealing with law and order and defence have kept a constant check on the organizations. [13]

To counter the influence of the government on the social life, and in attempts to win over the machinery of the government the political Islamic movements have been working towards infiltrating the bureaucracy and the other organs of the government. Once the government became aware of the strength of the alternative socio-political networks they took steps towards controlling its powers and ensuring that it remained limited to being a pressure group and not offer an alternative to the government. The scope of the works of the religio-charitable organizations was limited to supplementing the government social welfare schemes, rather than offer an alternative to it.

The responses to external variable of globalization and most importantly, the inconsistent policies of the sole superpower have been limited.

The Arab states used to be categorized before September 11 as rouge states and pro-West states according to U.S. standards. With the declaration of the War on Terror, the US has managed to usurp the power and right to become the single largest dictator in the region. The Arabs have been interpreting the US statements to read: "Do what the US is telling you what to do or you are next". The White House predicted that victory in Iraq would convince adversaries to fall into line, i.e. moderate their ways to avoid becoming the next U.S. target. It is a kind of domino theory in reverse. This leaves the Arab states with the options of sanctions, political isolation, containment, if not outright military subjugation. Most Arab states believe that democracy is not in their own interest if they want to stay in power, if any definition of democracy, accepted by the West, is applied in the Arab world, but most believe that no one can face the US and more importantly they cannot survive without U.S. support. Any reluctant role by the US toward supporting these regimes will affect their future in staying in power. Thus, most Arab states have started to implement some sort of political participation at different levels and in different paces. The whole idea of these initiatives is not their convinced belief on the importance of democracy, because they do not. [14]

Conclusion

From the late 1800s, when European colonization and military dominance was sweeping the globe, the region of West Asia and North Africa too was forced to undergo changes which have changed the equations between the state actors in the region and the social forces in the region. Mahfoud Bennoune quotes Albion Small to make a point that, 'conditions are what they are, events occur as they do, because, a long chain of antecedent conditions and occurrences have set the stage and furnished the motives'. [15] He also quotes Karl Marx to say that 'men make their own history, but they do not make it under circumstances chosen by themselves, but under circumstances directly encountered, given and transmitted from the past. [16] Colonization or the domination and control of one country over another, is marked by an increased interference by the state in every aspect on an individual's life. It is an indicator of the increase in centralization of control by the state, an attempt to make the colony dependent on the parent country for guidance in every aspect of its life.

The European colonial policies integrated the colony into the larger global economic, political and social system.

Colonial legacies refer to the impact or the aftermath of the economic, political, social and legal structures and management techniques the countries inherited at the time of their independence. It refers to the legacies of modernization, economic integration into the global economic setups and the evolution of political-administrative structures, which facilitated the transition of the society, economy and polity towards a modern European society.

As the world is shrinking owing to increased economic, social, cultural, political interactions, so have the development of the state and social systems in the region. Classification of a state system or a social system cannot be narrow or fixed. Colonization affected different levels of society and economy. The social reaction and the role of the social forces, under the colonial regimes, represented the reaction to the exploitative nature of the colonial policies. As the economy got more integrated into the larger global economy, it created economic, political and social structures which replicated the west. However, it also created a social and economic imbalance between the urban and the rural, the modern and the traditional, and the Westernized and the oriental and backward. The social forces reacting to the rural-urban, and the rich and poor divide were very different in nature, with only anti-imperialism being the common goal. The colonial state's attempt to take over the educational, religious, legal systems to either destroy them completely or to re-organize them brought about a feeling of insecurity and resentment within the society.

Though there is no denying the commonness of cultures, religion, socio-political movements and the anti-Israeli, anti-Western sentiments of the masses across the region, the differences too are important. Most Western historians and political analysts, when analyzing the evolution of contemporary polities in West Asia and North Africa, developed a methodology that would rationalize contemporary behaviour patterns in terms of the history of Islam in the region. For them the impact of the Caliphate has been the most important variable that shaped polities, mindsets and identities of the societies. The period of European filling of the vacuum after the fall of the Ottoman Empire to date, is rarely taken into account.

Scholars like John Esposito, point out that modernization for the Muslim world has not been a matter of making simple choices between Mecca and mechanization, static tradition and dynamic change, and secular leaders or intellectuals and ulama (the traditional religious elite). Countries as dissimilar as Afghanistan, Egypt, the Gulf states, Iran, Pakistan, Saudi Arabia, and Turkey demonstrate the complexity and divers nature of Muslim experience and experimentation, various patterns of modernization, and differing interpretations and implementations of Islam. The advent of an alternative Islamic activist elite reflects new realities in the Muslim world. [17]

This paper seeks to argue that whether we talk of the alternative elites, or we talk of the ruling elites in the region, the political role of civil society institutions is the key to understanding the dynamism of change in the region. Even if for the sake of convenience, we classify the alternative elites as the religious leaders, or Islamists, and the existing political elites as the secular government, the concept and institutions of civil society remain the balancing factor between the two. It has been through the institution of the civil society that the Islamists seek to curb the powers of the secular government. On the other hand, it is through the very civil society institutions that the government seeks to co-opt its socio-political opposition. Democratization is a process by which the system of checks and balances between the secular government and the Islamists takes place.

What needs to be kept in mind is that barring the minor differences in the degree of economic power of the political elites, all systems work towards the usage of civil society institutions as a tool to counter each other and to dominate the society. This struggle for domination will have peculiar shades in West Asia and North Africa. If the rentier economies of the region do not seek political pluralisms, the non-rentier economies too will not be too keen on democracy as an alternative polity.

Notes

1. El-Ghonemy, Riad, *Affluence and Poverty in the Middle East*, (Routledge, London and New York, 1998), p.30.
2. Jeremy M. Sharp, "U.S. Democracy Promotion Policy in the Middle East: The Islamist Dilemma" in *Foreign Affairs, Defence, and Trade Division Congressional Research Service* (The Library of Congress, June 15, 2006), p. 4.
3. Gause, G, The United States and Democratization in the Gulf: An Uncertain Balance, *Journal of Social Affairs,* Volume 21, Number 84 (Winter 2004), p 13.
4. ibid, p 21.
5. John L. Esposito, *Claiming the Centre: Political Islam in Transition*, Harvard International Review, p 49ff.
6. Barakat Halim, *The Arab World* (University of California Press, 1993), p. 15.
7. Abdel Azim Ramadan, "Fundamentalist Influence in Egypt: The Strategies of the Muslim Brotherhood and the Takfir Groups", in Martin E. Marty and R. Scott Appleby ed., *Fundamentalisms and the State* (Chicago: University of Chicago Press, 1993), p. 152.
8. James Pisctori, "Accounting for Islamic Fundamentalisms", in Martin E. Marty and R. Scott Appleby ed., Accounting for Fundamentalisms: The Dynamic Character of Movements (The Fundamentalism Project Series, Vol. 4), (University of Chicago Press, 1994), p. 369.
9. E.E. Shahin, *Political Ascent: Contemporary Islamic Movements in North Africa* (Westview Press, Boulder, CO, 1997), pp. 244-245.
10. See James Piscatori in Marty and Appleby, 1994.
11. ibid, p. 370.
12. On the issue of usury and the opposition to the banking system see Auda, Gehad. "The "Normalization" of the Islamic Movement in Egypt from the 1970s to the Early 1990s", in *Accounting for Fundamentalisms*, Vol. 4 of The Fundamentalism Project, ed. Martin Marty and R. Scott Appleby (Chicago: University of Chicago Press, 1994), pp. 391-92.

13. "Despite the lines of understanding between the Brotherhood and the Ministry of Interior which were established in the 1970s and early 1980s, the Ministry of Interior was keen, particularly under the ministry of Zaki Badr (1986-1990), to make the Brothers feel themselves under surveillance by the police........ The Interior ministry never missed an opportunity to attack the Brotherhood publicly as a sly organization that only sought power and was never true to Islam. It attempted to prove that there was a covert deal between the Brotherhood and the radical Islamists, a division-of-labour scheme for destroying the state. Furthermore, it made great effort to restrict the Brothers' access to the public through confiscating their publications or banning their public meetings." ibid, p. 391
14. Adnan M. Hayajneh, The U.S. Strategy: Democracy and Internal Stability in the Arab World, in *Alternatives: Turkish Journal of International Relations*, Vol.3, No.2&3, (Summer/Fall 2004), p. 25.
15. Bennoune, Mahfoud, *The Making of Contemporary Algeria, 1830-1987* (Cambridge University Press, Cambridge, 1988), p. 1.
16. ibid, p.1.
17. John L. Esposito, *Claiming the Centre: Political Islam in Transition*, Harvard International Review, p 49ff.

8

Internet, Dissent and Virtual Public Sphere in Saudi Arabia

M.H. Ilias

The proliferation of globalizing means of communication such as internet and satellite television has energized a multitude of new social expressions in the Gulf. New political meanings are also created collaboratively through the circulation of global media technology and the exchange of ideas attached to it within the local context. However, the contribution of the new media in shaping the political landscape of the Arab Gulf lies not simply in its potential to disseminate liberal ideas or instil radical religious ideologies but its ability to form a virtual 'public sphere', [1] where the attitudes and interests of ordinary Arabs are being increasingly defined and shaped. Of the new means of communication, Internet, through which people have access to multiple sources of information that allow them to have new perspectives and even to criticize the government policies, plays an increasingly central part, if not the most important, in the battle of hearts and minds. Of particular interest here is the different ways in which women and opposition use the medium for assertion and how the Internet influences the ordinary lives. Websites, blogs and social networking sites can be added to the elements identifying as supporting this micro-public sphere in the Gulf.

Given, rising inter-connectedness that makes multilateral flow of ideas and cross-border identification of similar groups theoretically possible, this development may not seem surprising. But the trend in the region has been a significant social advance, making possible the exploration of new avenues that were previously precluded. Many studies have noted that the rapid globalization of media and the new spaces it provides for different groups imply that diverse voices (of out and down groups), including women's, are increasingly being heard in various public spheres. [2] In these new communicative spaces, not only is the number of women working visibly increasing, but public discussions about so-far taboo subjects concerning women, such as domestic violence and Islamic law are also substantially rising. [3] Looking at the present political scenario, one can find ample indications of such assertiveness of many sidelined social actors.

With a high restriction on social organization polity in the Gulf signals the presence of a weak civil society. As independent groups are unimportant, associated life is weak. The public space between the nuclear family and the state is sparsely populated, therefore, civil society lends no durability to political systems by making some demands or pressures. Even though a variety of important groups have emerged, survived and transformed over the last three decades, almost all of them have the patronage of the state in one way or another. The state either goes to some lengths to prevent, pre-empt or destroy a variety of social organizations or incorporates many groups within its constituency, including those it has created itself. As Jill Crystal notes, 'although these groups are not private, they could certainly break with the state at the first opportunity, the first weakening of state control.' [4] Associations of journalists, lawyers, and academics are the most illustrious of such groups. 'State sponsored groups with public institutions, groups that maintain a strong corporate cohesion through public professional associations and that could retool quickly to become private groups.' [5] So is the case with the ruling family, which partakes in both formal government and civil society. [6] Domestic criticisms from the house of Saud are now well expressed-most of the times in a more liberal form. [7]

Finally, there is the issue related to the very definition of 'civil'. The issue becomes significant, especially with the powerful institutions of family or clan structure operating in opposition to the concept of civil. In this situation, only the new middle class, an emerging group of liberal technocrats with a penchant for representative government, has the potential to form a civil society, though they are yet unorganized. [8]

The idea of public sphere in the region tends to exclude any recognition of any civil society organization or institutional condition. At the same time, it must not be understood as both autonomous and sovereign with respect to the state. Instead, the public sphere must be understood as constituted solely by the circulation of independent ideas through the medium of internet with less 'external' mediations. Likewise, as happens elsewhere, the virtual public sphere has a middle class content. The participants are part of educated elite, whose capacity to mediate between society and governmental structure is still unsure. Finally, there is a doubt over public sphere's capability to facilitate the exercise of the rights of free speech and of participatory citizenship, as happens in the west, where free speech has been identified as an important component of the public sphere. It is again a matter of concern that the multiplicity of alternate socio-political expressions, which form a part of public sphere themselves, do not result in a serious structural transformations.

However, despite the weakness, as a new arena for participation in public life, the 'cyberspace' in the Gulf is essentially a re-conceived public sphere and the 'public life' in cyberspace is a very particular manifestation of society. Although it enjoys less autonomy compared to western societies, the internet acts here as a site for the creation of the public sphere-providing a framework within which the public issues of the day are discussed. Hence, the public sphere in the Gulf qualifies to be a typical Habermass-ian one, at least in the sense of its potential for being a domain of social life, in which such a thing as public opinion can be formed. In the absence of serious structural reforms, the formulation of such a space may lead to a democracy, where the participation people in the political process would no longer be represented by the constitutional apparatus, but embodied in the informal and 'sensible' democratic experiences. The entire discourse constructs this as an entity with high liberating prospects and democratic function.

Dealing with the dialogic aspects of internet in the Gulf societies demonstrates how a 'virtual-public sphere' is maintained by circulating shared cultural and political items. Many analyses have already brought the subtle political meanings of the internet with attention to the informal politics of everyday life. This 'freedom' of expression in the virtual space has a tremendous impact on women and minority groups in the Gulf, where perceptions of civil society are highly influenced by a sense of alienation, which is rooted in societies' peculiar kind of relationship with patriarchal governments.

The internet also holds great potential for widening the experiences, interactions and opportunities of the majority of citizens who are potentially excluded from normal power avenues. In a closely monitored Islamic society, where the presence of women in the public sphere is supposed to be regulated by Islamic precepts, their virtual self-narration has become a new form of transgression which can be understood as a search for a new identity. So the formation of public sphere may eventually lead to real democracy, where freedom and equality would no longer be represented in the institutions of law or state, but embodied in the very forms of concrete life and sensible experience.

Furthermore, the Net has become a major locale for popular culture. People use e-mail to keep in touch with distant family friends and use the internet for personal, religious or spiritual information, playing games online. The use of the Internet in the Gulf, thus, marks the formation of an organic techno-culture [9] created by Internet users from their own experiences and artistic resources. Different forms of techno-culture which are strongly accepted and represented within the society can serve as a barometer for health of the society. They find specific roots in lived cultures of ordinary people. As this subsection is quite informal and used by the ordinary people to communicate their emotions, feelings, worldviews and opinions, the construction of popular culture on the Internet also constitutes an index of what is important to society. So, apart from offering increasingly sophisticated way of communication the internet in the Gulf countries is also a space, where popular culture can be created, personalized, recognized and enjoyed. People turn to a subsection of the Internet for everyday construction of popular culture operating in the realm of pleasure and creative expressions.

Indeed, writings on such communicative spaces existing alongside the Internet are optimistic about the possibilities that the web, both as a tool for political organizing and as a means of exploring alternatives functions. However, most arguments for the democratic potential of the Internet are based on a naïve dismissal of the relations of power that construct and permit social interactions. They always fail to examine so-called democratic principles and practices in terms of their exclusionary tendencies.

There is, of course, a small cache of literature developing around the notions of the digital inequality. In liberal democratic countries, cyberspaces and micro- public spheres they embody are a realm of exclusion on the basis of hegemonically constructed 'male universals'. [10] By its very design, the internet has a reputation for being biased towards the interests and styles of men. [11] The participation in the cyberspace is a socially defined one, sharply determined by the phenomenon of digital divide. The citizenship has been re-worked along lines of patriarchy. So understanding cyberspace as a masculine realm is crucial for analyzing its democratic potential. This argument is very significant, when it comes to the Internet and participation in the Arab Gulf, where the participants are part of the educated male elite, who would mediate between society and governmental, economic and other structures. Though the concept public sphere matches with the situation in the Gulf, the lack of gender and class consciousness in it has fired the imaginations of feminist and marginalized groups in the region. Dina Matar argues that the appropriate term to describe the specific communicative spaces of the marginalized in West Asia is counterpublic. Subscribing to Fraser's argument [12], she says that such spaces 'can be seen as the spaces in which different marginalized groups seek to contest exclusion and hegemonic practices.' [13]

There has been a burgeoning interest in a strange merger, Islam and the Internet, over the last two decades. The liberating potential of this merger has been a serious point of concern in the political discourse and has spawned a tremendous amount of interesting works. In Saudi, a broad range of liberal and militant Muslim expressions can also be located online. They can contain news, views, informal chats and social networking opportunities that go beyond the traditional ideological and religious frames of reference of many Islamic organizations. The complex spectrum of dialogues, networking and various applications of the media speak, of course, of the presence of a Cyber Islamic Environments. [14] Gary R Bunt draws attention to this aspect of the cyberspace marked by the proliferation of Islamic websites, chat rooms, e-mails lists and other related media activity-including expressions of beliefs and the articulation of agendas-as a phenomenon heralding a maturity of Cyber Islamic Environments. [15]

This work's major concern, however, does not hinge on the representation of previously excluded groups in the newly emerged public sphere in the Gulf. But it tries to examine how domination and dissent have moved from real to virtual space. As happens elsewhere in the Arab World, the new technologies and new means of communication have provided many dissenting groups with an intermediate space and new means of disseminating information and sharing experiences on a 'virtual space' beyond their limited conceptual and physical spaces.

Dissent: From Street to Net

Even though the al-Saud regime denies the existence or allows no room for it, the opposition is intimately tied to the fabric of religious, regional and economic networks. Looking at the history of dissent, one can see it was the Gulf War I, which opened the floodgate of opposition in the contemporary period. The stationing of the US troops in the country during the war in particular, transformed an inchoate resurgence of issue-oriented responses into organized opposition movement. As Okruhlik notes, 'the universities became the major theatre of dissent; mosques became centres of sermons, criticizing the government in subtle manner. Secret tapes and underground leaflets were circulated in the streets and mosques.' [16] And with the wide application of the internet, the strategy of political opposition moved from subtle criticism to a more open and unveiled attack on the regime.

According to Edmund Ghareeb, Arab émigrés living in the US and Europe were the pioneers on the Internet. [17] As the creators of first websites they brought 'their cultural, political and Islamic interest and contents to cyberspace and helped to define it.' Among the opposition groups, the first to enter into this new arena was the Defence of Legitimate Rights (CDLR), which sent regular e-mails and ran a sophisticated website in order to expose corruptions and to portray the regime as un-Islamic. Following a split in the organization in 1996, the Movement for Islamic Reform in Arabia (MIRA) was set up by Saad al-Faqih, a Saudi exile living in London. Websites of both CDLR and MIRA got clicks from a diverse-range population of Saudis, namely, students, scholar and journalists living abroad. They obviously benefited from the cover of

European immunity extended to many exiled Islamist movements, especially in the United Kingdom. [18]

One of the main characteristics of the new media is that they are not limited to addressing only a local, national or regional audience but are reaching out to a wider audience in the Gulf and among the immigrant communities from Gulf in Europe, the Americas and Australia. So, the extensive use of the internet in the late 1990s and early 2000 made possible a wide recruitment of sympathizers all around the world, though organization and mobilization from exile had their own limitations. [19] Furthermore, with the convergence of interests of different groups, many sources of dissent propagated through the medium of internet also began uniting on three central points: 'call for redistribution of wealth, procedural social justice, and regime accountability; in essence, the rule of law'. [20] Despite the Government attempts at censorship, the internet created new patterns of interaction among the dissenting groups and opened up the scope for a new sort of web-based activism.

It is not only oppositional politics of various kinds that find a presence on the Saudi internet. The internet also provides the State with a new means to reach- out to the people. The authority's use of the internet remains not limited to propagating officially sanctioned version of Islamic thought, Wahabism. [21] Through the official sites, the Government offers counter arguments to the popular sites maintained by the dissenting groups. In religious missionary terms, some parts of the regime have actively embraced e-development so that the official religious authority has a large presence online. The traditional official clergies too have turned to it. The official ulemas use internet to issue and propagate fatwa that always justify the controversial positions and policies of the regime. However, in the wake of recent developments like Iraq War, the state-appointed clergy has been overpowered by a popular level alternative clergy that is articulate and vocal. They appear with counter-fatwas to those of official clergies in many politically sensitive issues. There is, in fact, a rapid increase in the number of takers for popular Islamic authorities and their fatwas.

Even though criticism against the monarchic regime in Saudi seldom erupts into public confrontation, political, economic and social problems, for last two decades, have provided fertile field for dissent-that can no longer be managed from above. Because of the lack of serious structural reforms, the call from the most radical flank is finding audience among population. Faced with fierce repression, people are developing new ways of articulating dissent. Among the opposition groups in the Gulf, Saudi opposition stands different from others, both because of the extreme limitations on conventional expressions of dissent within the country and the opposition's increased access to the global flow of information. [22] They are supposed to be the first of the opposition groups in the Middle East to make extensive use of new technologies in communicating their message to their followers. [23]

A close look at the proliferation of anti-government websites or blogs would reveal that, it is not a natural occurrence or not simply a function of the sudden availability of new technologies or the existence of a large number of disturbed youth, although these are contextual realities. Rather, these issues speak of a fundamental problem of the definition of 'political'. Interestingly enough, it also marks a significant move from the classical forms of Arab dissent to the new patterns of experience. Traditionally, Arab streets are regarded as an expression of public opinion and collective sentiments. For many decades, the street politics remained the modern urban theatre of dissent par-excellence. [24] Arab anti-colonial struggles attest to the political legacy of the Arab streets. As the chief locus of politics for the ordinary people, streets aspire the voices of those who are structurally absent from the position of power. This crowd includes not only marginalized elements like urban poor and the unemployed youth, but also some anti-establishment groups like students, workers, state employees and shopkeepers. [25]

Over the last two decades, especially after the Gulf War I, the Arab street has become an extension of the 'Arab mind' which reflects the collective dissent of ordinary population along with the culture and collective conduct. As long as the local Arab regimes ignore popularly held views, the street continues to be the most vital locus for the audible expression of collective grievances. But with primordial tribal structure on one side and totally atomized modern life on the other Gulf society lacks such a physical space for the expression of collective dissent. Unlike in other parts of the Arab World, mosques seldom serve to be the site for new kinds of social and political organization and expression. It is to this political vacuum, where the Internet steps in. The battle for Gulf minds, thus, is not being fought by radicals in the mosques. It is being fought on the net. While formal politics is constrained by dynastic sensibilities and Islamic discourses, Gulf youth are developing powerful political voices, analyzing national and international issues and public and private concerns via Internet.

The other transformation is related to majlis or the traditional multi-purpose informal gathering of the Arabs. Popularity of internet as a means of personal communication characterizes a major shift in theatre of dissent. In each state there have been different forms of traditional social organizations including mosques, religious institutions, religious study groups and funeral associations. Participation of all groups (especially of women and minorities) in such traditional forms of social organizations appears something hindered by the peculiar design (mostly patriarchal) of the society. Most of them are marked with the anecdotal exclusionary practices; a case which is hard to substantiate. Of which, routine semi public meetings (like Majlis) serve to be a space for expressing dissent somewhat openly. They are often held during early-evening hours at private homes, where 'male' Arabs will gather to talk politics. Saudi has a pre-existing culture of consultation and discussion inherited from the Bedouin and Arab traditions of Majlis, the 'sitting' or council where decisions were ideally promulgated. As a means of one-to-one criticism, internet appears to replace the traditional social space of Majlis. In short, the sites of dissent are no longer the secret gathering but internet nodes, specific websites, and offices outside the country that transmit information to sympathizers inside.

The internet has the capability to breed and spread new forms of globality. Particularly in Saudi Arabia, it represents instances of the growing electronic connectivity among people (Saudis) living in faraway places. Interactive sites are especially valuable in maintaining community and connection across space, and in neutralizing the physical borders. The dissent does not work in a vacuum, though operating from faraway places. Websites create a new way to recruit anywhere, anyone of Saudi descent without recognizing the frontiers of groups and communities. The new means of communication and the global information revolution pose new challenges to the regime's ability to control electronic dissent. [26]

It is not street alone that gets replaced. Next to the Arab Streets, the other means of religious teaching and preaching like mosque sermons, state radio and television programmes also got dwindling acceptance. So is the case with cassette as a tool for ideological indoctrination and a vehicle for the transmission of fundamentalist directives. The cassette tape as a means of communicating religious and political messages became popular in the Gulf in the mid 1980s thanks to Iranian revolution. [27] The use of cassettes in Iran contributed to the success of revolution. During this period, sermon tapes provided one of the prime means by which Islamic moral/ethical traditions were recalibrated to a new political order. [28] Cutting across the denominational lines, the cassette sermon as a symbol of Islamic fanaticism fired the popular imagination. The circulation of Ayatollah Khomeini's recorded messages played a key role in the mobilization of radicals in the region. [29] But Islamic cassette sermons are generally associated with a miniscule few groups-of underworld of militants and radical preachers. Cassette sermon's inherent limitation and lack of possibility to initiate dialogue might be the prime reason for its rejection. [30] In the 1990s, e-mail and fax contacts were believed to have been instrumental in introducing new means of governance and protest in Saudi Arabia. The catchphrase 'government by fax' aptly translates the overdependence of the state on these means. [31] Petitions by the opposition groups also were submitted that way.

Unlike the other tools, the 'virtual opposition' on the internet may not have direct links with the street and public opinion in the homeland, despite its capacity to provide a cyber environment of freedom of assembly, spontaneous expressions and dialogues. But, it is successful in mobilizing international public opinion against the Saudi rulers to open up the system for a greater accountability, contest, participation, and above all else more humane treatment of opponents. Hence it can not be completely discounted. [32]

These media plays a key mediatory role within an expanding arena of popular Islamic argumentation and deliberation among middle and upper class Muslims. The role of traditional Islam as a legitimating ideology of the Arab Gulf states may be still operative. Nevertheless, the new media technologies have brought a change in the pattern of religious discourses and the ways in which they have been received. The traditional ulema's engagement with new technology is the most significant and interesting phenomenon. Also to add, there is the emergence of a new class of preachers with target audiences (mostly educated class) different from those of the classical ulema. This new Islamic 'cyber-evangelists' make their message relevant in ways different from traditional ulema, making their topics more appealing to the educated public.

Perhaps more striking is the newfound popularity of websites and blogs that represent new communication genre for variety of purposes like issuing fatwas. People often use the internet to find answers to questions related to faith and practice. The proliferation of Islamic websites, blogs, you tube clippings e-mail-lists and other related sites for expressions of beliefs and articulation have increased tremendously. Sermons are broadcast in 'live' or recorded formats, or transcribed and circulated by e-mail, discussion rooms and the web. People seek online theological guidance on even otherwise negligible issues. The extensive application of the internet as a means of disseminating religious opinions, thus, signifies a technologically adept integration of religious symbolism and traditional notions.

The dissent on the Internet, however, is not limited to the spread of radical elements only, but it cuts across cleavages of class, gender and school of Islam. Radical Islamists, however, have clearly been the most articulate and powerful of the various virtual social forces in Saudi Arabia. They are better organized and more cohesive than other social forces in the country. [33] For the radicals, the internet has offered a new opportunity in addition to much needed international support and solidarity, including that of people living in exile. In Saudi, its effectiveness as a platform for radical debate has been demonstrated well. There are hundreds of blogs showing proclivity to the radical or fundamentalist versions of Islam; many others propagating more mainstream visions of Islam.

Saudi Blogosphere and Emerging Counterpublic

As we discussed earlier, the use of Internet in the Gulf generally represents a subsection of the products of internet which are appropriated by people in their daily lives and remodelled as the raw material through which they connect to others. However, blogosphere, as a variant of cyberspace, sets in motion an interesting socio-political practice and participation. It is a newly-found social space, along with the old social spaces such as souks and bazaars. Especially in the context of recent political development, intensifying political protests and reforms, Saudi blogs have taken on the important and serious role of offering a platform for discussion, debates and dissent in a volatile and vibrant environment. The popularity of blogs in the region lies not only in the fact they offer more alternative source, largely free of government control, but more importantly because they are reflecting views and opinions held by the ordinary people. They are in fact not reflected in the mainstream media.

Most Saudi Arabian blogs remain as an avenue for expressing opinions and ideas and polemics for diverse groups. There may be element of exaggeration or subjectivity [34] seen with each blogs, but they remain to be the most effective popular channels of communication. Blogs, then, have proved to be an invaluable tool, not just for regular communication, but a new communication genre for variety of purposes like political mobilization, opinion building and even for fund raising. What sets blog apart, from other internet source is their personal way in communicating to mobilize people behind a cause.

Diasporic use of the blog is another worth-noting phenomenon which is recognized within the global blogging networks. It represents an example of new forms of translocal and distanciated community. So the generic term Saudi blogging includes the activities of those who write outside Saudi Arabia. Like many other Arab Gulf countries, where politics has a constrained arena to play, Saudi blogosphere also centres on the dynamic relationship between Saudi and its diasporas, activity inside Saudi and outside.

As a sort of citizen journalism, blogs are reshaping current media practice in Saudi Arabia. Much of the Saudi blogs functions as filters, because they smuggle information from outside sources and try to present it in a more restricted environment. They provide users with an audience and relatively audible voice; they also offer a virtual space where information ignored by the mainstream media can be published. Popular attention to blogs has grown because of the increase in the number of blogs posted and the interesting issues they handle. With the regime tightly controlling the activities of the official media, young people are increasingly turning to the blogs to express dissent. The tone may be, to a great extent, Islamist, anti-American or anti-government, questioning the Saudi regime's moral fabric to speak in the name of Islam. [35] The blogs gained boost in popularity during the Iraq War and have emerged, since then, as an important alternative source of news and visuals. They provided not only the news of the event but also instantaneous comments and perspectives on issues.

There is, of course, much to be said about attempts at control and censorship by the authority. Facing the new challenges and the success of the blogs the state implemented many sophisticated filtering systems to block all blogs that could jeopardize the moral foundation and the security of the Kingdom and to arrest respective bloggers. However, despite the political risks, this general mood is shared by hundreds of blogs. Topics ranging from fatwas on politically sensitive issues to domestic violence [36], accountability of the regime to human rights violation, which were always left untouched earlier, find due expression in the new context. In a society like Saudi Arabia, where women had no public forum and no opportunity to express themselves, blogs became a way of making themselves publicly visible and expressive. Through their personal narration, women bloggers from Saudi Arabia transgress several socio-cultural boundaries. With many tender themes of love and sex, blogs always push the boundaries of permissible expression. Throughout the Gulf, blogs have proved to be an invaluable tool, not just for regular communication, but also free expression, especially for women.

It is more significant as blogs also offer an escape from the hierarchy and obligations of religious structure. This may also be true of social networking sites. The presence of Saudi women in one of the most popular sites, facebook is a testimony to this popularity. Obsession with facebook is categorically no longer the preserve of teenagers and students, and has been adopted by a growing army of housewives, determined to link up with old acquaintances and school mates.

Conclusion

The introduction of new means of communication has, indeed, caught scholars flatfooted. They attempt to catch the entire phenomenon with old butterfly nets. For many, this is just an extension of globalization and the old frameworks will be adequate to define it. Many flirt with political Islam and think the Internet has become the major source of propagation for the fundamentalist ideals. There may be an element of truth in it. The internet has, of course, become a significant element of propagation and identification for radical Islamic organizations. If you are a cybernaut, you now have much more influence over young Muslim minds than a scholar who has spent thirty or forty years studying the traditions. However, what escapes from these old nets is a differently situated experience.

The region has shown quite diverse responses to the new media. It embraces a variety of new and evolving media technologies, many of which have greater social and political implications. As a new media, which is far more immune from the controls of the state, the internet helped shaping public opinion and influencing the attitude of ordinary people in an unprecedented fashion. Many see this trend as contributing to increased democratization though it does not reflect in the development of democratic institutions. It is true that there is a suspicion over the capability of cyberspace to bring new forms of participatory democracy or contribute to a massive change in political process.

There is a commonly held scepticism about the competence of virtual public sphere to support the wide social and cultural diversity and pluralist accommodation. It is readily apparent that the situation is far from anything like a public sphere, especially with regard to its potential to give birth to political institutions and new forms of associations in civil society. But the conception of the public sphere here must be generalized beyond its European models, if we are to understand what is happening on the Saudi Internet. We generally overemphasize a specific model, while not recognizing a variety of possible alternative expressions.

Here recent literature on concepts the public sphere supports the idea of the presence of a virtual one by broadening how we think about public sphere beyond its European models. In order to make sense the idea, we need a conceptually broader definition of the public sphere that takes into account manifestly different historical condition.

The second argument is about the elitist nature of public sphere. No one can deny that such a virtual public sphere engages the emerging new class of well-educated and well-travelled Saudis only. The present virtual public sphere may be an elitist one in content, addressing primarily the well-to-do and well educated groups. However, it speaks of new realities which are likely to have profound political implications for the Saudi society. It may eventually win support among the masses and increase understanding of the nature of public opinion. This is evident from the activity of blogging which has fertilized debates on many sensitive issues regarding the everyday social life.

Notes

1. Formally, the public sphere is a concept put forward by German critical philosopher Jurgen Habermass the public sphere means to indicate the existence of any space between 'the private' and 'the state', and is a locale within which the state can be

criticized. Subscribing to Habermass' view, Corner defines public sphere as being 'the space within a society, independent both of state power and of private, corporate influence, within which information can freely flow and debate on matters of public, civic concern can openly proceed. See Jurgen Habermass, 1992 "Further Reflections on the Public Sphere", in Calhoun, *Habermass and Public Sphere* (Cambridge: The MIT Press, 1999), pp. 421-426, 422 and Joseph Corner, "Television: form and Public Address", in Edward Arnold et al (eds.), *The Media in Australia :Industries, texts, Audiences* (Sydney: Allen & Unwin, 1995), p. 42. Nancy Fraser has criticized the original conception of public sphere for it alleged exclusion of women. In an appreciative criticism, she argues that in original Habermassian formula, the participants in this sphere were a part of the educated male elite, who would mediate between society and governmental, economic and other structures. See Nancy Fraser, "Rethinking the Public Sphere: A Contribution to the Critique of Actually Existing Democracy", in op. cit., Calhoun, 1999, pp.120-23, 122.

2. For further details of the discussion see Dina Matar, "Heya TV: A Feminist Counterpublic for Arab Women", *Comparative Studies of South Asia, Africa and the Middle East*, Vol. 27, No.3 (2007), pp.13-24, Mamoun Fandy, "Cyber resistance; Saudi Opposition between Globalization and Localization", *Comparative Studies in Society and History,* Vol. 41, No.1, (January 1999), pp. 124-147 and Gwenn Okruhlik, "Networks of Dissent: Islamism and reform in Saudi Arabia", *Current History*, Vol.101, No. 651 (Jan, 2002), pp.22-28.
3. Op. cit., Dina Matar, 2007, p.13.
4. Jill Crystal, "Civil Society in the Arabian Gulf", in A.G. Norton (ed.), *Civil Society in the M. East* (Leiden: E.J. Brill, 1996), pp. 259-286, 262.
5. Ibid, p. 283.
6. Op. cit., Mamoun Fandy, 1999, p. 34.
7. Ibid.
8. Exorbitant oil revenues have given the state power to weaken social groups by co-opting the social organization collectively or by fragmenting them through selective co-option of key members. Nonetheless, despite their best efforts, incipient pressures from Islamists, human rights, tribal, technocratic and

other groups have in fact have appeared in the Gulf. See op. cit., Jill Crystal in Norton, 1996.

9. Techno-culture is a new form of popular culture seen on internet. Habermass identifies techno-culture which is otherwise suppressed by high culture as constituent element of public sphere. Techno-culture has now become the springboard for new expressions of popular culture in the Gulf.
10. Political blogs with hawkish views and most of such bloggers are young, well educated, high income males, who are internet veterans. See Ann Parallel Travers, "Subaltern Feminist Counterpublics in Cyberspace", *Sociological Perspectives*, Vol. 46, No.2 (Summer 2003), pp. 223-237, 223.
11. Judy Wajcman, "Gendered by design", *Internet Issue Brief,* Vol. 1, No. 2 (July, 2004), pp.11-14.
12. Fraser's use of the term counterpublic has become central to feminist critiques of the public sphere. She argues that Habermas' conception of the ideal public sphere was far too narrow, and subordinated groups (women and minorities etc.) create 'counterpublics' where they come together in order to challenge the hegemony and assert identities. See Nancy Fraser, in op. cit., Calhoun, 1999, pp.121, 23.
13. See op. cit., Dina Matar, 2007.
14. 'Cyber Islamic environments' is an umbrella term/common rubric, which can refer to a variety of contexts, perspectives and applications of the media by those who define themselves as Muslims. See Gary R Bunt, 2003, *Islam in the Digital Age: E Jihad, Online Fatwas and Cyber Islamic Environments,* (London: Pluto Press, 2003), pp. 4-5.
15. Ibid., pp. 2-3.
16. Op. cit., Gwenn Okruhlik, 2002, p. 24.
17. Edmund Ghareeb, "New Media and the Information Revolution in the Arab World: An Assessment", *Middle Eastern Journal,* Vol. 54, No. 3 (Summer 2000), p. 415.
18. Larbi Sadiki, 2007, "Saudi Arabia, Re-Reading politics and religion in the Wake of September 11", in Shahram Akbarzadeh & Abdulla Saeed, *Islam and Political Legitimacy* (eds.), (London: Routledge & Curson, 2007) p. 42.
19. Ibid., pp. 42-43
20. Op. cit., Gwenn Okruhlik, 2002, p. 24.
21. Ibid., p. 25

22. Op. cit., Mamoun Fandy, 1999, p.126.
23. Ibid.
24. Asef Beyat, "The Street and the Politics of Dissent in the Arab World", *Middle East Report, No*. 226 (2003), pp.11-12.
25. Ibid., p.11.
26. Op. cit., Mamoun Fandy, 1999, p. 130.
27. Before cassette it was the turn of radio, people like President Jamal Abdal-Nasir of Egypt have used this tool skillfully in strengthening the popular base in the Arab world.
28. Charles Hirschkind, *The Ethical Soundscape: Cassette Sermons and Islamic Counterpublics* (New York: Columbia University Press, 2006), p. 2.
29. Ibid., p. 2, 4.
30. Cassette enables only an extension of one-sided authoritative discourse. Dialogues are difficult to pick up in such media.
31. Paul Dresch & James Piscatori, *Monarchies and Nations: Globalization and Identities in the Arab Sates of the Gulf* (London: I.B. Tauris, 1988).
32. Op. cit., Larbi Sadiki, 2007, pp. 42-43.
33. Op. cit., Gwenn Okhurlik, 2002, p. 27.
34. Blogs have the potential to have a strong sense of me-ness, given the deeply personal nature of the online diary-keeping or journal writing function afforded by them. Yet this information is public in that it is disseminated to a vast audience of lurkers and commentators, making it mass communication.
35. Joshua Teitelbaun, "Dueling for Da'wa; State vs. Society on the Saudi Internet", *Middle East Journal,* Vol. 56, No. 2 (2002), p. 226.
36. Aysha a Saudi blogger, who has recently returned to her country with her husband and child, after two years in the US, comments on how men try to micro-manage every aspect of their wives' lives-and what some women do about it. See "Saudi blogging round-up", available at www.bbc.co.uk/go/pr/-/2/hi/middle_east/7631927.stm (October 1, 2008).

References

Ann Travers, "Parallel, Subaltern Feminist Counterpublics in Cyberspace", *Sociological Perspectives*, Vol. 46, No. 2 (Summer 2003), pp. 223-237.

Asef Bayat, "The Street and the Politics of Dissent in the Arab World", *Middle East Report*, No.226 (Spring 2003), pp.10-17.

Charles Hirschkind, *The Ethical Soundscape: Cassette Sermons and Islamic Counterpublics* (New York: Columbia University Press, 2006).

Dina Matar, "Heya TV: A Feminist Counterpublic for Arab Women", *Comparative Studies of South Asia, Africa and the Middle East*, Vol. 27, No. 3 (2007), pp. 13-24.

Edmund Ghareeb, "New Media and the Information Revolution in the Arab World: An Assessment, *Middle Eastern Journal*, Vol. 54, No. 3 (Summer 2000), pp. 395-418.

Gary R Bunt, *Islam in the Digital Age: E Jihad, Online Fatwas and Cyber Islamic Environments* (London: Pluto Press, 2003).

Gwenn Okruhlik, "Networks of Dissent: Islamism and Reform in Saudi Arabia", *Current History*, Vol.101, No. 651 (January 2002), pp. 22-28.

J. Corner, "Television: Form and Public Address", in Edward Arnold et al (eds.), *The Media in Australia: Industries, Texts, Audiences* (Sydney: Allen & Unwin, 1995).

J.E. Katz, R.E. Rice and P. Aspden, *The Internet, 1995-2000: Access, Civic Involvement, and Social Interaction* (MIT Press: Cambridge, 2001).

Jill Crystal, "Civil Society in the Arabian Gulf", in A.G. Norton (ed.), *Civil Society in the Middle East* (Leiden: Brill, 1996), pp. 259-286.

Joshua Teitelbaun, "Dueling for Da'wa: State vs. Society on the Saudi Internet", *Middle East Journal*, Vol. 56, No. 2 (2002) pp. 222-239.

Judy Wajcman, "Gendered by design", *Internet Issue Brief*, Vol. 1, No. 2 (July 2004), pp.11-14.

Judy Wajcman, *TechnoFeminism* (Polity Press: Cambridge, 2004).

Jurgen Habermass, "Further Reflections on the Public Sphere", in Calhoun, *Habermass and Public Sphere* (Cambridge: MIT Press, 1992), pp. 421-426.

Larbi Sadiki, "Saudi Arabia, Re-Reading politics and religion in the Wake of September 11", in Shahram Akbarzadeh & Abdulla Saeed (eds.), *Islam and Political Legitimacy* (London: Routledge & Curson, 2007), pp. 29-49.

Mamoun Fandy, "Cyber resistance; Saudi Opposition between Globalization and Localization", *Comparative Studies in Society and History*, Vol. 41, No. 1 (January 1999), pp. 124-147.

Mansoor Moaddel, "The Saudi Public Speaks: Religion, Gender, and Politics", *International Journal of Middle Eastern Studies,* No. 38 (2006), pp.79-108.

Mohamed El-Sayed Said, "Global Civil Society: An Arab Perspective", in Mohamed El-Sayed Said, *Global Civil Society* (London: Sage, 2005), pp. 60-71.

Nancy Fraser, "Rethinking the Public Sphere: A Contribution to the Critique of Actually Existing Democracy", in Calhoun, *Habermass and Public Sphere* (Cambridge: MIT Press, 1992), pp.120-23.

Paul Dresch, and James Piscatori, *Monarchies and Nations: Globalization and Identities in the Arab Sates of the Gulf* (London: I.B. Tauris, 1998).

9

Political Legitimacy of Monarchy and Civil Society in Jordan

Shelly Johny

Studies on the development of civil society initiatives in various West Asian countries gained added importance in the 1990s when similar movements calling for greater political participation were witnessed in Eastern Europe and Latin America. Jordan was among the most prominent case studies especially in the context of political reforms launched by the monarchy in that country in 1989. As will be looked in greater detail later, civil society in Jordan is not a force that merely occupies the space between state and society, but has linkages with political actors which contributes to the expansion of the democratic space in the country. This paper will try to look at how political parties like the Muslim Brotherhood view civil society initiatives and utilize the latter to achieve their overall objectives. It is also necessary to look at how the pace of democratization has progressed in Jordan since reforms were introduced in 1989. The different kinds of restrictions that the state has placed on both electoral politics and civil society initiatives have been already explored in detail. Therefore, the focus here is how such attempts by the state have affected the interactions between the various entities in the political and social spheres.

Civil Society in Jordan

One of the problems associated with trying to study the nature of civil society in the state of Jordan is an understanding of what exactly constitutes civil society in that country. A look at the debate on Jordanian civil society shows that there are two distinctive understandings on the issue. Scholars like Quintan Wiktorowicz are of the view that civil society in Jordan be defined as it is usually in West Asia as a variety of associations and non-government organizations that work in organizing social and cultural activities in different sections of society and occupy the space between the state and the public. Looked at from this viewpoint, the political reforms introduced in 1989 are seen in a critical manner as an attempt by the state to seemingly allow greater political freedoms while through that effort seeks to better monitor and regulate the activities of different associations, organizations and formations in Jordan. The elaborate mechanism in place that makes it a complex process to create and register an association and conduct activities under its banner actually make it virtually impossible for the registered association or organization to act as an entity that can raise political issues that are inimical to the interests of the state and argue for the advancement of existing political rights. The state reserves the exclusive right to withhold recognition of any association that it sees as threatening the stability of the regime. [1]

The second approach has been favoured by Richard T. Antoun who sees civil society in Jordan from an anthropological perspective. According to him, tribal structures and tribal codes of conduct play a very important role in managing the affairs of the society in Jordan. These structures help in regulating social life, solving disputes and arranging marriages in the lesser urbanised setups in Jordan. This view sees tribal structures with a strong presence at the grass-root level as civil society elements in the context of Jordanian society. [2] Both these views are relevant for the purpose of our study. They actually reflect the duality that continues to exist in Jordanian society as one divided between more politically conscious Palestinians who are mostly participants in professional associations and the more tribally oriented Transjordanians. While these distinctions have slowly started to blur they continue to have a bearing on how

Jordanians see themselves as divided into two different ethnic communities.

One of the consequences of the political reforms in 1989 has been the creation of a plethora of voluntary organizations representing various interests in Jordan. The state has created a series of checks and balances to ensure that these organizations and associations do not become a threat to the government. But at the same time, these organizations have come to represent such a diverse range of interests and demands which the state will increasingly find it hard to placate with a patronage system that was suitable for sustaining the monarchical form of government in the pre-1989 situation. The revolution in communications has also made segments of society, especially the educated, aware of the need for change in a highly conservative and static environment. It is needed to note here that while Richard T. Antoun's observation about the relevance of tribal structures holds true for a society like Jordan, such elements are beholden to the Hashemite royal family and are less likely to press for political reforms.

A study on civil society cannot ignore its impact on attempts to further democratic rights in a country and thereby there is a need to look at the links between civil society and politics in Jordan. Civil society in Jordan shares some of the same characteristics with civil society initiatives in other parts of West Asia. Unlike Western notions of civil society, many of the civil society movements in West Asia include movements or organizations that are ideologically close to or are even fronts of political-religious parties like the Muslim Brotherhood. To that extent, civil society in West Asia partly reflects attempts by political or religious parties to utilize all the resources at their disposal and exploit whatever space that has been provided by the state. This results in a situation where civil society becomes an extension of the battles that are carried out in the political realm. In the case of Jordan, there are various civil society organizations that are ideologically linked to the Muslim Brotherhood. Professional associations have also actively conducted campaigns related to the issue of Palestine. [3] A politicization of the space of civil society has its influence on state-civil society relations as is evident in the post-1989 period.

State and Democratization Process in Jordan

It is now generally understood that Jordan went in for political reforms because of the weakening of the 'rentier' economy system that had sustained the state until then. Under this system, which linked Jordan to the rentier-state systems that prevailed in the oil-rich Gulf region, the Jordanian government received a disproportionate part of its revenue or 'rents' from the flow of income from its expatriates working in the Gulf countries and in the form of direct aid from oil-rich Gulf countries directly rather than by taxation of the population. The lack of taxation meant less need for the Jordanian regime to be accountable to the public and create representative institutions. These revenues declined in the wake of economic downturn following low oil prices during the 1980s. This crisis was further compounded during the Iraqi invasion of Kuwait and the subsequent Gulf War in 1990-1991 as Iraq was the biggest market for Jordanian agricultural and industrial products and also a source of cheap oil. The UN trade sanctions against Iraq severely affected the Jordanian economy. [4] The Jordanian state turned to the International Monetary Fund (IMF) for help. But it had to cut down on its public expenditures or subsidies according to the IMF guidelines. The political unrest in the country following these measures which resulted in increasing fuel prices in 1989 forced King Hussein to introduce political reforms and return to parliamentary politics to pre-empt greater threats to the regime. Thus the political liberalisation process was introduced by the state for its own survival rather than as a consequence of genuine societal change. [5]

As mentioned earlier, civil society in West Asian countries like Jordan cannot be de-linked from politics of the country.

How these links become vital in the context of Jordan will be explored later. As the political reforms were introduced as a part of regime survival, the state has created a large number of restrictions on political participation in order to ensure that a viable opposition to the policies of the monarchy do not come up. It is worth putting added attention here on the Muslim Brotherhood in this paper as it the largest and most organized movement in the country capable of putting up stiff opposition to the policies of the government. [6] The movement is one of the oldest to be allowed to function in Jordan since the time of King Abdullah, the first king of Jordan. [7] In the parliamentary elections of 1989, political parties were not allowed to contest and individuals contested in their personal capacity. In spite of such restrictions, Islamists including members of the Muslim Brotherhood won thirty-two seats from a total of eighty seats.

However, the Muslim Brotherhood was prevented from implementing its programmes like the segregation of the sexes in schools, the prohibition of alcohol and preventing peace talks with Israel. Even though the Islamists managed to appoint the parliament speaker, parliament could pass only those laws which had the approval of the king. While the Political Parties Law passed in 1992 legalized political parties, there were also a number of restrictions on them. It prevented political parties from having organizational or financial links to any outside entity. This created potential pressure mechanisms for the regime on organizations like the Muslim Brotherhood and Palestinian groups like the Popular Front for Liberation of Palestine (PFLP) and Democratic Front for Liberation of Palestine (DFLP) which had links with their branches in other parts of West Asia.

To create a more compliant parliament, the government introduced the 'one-person, one-vote' system for the national parliamentary election of 1993. In the earlier election, each citizen could vote for as many candidates as there were seats in the electoral district. By introducing this measure the government ensured that people would vote for tribal candidates who were pro-monarchy rather than the Islamic Action Front (IAF), the political party of the Muslim Brotherhood. The formation of electoral districts also favoured the central and southern tribal areas of the country. As expected by the government, the Islamists won only twenty-two seats. Apart from the IAF, no other party won more than five seats and candidates from official parties won only thirty-four of the eighty seats with the rest won by independents. Besides the political process the government has also restricted criticism by the press of government policy through the Press and Publications Law. [8] Permission has to be sought from the government for conducting protest marches and demonstrations. [9] The restrictions placed on political parties led to their boycotting of the 1997 parliamentary elections. [10] Even though the IAF contested the 2003 and the 2007 parliamentary elections, it won much lesser seats than 1989 and 1993. In 2003, they won seventeen seats out of a total of one hundred and ten [11] and in 2007 it suffered its worst electoral defeat winning only six seats. [12]

Politics and Civil Society in Jordan

The restrictions put on the parliament and freedom of expression has created frustration among political parties especially the IAF on the political process in Jordan. Members of the IAF and the Muslim Brotherhood have increasingly begun to feel that they have begun to lose public support because of their inability to speed up the process of democratization and introduce political reforms. Hopes that the process of democratization would get renewed strength after Abdullah became king in 1999 was dashed when he continued with the policy followed by King Hussein in his last years and restricted the scope for change in the political space. It is in this context that civil society has become quite relevant for religious political parties like the Brotherhood. The Muslim Brotherhood has provided a broad range of social services like schools, hospitals and charities to the society in Jordan long before the democratization process began in 1989. This is a similar pattern followed by political Islamist movements in countries as diverse as Pakistan, Lebanon and the Palestinian territories and in return movements like the Jamaat-i-Islami, Jamiat-Ulema-i-Islam, Hezbollah and Hamas have achieved good dividends in national elections in those states.

A restriction of the political space and even losses in the parliament can be balanced by the range of services that the Muslim Brotherhood provides at the social level. While the present setup of the electoral systems does not allow the Brotherhood to reap benefits from its activities in the social sphere, it is this movement which will stand to gain the most if genuine democratic reforms are introduced. In fact the social and cultural realms are seen as extended battlegrounds by Islamist movements. This phenomenon has gained added strength in the context of the withdrawal of the state from providing public services due to the weakening of the rentier system and implementing of the structural adjustment programmes of the IMF which calls for cutting down of state subsidies. This has created a tremendous impact on society as large sections of it were dependent on state-implemented projects and schemes since the beginning of the nation-building exercise. The Muslim Brotherhood has sought to fill this vacuum. There are a number of social and cultural organisations which strive to promote and spread conservative Islamic values in the wider society. For example there are non-governmental organisations linked to the Muslim Brotherhood like the al-Afaf Charitable Society which try to encourage marriage and setting up of families according to the Islamic value system. Such organizations view westernization as a cultural onslaught on the indigenous cultural value system. [13] An anti-western Islamist social and cultural thought can be pitted against the government in the future because of the perceived pro-Western orientation of King Abdullah as compared to Hussein who had strong appeal among the tribal

Bedouin population.

While the state is ever vigilant to prevent the articulation of opposition in social and cultural activities the very fact that the Muslim Brotherhood is active in these areas means that it can preserve its strength in society for future political gains. Islamist social and cultural organizations also have popular appeal as they are seen in contrast to the corruption that widely prevails in government circles. In a practice termed as *wasta*, ones personal connections to influential figures can help in gaining access to government facilities. Islamists are seen as selfless and genuine in comparison to the politicians close to the regime. [14] Thus it can be said that in spite of the odds against them due to the setup of the political system, the Muslim Brotherhood fared quite well in the first two parliamentary elections held since 1989.

This does not mean that voluntary organizations and associations are free from strict laws governing their activities. The Law of Societies and Organizations and Political Party Law prevent voluntary organizations from being part of any political activity. [15] But as far as the Muslim Brotherhood is concerned, it is involved in the preservation and conservation of conservative Islamic values which have widespread appeal in a society like Jordan and the state cannot put an objection to it. Civil society will continue to be of relevance to domestic politics in Jordan. But ultimately the pace of democratization in Jordan will not just depend on the unity of forces that will force the monarchy to liberalize but also on whether the monarchy sees it as a threat to its existence and wider regional events that have an impact on events inside Jordan.

Regime Legitimacy and Impact of Regional Politics on Jordan

The rulers of Jordan have faced a crisis of political legitimacy since the very beginning because of the nature in which the state of Jordan was created. The modern day state of Jordan was carved out of the province of Greater Syria to serve the imperial interests of Great Britain in West Asia. It was only incidental that Abdullah, the son of Sherief Hussein, the Hashemite ruler of the Hejaz province in Arabia was made the ruler of the new country, which was only a temporary arrangement at the time. [16] Transjordan had a very small population and little resources at the time of its creation. Unlike political entities like Egypt, Syria and Iraq which were former Ottoman provinces, the inhabitants of Transjordan did not see themselves as citizens bound to a concept of nation state. Thus, the rulers of Transjordan faced a crisis of legitimacy at two levels which continued to bedevil the rulers in future years. At the first level was the legitimacy of the state of Transordan itself as it was seen by many in the Arab world as a creation of British imperialistic designs. At the second level was the legitimacy of the individual Hashemite ruler of Jordan. It was to bolster the legitimacy of the state of Jordan that Abdullah annexed the West Bank and East Jerusalem with British approval. [17]

While the step increased the importance of Jordan it created political problems for Abdullah with thousands of Palestinians as refugees in his country. Abdullah's involvement in Palestinian affairs cost him his life in 1951. The greatest challenges that the Jordanian monarch faced was during the reign of his successor Hussein. The Palestinian problem became all the more grave after the 1967 war due to the loss of the West Bank and East Jerusalem and a new wave of refugees who sought shelter in Jordan. The defeat of the Arabs in that war led to the radicalisation and militarization of the Palestinians. Various Palestinian guerrilla groups were formed and they created a state within a state in Jordan. This was a direct threat to the authority of the Hashemite monarchy and resulted in a civil war (1970-71). The Hashemite monarchy successfully crushed the rebellion and defeated a Syrian invasion force that had come in support of the Palestinians. [18] The Palestinian groups were expelled from Jordanian territory and Jordan refrained from joining the Arabs in the next Arab-Israeli War of 1973 in its own interests.

Using diplomacy, Hussein developed strong links with all the major West Asian Arab countries. [19] Jordan entered into peace negotiations with Israel in 1993 and finally signed a peace agreement with that country in 1994. Thus Hussein managed to attain not just the loyalty of his subjects but also acceptance within the region. But Jordan because of a number of factors continues to be affected by developments at the regional level. This is mainly because of internal factors and the geographical position of Jordan, positioned in between the major countries of West Asia, which makes it inevitable that it gets affected by turmoil in other parts of the region. In fact, the Palestinian issue has heavily affected the democratization process in Jordan. Domestic criticism of the peace agreement with Israel is cited as the main reason for the slowing down of political liberalization in Jordan during the time of King Hussein.

Similarly, the worsening of Israel-Palestine relations during the Second Intifada that began in 2000 and its impact on Jordan led to a state policy which preferred security over political reforms. [20] The Palestinians who constitute close to more than fifty per cent of the population continue to be an important factor in Jordanian domestic and foreign policy. [21] The recent Israeli air attacks and ground incursions against Gaza can increase domestic opposition to Israel within Jordan and public pressure on the monarchy to do something about the situation. Domestically, more worrying to the monarchy is the strong showing of Hamas in the Palestinian elections of 2006 and its grabbing of power in Gaza. The obvious fear for the regime is the encouragement that it can give to Islamists within the kingdom.

Jordan has also been affected by the turmoil in Iraq. Radical Jordanian Islamists like Abu Musab Zarqawi have gone to fight American troops in Iraq and take part in the Sunni-Shia sectarian violence in the country. They have also conducted terrorist attacks in Jordan itself. [22] There were concerns about the impact that radical Islamists could have on the Muslim Brotherhood whose leaders took part in the condolences to Zarqawi after he was killed in Iraq. [23] While the Jordanian monarchy has enjoyed stability since some time, it is mindful of any threats to its existence. A spill over of instability from the neighbouring countries can force the monarchy to reverse the democratic process and restrict civil society initiatives.

The regime is well aware that the tribal Bedouin population of Jordan has previously been less inclined to oppose the government and has successfully prevented the Muslim Brotherhood from gaining substantial seats in the last two parliament elections. However, in the course of the implementation of IMF structural-adjustment programmes, the Jordanian tribes are finding that they are losing out on a large number of benefits that they used to receive earlier and are not being seen as the major support bases by the regime in the same way as before. [24] In the future, it is likely that this segment of society might organize itself in oppositional terms to the government in politics as well as civil society initiatives. From the perspective of the Muslim Brotherhood, it finds itself in a more restricted situation than in the pre-1989 situation. Also, a large number of the supporters of the Muslim Brotherhood are Palestinians in an environment where supporting an Islamist movement is politically and socially more acceptable than adopting an overtly Palestinian point of view. Presently, there have been rivalries and tensions between the leaders of the Palestinians and Transjordanians in the IAF. [25] If the state places further restrictions on activities in the space provided to civil society besides the sphere of electoral politics, a united and renewed Muslim Brotherhood could put stiff resistance to the government.

Conclusion

Civil society in Jordan has gained added impetus in Jordan ever since the liberalization efforts introduced in 1989. Civil society formations include a host of voluntary organizations, professional associations and non-governmental organizations. There is also the view that tribal structures also perform the role of civil society in the context of Jordanian society. While the state has imposed lots of restrictions on the activities of civil society initiatives the latter has created a space for itself to a certain extent. Because of the environment that exists in Jordan, politicization of the civil society arena cannot be avoided, and many of the voluntary organizations are ideologically linked to known political parties like the Muslim Brotherhood. Political parties utilize whatever space that has been provided by the state and see social and cultural activities as extended fronts of the political background. Civil society is likely to become more relevant because of the setbacks that the Muslim Brotherhood has suffered in electoral politics. Ultimately, further attempts by the state to restrict political and civil society spaces can heighten tensions between political parties and voluntary organizations on the one side and the government on the other.

Notes

1. Quintan Wiktorowicz, "Civil Society as Social Control: State Power in Jordan," *Comparative Politics*, Vol. 33, No. 1, (Oct., 2007), pp. 43-61.
2. Richard T. Antoun, "Civil Society, Tribal Process, and Change in Jordan: An Anthropological View," *International Journal of Middle East Studies*, Vol. 32, No. 4, (Nov., 2000), pp. 441-463.
3. Jillian Schwedler, "More Than a Mob: The Dynamics of Political Demonstrations in Jordan", *Middle East Report*, No. 226, (Spring, 2003), p. 18.
4. Alan George, *Jordan: Living in the Crossfire*, (London, Zed Books, 2005), p. 34.
5. Rex Brynen, "Economic Crisis and Post-Rentier Democratization in the Arab World: The Case of Jordan", *Canadian Journal of Political Science*, Vol. 25, No. 1, (March, 1992), pp. 69-97.
6. Glenn E. Robinson, "Defensive Democratization in Jordan", *International Journal of Middle East Studies*, Vol. 30, No. 3,

(Aug., 1998), p. 402.
7. Mary C. Wilson, *King Abdullah, Britain and the Making of Jordan*, (Cambridge, Cambridge University Press, 1987), p.166.
8. Quintan Wiktorowicz, "The Limits of Democracy in the Middle East: The Case of Jordan", *The Middle East Journal*, Vol. 53, No. 4, (Autumn, 1999), p. 616.
9. Op. cit., Wiktorowicz, 2007, p. 50.
10. Beverley Milton-Edwards and Peter Hinchcliffe, "Abdullah's Jordan: New King, Old Problems", *Middle East Report*, No. 213, (Winter, 1999), p. 29.
11. http://www.nytimes.com/2007/11/11/world/middleeast/11jordan .html?pagewanted=1&_r=1&sq=Jordan&st=cse&scp=20
12. http://www.washingtonpost.com/wp-dyn/content/article/2007/11/26/AR2007112602041.html
13. Quintan Wiktorowicz and Suha Taji Farouki, "Islamic NGOs and Muslim Politics: A Case from Jordan", *Third World Quarterly*, Vol. 21, No. 4, (Aug., 2000), pp. 691-692
14. Op. cit., Robinson, 1998, p. 399.
15. Op. cit., Wiktorowicz, 2007, p. 53.
16. Op. cit., Wilson, 1987, p. 53.
17. Ibid, p. 2.
18. Peter Gubser, *Jordan: Crossroads of Middle Eastern Events*, (Boulder, Colorado, Westview Press, 1983), p. 104.
19. James Lunt, *Hussein of Jordan: A Political Biography*, (London, Macmillan London Ltd., 1989), p. 231.
20. Philip Robins, *A History of Jordan*, (Cambridge, Cambridge University Press, 2004), p. 202.
21. Yitzhak Reiter, "The Palestinian-Transjordanian Rift: Economic Might and Political Power in Jordan", *The Middle East Journal*, Vol. 58, No. 1, (Winter, 2004), *p*. 74.
22. http://www.atimes.com/atimes/Middle_East/JL24Ak02.html
23. www.articlearchives.com/crime-law-enforcement-corrections/human-rights/900586-1.html - 51k
24. Anne Marie Baylouny, "Militarizing Welfare: Neo-Liberalism and Jordanian Policy", *The Middle East Journal,* Vol. 62, No. 2, (2008), p. 278.
25. Op. cit., Robinson, 1998, pp. 400-404.

10

Role of Israeli Civil Society in Conflict Transformation

Moinuddin Ahmed

Introduction

Israel differs in many aspects from its neighbouring states in West Asia. In fact, many observers have spoken about the uniqueness of this country. The milieu of its emergence and the circumstances of its existence gave it a new distinguishing feature: presence of a well equipped and a highly trained military. Israel has established a gigantic military apparatus because of the threat it perceives from its neighbouring countries as well as from the armed Palestinian groups in the Occupied Territories. Moreover, Israel is generally alleged of breaking peace in the region because of its willingness to use military might against the slightest provocation by its external adversaries. Can a state that feels so insecure of its external environment tolerate internal opposition in the form of civil society? Before we answer this fundamental question about the existence of civil society in Israel, let us try and understand the phenomenon at the conceptual level.

Civil society does not lend itself to theoretical simplicity. Understanding about civil society and its manifestation varies widely. One of the most acceptable imageries of civil society is that of a congregation of people involved in non-state and non-private affairs. Any group formed outside the realm of the state or the influence of family can be termed as a civil society group. As soon as people enter public sphere they can form a civil society group. People constituting the civil society may not always be involved in demanding something, but a group is more often recognized when it starts asserting its demand.

The language of civil society was picked up by the western intellectuals of various political persuasions to articulate their discomforts with modern society and government. It is an idea that has drawn different definitions from diverse spheres of academics in different parts of the world. While American scholars consider civil society as an answer to anomie, Europeans recognize it as an answer to interventionist government. In India, civil society is considered to facilitate pluralist democracy. [1]

Although there is not any single definition of civil society, most definitions are interconnected with the concept of democracy. According to a United Nations report, civil society together with state and market is one of the three spheres that constitute democratic society. [2] Civil society does so by promoting democracy seizing political initiatives and thus trying to enlarge the space for political participation. [3] In other words, civil society acts within the space located between the state and the private sphere of the individual, in which governance and development goals are contested. Civil society therefore interacts closely with the state. [4] For Antonio Gramsci, civil society could provide the possibility of liberation; a terrain where rising social groups may challenge the power of the state and the dominating classes associated with it. Throughout the New Left tradition, civil society is seen to involve modes of education and negotiation, attitudes of tolerance, patterns of discourse and vehicles of association. [5]

Having such a remarkable potential, the concept of civil society has been able to attract enormous interest of the peace builders who use the civil society as a tool for conflict transformation. Expectations from the civil society increase, where a society seeks to exercise its own power, while challenging decision making of the political elite. The potential of civil society has proved to be a mighty one in the countries where people and have questioned state actors who have not lived up to their expectations. The turbulent history of Israel/Palestine and the dismal performance of the negotiating parties—the Israeli government and the Palestinian representatives—in reaching a peaceful solution have given little hope to those who want to see the end of misery for people on both the sides.

Dialogues have failed and mediators have also been unsuccessful; peace seems to be a distant dream and the overwhelming presence of Israeli military in the Occupied Territories makes the situation even worse. A numbers of commissions, white papers, recommendations, accords and UN resolutions have also fallen flat on one of the most contested piece of land on earth. The Israel-Palestinian conflict has proved to be one of the most challenging tasks for the peace builders. In this context, the role of Israeli civil society becomes extremely important in shaping the future of the conflict and to place it on a track, where every possible tools of conflict transformation can be used for peace building.

At times it becomes hard to imagine the peace building efforts of civil society in Israel in view of the circumstances in which Israeli military was established in 1949 as a requirement of 'a militia of civilians trained and equipped for combat and capable of being mobilized at a very short notice.' [6] The result was the creation of something that many observers have chosen to call a 'citizens' army' with its strength based largely on reserve formations. This had important consequences as far as the civil-military relations were concerned, producing what Dan Horowitz has characterized as a 'civilianized military in a partially militarized society'. [7]

This does not mean that the country is devoid of any civil society organization and has never seen demonstrations and oppositions to the government policies, yet most of the civil society organizations in the country are formed by the people who were directly or indirectly related to military. The Israeli civil society after its emergence in the 1970s has been able to encourage several peace initiatives. The uniqueness of the working of these grass-root organizations in Israel lies in the fact that they work in an environment where the government's policy making is highly influenced by the stranglehold of the military in the country.

Looking at the present situation there are heightened expectations from the Israeli civil society to something remarkable for the in the Israel-Palestinian conflict. There is no doubt that the Israeli civil society is capable of making things happen now as it was successful in pushing the government to unilaterally withdraw from the south of Lebanon in May 2000. But we have to bear in mind that although Lebanon was a success story, where the military was called back from being stationed in a sovereign country, the case here is entirely different. The Israel-Palestinian conflict looks simple if it is put simply as a problem of occupation, but here, complexities are unearthed after virtually every peace initiative.

At present, Israeli civil society is divided along identity and ideological lines: on the one hand there are exponents that sustain cultural pluralism and openness (including Jewish Israeli and Arab Israeli groups); on the other hand, there are advocates of an exclusivist identity. [8] This tendency makes civil society in Israel weak and not as active as in the past, leaving room for a stronger engagement of the military, that has become increasingly empowered to influence the ongoing conflict. [9] Therefore, the Israeli civil society is faced with two crucial tasks: first, to defy the influence of military in order to succeed in bringing conflict transformation and second, the onerous charge of building confidence among the Palestinians. It is indeed an uphill task for civil society to perform when the Israeli military's confidence is sky high.

Israeli Civil Society under the Shadow of Military

Civil society emerged in Israel only in 1970s, in so far as the first two decades of the life was focused on centralization and collectivism. [10] In the late 1980s and in the 1990s along with economic liberalization and the outbreak of first Intifada, many associations flourished in Israel, promoting different values and needs: not only peace, but also civil rights and newer issues in Israeli public discourse such as non-discrimination, environment etc.

In the first two decades of the independence, Israeli society was passive in response to the all embracing rule of political system i.e. the political parties and constitutive institutions of the organized Yishuv (pre-state Jewish community in Palestine). Israeli society was led by relatively coherent ruling state instruments to assimilate the newcomers into a hegemonic Israeli culture marked by a high level of mobilization and a strong claim of collectivity. The highly centralized economy and land resources—mostly owned by state—further underlined the dominant role of the state in society. With national security being continuously threatened, the issue of security occupied the core collective consciousness urging solidarity and national cohesion in which military service played a primary role. [11]

One of the first few steps that were taken by the David Ben-Gurion, the first Israeli prime minister was to centralize the pre-state entities—small militias such as Haganah, Palamach and Irgun—under one umbrella, which, according to him were the highest expression of Zionism. The significant features of this process were further emphasized by the introduction of such notions as professionalism and de-politicization, which, in turn were taken up by the military as part of its own organizational image. [12]

The complex military interface with the society, economy and politics—its various roles in education, settlements in frontier areas, military government over the Arab population in Israel (1948-1966) and the Occupied Territories (since 1967), and the strategic intelligence and planning, policymaking core institutions—all combined to shape a 'cultural code of civilian militarism,' with institutional violence as an 'organizing principle.' [13] In these circumstances, the public space became completely dominated by the military, which placed tremendous pressure on the civil society to maintain a domain where free, pluralist and rational discourse could be conducted for common good through communicative actions and mediation of interest groups.

Since the early 1970s, Israeli society has undergone a process of social and ideological polarization and the rise of distinct interest groups as a consequence of wars, economic liberalization, and immigration from Soviet Union with the end of the Cold War. [14] This period witnessed a transformation of Israeli society from collective to individual orientation. Social segmentation and multiculturalism also became apparent in 1990s. The declining political hegemony of secular 'Israeliness' represented by the Labour movement and its institutions gave way to separate multi-cultural autonomies with their particular institutional system, concept of rules, and the desirable resource allocation. [15]

These changes gave rise to a burgeoning civil society – hitherto content with the passive role of legitimizing and constituting a state regime—willing to assume an increasingly active role in manifesting expectations for accountability and moral behaviour on the part of the political system. Yet, interest groups, voluntary associations and institutions preferred to address their grievances through exclusive channels rather than in broad civic frameworks. Many of these activities are based on particular network of kinship and friendships, which preclude certain segments of society and thus fail to expand the domain of civil society. Public protests and demonstrations became more frequent and massive in scope, especially after the Lebanon war in 1982. However, they were aimed at immediate objectives and disappeared from the public arena after a relatively short burst of activity without creating a permanent public space beyond state control. Moreover, this mode of action set civil society on adversarial terms with the state as the appropriate address for its complaints, instead of constituting civic norms and patterns of action. [16]

Thus, in spite of the broadening participation of Israelis in professional and communal associations, civil society in Israel remained essentially established or corporative, fragmented and passive, with some segments demonstrating intolerance towards other civil sectors and organizations. Furthermore, official regulative apparatus further weakened the civil society, restricting its freedom of action and encouraging its members to prefer unity and avoid disagreements. These characteristics are particularly apparent in the almost total absence of protest movements from the Israeli political arena, despite deep social frustration. [17] Nonetheless, since early 1990s, the proliferation of private media, the mushrooming of think tanks and human right associations NGOs, and emergence of organizations for intercultural dialogue (in addition to long-term protest movements), have contributed to an open and critical public discourse.

Civil society in Israel is particularly strained in affecting policymaking on national security, which had traditionally been kept out of public sphere and discourse, including by the law of Military Censorship. Israeli society largely complied with these restrictions in the name of 'rallying around the flag', especially in the time of crisis and war. [18] Although this consensus seriously eroded in the controversy over the Lebanon War and the apparent bankruptcy of the military 'Civil Administration' in the Occupied Territories during the first Intifada (1987-1991), it remained a major feature of Israeli society. [19]

Similarly, despite the blows to IDF prestige as a result of major military crises since the Yom Kippur War, sustained threats to Israel's collective and individual security has kept alive the public's esteem for military leadership. This has helped the IDF preserve its status as the ultimate guarantor of Jewish national survival, as a national symbol and as the most credible state institution. Moreover, the decline of traditional constitutive social and political institution since the early 1970s allowed the senior military officers to become an integral part of social and political elite. This is best manifested in recruitments of senior officers by political parties and their rapid attainment of key official positions in the government and legislature, and executive positions in the private economy, local government, and the educational system. [20]

Israeli Civil Society and Conflict Transformation

Conflict transformation depends primarily on state actors, such as the political authorities of both the sides of the conflict, the Arab countries, foreign powers and the UN. The United Nations with its several Resolutions in the past sixty years could not manage to bring peace in the region. The Israeli elites along with their Palestinian counterparts have taken certain steps for conflict transformation but have not achieved long-term positive results. According to Hermann, 'conflict transformation in Israel has traditionally been considered the exclusive competence of the government and the military, which has retained the monopoly on these critical issues at least until the 1970s. Israeli elites were considered as the only legitimate actors to deal with peace and war. Activities carried out by the civil society organizations were viewed as against the state's interest and as such discouraged, while political parties were the only recognized channels for public expressions and demands.' [21]

Open civil discontent towards this traditional security thinking erupted in the mid-1970s. During these years, the largest right-wing fundamentalist group Gush Emunim (Block of the Faithful), and the largest peace movement to date, Shalom Achshav (Peace Now)—on opposing ends of the Zionist camp—were both founded along with smaller civil society groups in this period. Gush Emunim believes the West Bank, Gaza Strip and the Golan Heights to be Israeli territories and considers that Jewish people have the right to settle in these territories. The movement's mobilizing structures have included state-funded religious schools, military units, and both formal and informal social networks. Skilful exploitation of available political opportunities, mobilizing structures and ideological framing have allowed the movement to implement its programme of settlements within the Occupied Territories in the face of substantial domestic and international opposition. The ensuing radicalization of the movement resulted into violent acts during pivotal phases of peace process such as Camp David I negotiations, implementation of the Oslo Accords, and Israel's unilateral withdrawal from Gaza in 2005. [22] Another group by the name - Women in Green or Women for Israel's Tomorrow - has been active there since 1993 as a registered non-profit organization. It is keenly taking part in weekly street theatre and public demonstration, writing articles and making posters, and carrying forward it agenda through advertisements in newspapers and public lectures. It is opposed to a two-state solution and the return of land occupied during the 1967 War. It also aggressively supports Israeli settlement of the territories, which it proposes should be annexed. [23]

On the other end of the spectrum, Peace Now asserts the right of both Jews and Arabs to live within secure borders, recognizes the Palestinian right to self-determination and advocates the creation of a Palestinian state in the territories occupied as a result of 1967 war. Peace now operates through public campaigns, advertisements, petitions, distributions of educational materials, conferences and lectures, surveys, dialogue groups, street activities, vigils and demonstrations. A particularly important ongoing project of Peace Now is the Settlement Watch, [24] which monitors and protests against the building of settlements along with studying settler attitudes regarding possible evacuation and compensation. Shortly after the beginning of the second intifada, the movement was instrumental in creating the Israeli Peace Coalition, which evolved into the Israeli-Palestinian Peace Coalition, composed of political and public figures as well as grassroots activists from both the Israeli and Palestinian mainstream. [25]

Labour's 1992 victory and the signing of the Oslo

Declaration of Principles in 1993 represented a turning point in the attitude of the Israeli government towards the peace talks and had significant repercussions on the civil society realm. A section of civil society judged the shift in the government's strategy as extremely dangerous, joining forces with right-wing parties to organize massive anti-Oslo campaigns. At this time right-wing groups of both the sides were at their nadir: Jews were killing Arabs and vice versa. This did not end here, as on November 4, 1995, Prime Minister Yitzhak Rabin was assassinated by a young Jewish Law student at a peace rally in Tel Aviv.

After Rabin's assassination and following the victory of Benjamin Netanyahu's Likud Party at the 1996 elections, civil society right-wing activism however considerably decreased. [26] During those years, civil society organizations on the Zionist as well as anti-Zionist left—often defined as peace camp or peace movement—were characterized by a variety of tactics, ranging from humanitarian missions and human right campaigns to more political activities, but their common objective was the promotion of a win-win solution for the parties involved in the conflict. They recognized the Palestinian right of self-determination and the PLO as the legitimate representative of the Palestinian people. [27]

However, joint activities particularly of the Zionist peace groups and the Israeli Arab civil society groups, have always been hampered by the fact that the former openly identified with the Zionist ideology and never embraced pacifist anti-militaristic position. [28] The road to Oslo became one of the landmark cases in working together on civil society organizations where a series of workshops and dialogues between Israeli and Palestinian academics, though facilitated by the Norwegian government, paved way for signing of the Oslo Accords. Another significant step in this regard was the problem solving workshop facilitated by Herbert Kemlan at the University of Harvard with the Israelis and the Palestinians. Although participants attended the workshop as private citizens, it is significant that many of them were members of the official Palestinians and Israeli negotiating teams.

It is important to note that even if the principles and efforts of the peace movement significantly contributed to the Oslo process, Israeli decision-makers refused to give it any credit and relegated it to the margins of negotiations. This contributed to the gradual slowdown of the movement between the early 1990s and the collapse of the Oslo Accords in the summer of 2000. The decline in the movement's activity was accompanied by other trends: a progressive institutionalization of the movement, support by the external donors such as the EU and other international founding agencies, the emergence of new groups that were by no means grassroots oriented, such as The Jerusalem Link [29] and the Peres Centre for Peace, [30] and the creation of an ad hoc coalition of peace and human rights groups, such as the Israeli Committee against House Demolition and the Coalition of Women for peace.

The advent of the 21st century came with radical changes in the dynamics of world politics. The diplomatic relations between countries were made and broken keeping in mind the 'new world's' most challenging enemy i.e. terrorism. West Asia became the focal point with the events of September 11, 200. All eyes turned towards the region with the US declaration of 'war on terror' in which Israel remained a prime strategic partner. The Israel/Palestine conflict bore a clear impact of this development. Slogans like 'Islam vs. the West,' 'West and the Rest' and many more captured the thought process of people around the world. In the circumstances, civil society organizations in Israel found themselves in a sticky situation in the midst of diverse reactions from various sections of the Israeli society over the events the incident of 9/11. [31] The relationship between Ariel Sharon and George W. Bush enhanced further in the wake of these attacks; Sharon saw common cause with the American in his own fight against Palestinians. He often referred to Arafat as 'Israel's Osama bin

Laden'. [32]

Right-wing groups and settler activists were re-empowered and reacted both through civil activism and violent acts against Palestinians and their properties. In the peace camp instead, the collapse of negotiations and the upsurge of violence resulted in a considerable reduction of civil activities and external financial support. As a consequence of Palestinian suicide bombing in particular, the narrative of political dialogue advocated by the peace movement lost public resonance and legitimacy. [33] However, Ariel Sharon's plan of unilateral disengagement from Gaza Strip provoked strong reactions by right-wing activists, who conducted a campaign to convince Likud members to vote against the plan. The much weakened as well as hardened peace movements supported Sharon's plan and staged demonstrations and initiatives to counter the activities of settlers and their supporters. [34]

Sharon was able to get the Disengagement Plan passed from the Knesset stating that Israel 'will evacuate the Gaza Strip, including all existing Israeli towns and villages, and will redeploy outside the Strip.' But regardless of withdrawal, 'Israel will guard and monitor the external land parameter of the Gaza Strip, will continue to maintain exclusive authority in Gaza air space, and will continue to exercise security activity in the sea of the coast of the Gaza Strip.' [35] However the peacemakers and majority of the observers believed that the plan spelt further occupation for Gazans. [36] They argued that according to the 'disengagement' plan, Israeli forces would keep control over Gaza's borders, coastline and airspace, and will reserve the right to launch incursions at will. Also Israel would continue to wield overwhelming power over the territory's economy and its access to trade. In addition to controlling the borders, coastline and airspace, Israel would continue to control Gaza's telecommunications, water, electricity and sewage networks, as well as the flow of people and goods into and out of the territory. Gaza would also continue to use Israeli currency.

Though there may be a difference in approaches and the ideologies of the different civil society organization in Israel, one aspect that remains common to all is the awareness about their limitations. They have never tried to cross the limits that challenge national interests. They have never been fully associated with international movements and campaigns, fearing that this would cast doubt on their patriotism and loyalty to the Israeli-Jewish collectivity. [37] Recent developments in Israeli civil society suggest a gradual disengagement of Israeli civil society organizations from the political sphere and the big questions of war and peace, 'towards an isolated, separated, apolitical, post material perspective', locking their activities 'into narrow frameworks, communities and even sectors.' This tendency could represent a chronic difficulty for Israeli civil society 'to serve as a harbinger for peace'. [38]

Conclusion

Most of the times we tend to think of inter-state conflict in the context of the nation state system. In a majority of cases the attempts to resolve conflict have relied on the traditional instruments of statecraft, namely force, mediation, negotiation, propaganda and economic sanctions and incentives. International relations are primarily based on power politics where powerful nations do not hesitate to use their economic and military might to pursue their respective agenda. But the experience of complex interdependence in the world today gives us a sigh of relief and makes us to think beyond a system focused primarily on the nation-state.

Citizens outside as well as inside the government are both instigators and transformers of the conflict. Civil Society seeks to educate people about issues that become start affecting lives of the people. Hence the civil society picks up the baton and raises its voice against the injustice. With a huge amount of expectations from the Israeli civil society to bring peace in the region, it can be said that so far there have been certain efforts but most of them have been in vain. This has been because of the nature of these organizations, which are more reactive than proactive, particularly on the Israel/Palestine issue. The Israeli civil society starts off with a flash but whenever there is strict opposition from military or there is an attack from the Palestinian militants they tend to sit back and wait for the storm to settle down before starting again.

Their efforts during the Lebanon war can be taken as a great example where they challenged the 'security zone' concept and pressured the Israeli government to pull back the military. But as far as the Israeli/Palestinian issue is concerned, the Israeli civil society has to answer the questions that are related to their existence, their nationality and their patriotism. Here Israeli civil society has to understand that their counterparts in the territories, who are also constrained to prove their effectiveness, are facing similar kinds of problem. Civil societies in both Israel and Palestinian territories have worked together for the past two decades defying the challenges by the right-wingers. The problem that civil society organizations of both the sides face is the external influence. The policy making in Israel is also influenced by the 'Zionist lobby' outside the country which adds to the opposition of military to any peacemaking efforts.

Many recommendations can be made regarding ways in which civil society in Israel and the Palestinian territories can be enhanced while sitting pretty thousands of miles away from the region. However, the exclusivity of the problem that is bombarded with justifications and claims and counter-claims from both the sides does not allow anyone to make any guesses. One can nevertheless say that there is immense scope for civil society activism in a democratic country like Israel. Democratic process must be put to good effect so that the regime is pressurized to guarantee peace.

The civil society organizations also have to use media to good effect. The lack of media exposure of civil societies is one of the major causes for its limited impact. The failure of the media to ignore peace news while giving special privilege to the conflict news has also added to the deficiency of reach of the civil society organizations. This is true that so far these organizations have faced great hardships as far freedom of press is concerned. According to Freedom House, both Israel and PNA place severely restrictions on press freedom and often impede journalists' ability to report safely and accurately on events in the West Bank and the Gaza Strip. Journalists reporting from the Occupied Territories are required to carry Israeli-issued press cards; for Palestinians and Arab journalists, these cards are very difficult to obtain. As a concluding remark it can be said that the Israeli civil society, although not had a big success as yet, remains a ray of hope for conflict transformation in the Israel-Palestinian conflict.

Notes

1. Carolyn M. Elliot, "Civil Society and Democracy: A Comparative Review Essay", in *Civil Society and Democracy: A Reader* (New York: Oxford University Press, 2007) p. 4.
2. Rooy, A. Van, *Civil Society and the Aid Industry: The Politics and Promise* (London: Earthscan Publication Limited, 1998) p. 19.
3. John A. Hall, "In Search of Civil Society", in John A. Hall (ed.) *Civil Society: Theory History, Comparison*, (Cambridge: Polity Press, 1995) p.1.
4. "Civil Society and Peace Building: Potentials, Limitations and Critical Factors", *Document of the World Bank* (Social Development Department), December 20, 2006). p.3. See:http://siteresources.worldbank.org/EXTSOCIALDEVELOPMENT/Resources/244362-164107274725/3182370-1164110717447/Civil_Society_and_Peacebuilding.pdf.
5. Op. cit., Elliot, 2007, p. 7.
6. Edward Luttwak and Dan Horowitz, *The Israeli Army* (London: Allen Lane, 1975), p. 76.
7. "The Israeli Defense Forces: A Civilianized Military in a Partially Militarized Society", in R. Kolkowicz and A Korbanski (eds.), *Soldiers, Peasants and Bureaucrats* (London: Allen and Unwin, 1982), pp. 77-107

8. U. Ben-Elizer, "The Civil Society and the Military Society in Israel", *The Palestine-Israel Journal of Politics, Economics and Culture*, Vol. 12, No.1 (2005), available at http://www.pij.org/details.php?id=329.
9. Ibid.
10. T. Hermann, "Civil Society and NGOs Building Peace in Israel", in E. Kaufman, W. Salem and J. Verhoven (eds.), *Peace building in the Israeli-Palestinian Conflict* (Lynne Rienner Publishers, 2006), p. 61.
11. Baruch Kimmerling, *The Invitation and Decline of Israeliness* (London, University of California Press, 2001), pp. 67-73.
12. Yoram Peri, *Between Battles and Ballots: Israeli military in Politics*, (Cambridge: Cambridge University Press, 1983), p. 39-40.
13. Op. cit., Kimmerling, 2001, p. 209.
14. Moshe Lissak and Dan Horowitz, define Israeli society as a multi cleavage society. See *Trouble in Utopia: The Overburdened Polity of Israel*, (New York, State University of New York Press, 1989), p. 32-97.
15. Op. cit., Kimmerling, 2001, pp. 110-112.
16. Joel S. Migdal, *Through the lenses of Israel: Exploration in State and Society* (New York, State University of New York Press, 2001), pp. 116, 119-120.
17. Avraham Sela, "Civil Society, the Military, and National Security: The Case of Israel's Security Zone in South Lebanon, (Project Muse, Israel Studies, Vol. 12, No. 1, Spring 2007, Indiana University Press), p.2. Available at http://muse.jhu.edu/login?uri=/journals/israel_studies/v012/12.1 sela.pdf.
18. Asher Arian, *Security Threatened: Surveying Israeli Opinion on Peace and War* (New York: Cambridge University Press 1995), p. 74.
19. ibid. p.75.
20. Oren Barak and Gabriel Sheffer, "Israel's Security Network and its Impact: An Exploration of a New Approach," in *International Journal of Middle East Studies* Vol. 38, No. 2 (2006), p. 235. Available at http://journals.cambridge.org/action/displayAbstract?fromPage=online&aid=430688.
21. Op. cit., Hermann, 2006, p. 61.

22. M. Munson, "Gush Emunim and the Israeli Settlers of the Occupied Territories: A Social Movement Approach", *Strategic Insight*, available at http://www.ccc.nps.navy.mil.si/2008/Apr/munsonApr08.asp.
23. See http://www.womeningreen.org.
24. Settlement Now is one of the wings of Peace Now that keeps a close eye on the settlements in the occupied territories. It maintains all the data regarding the settlements, its inhabitants as well as the cost of the settlements that is borne by the Israeli government in terms of the security forces, check posts and other measures that costs quite a good amount of money to Israel. Settlement now also makes account of the reports, legal actions and the maps related to the settlements. All the details related to Settlement Now can be obtained from its official website: http://www.peacenow.org.il/site/en/peace.asp?pi=57.
25. See Peace Now website http://www.peacenow.org.il/site/en/homepage.asp.
26. Op. cit., Hermann, 2006, p. 63.
27. See Nona Mikhelidze and Nicoletta Pirozzi, "Civil Society and Conflict Transformation in Abkhazia, Israel-Palestine, Nagorno Karabakh, Transnistria and Western Sahara", Microcon Policy Working Paper 3, November 2008, available at http://www.microconflict.eu/publications/PWP3_NM_NP.pdf.
28. Ibid. See also, "The Future Vision of the Palestinian Arabs in Israel" (2006), available at http://bitterlemons.org/docs/future-vision-english.pdf.
29. The Jerusalem Link is the coordinating body of independent women centers: Bat Shalom – The Jerusalem Women's Action Center located in West Jerusalem and *Merkez al-Quds lal-Nissaj* – The Jerusalem Center for Women located in East Jerusalem. It campaigns for as viable solution of the conflict based on the recognition of the rights of the Palestinians to self-determination, an independent state alongside the state of Israel, Jerusalem as the capital of both states, and a final settlement of all relevant issues based on international law. See http://www.batshalom.org/jlimk_about.php
30. The Peres Centre for Peace is an independent, non-profit, non partisan, non-governmental organization founded in 1996 by Shimon Peres. Its peace building activities are based on five main pillars: People-to-People Dialogue and Interaction,

Capacity-Building through Cooperation, Nurturing a Culture of Peace in the Region's Youth Business and Economic Cooperation, Humanitarian Responses. See http://www.perescenter.org/.

31. See, U. Ram, "Four Perspectives on Civil Society and Post Zionism In Israel", in *The Palestine-Israel Journal of Politics, Economics and Culture*, Vol. 12, No.1 (2005), available at http://www.pij.org/details.php?id=328
32. Akiva Eldar, "Arafat-bin Laden Equation Won't Stick", *Ha'aretz*, September 24, 2001.
33. Op. cit., Hermann, 2006, pp. 52-53.
34. Ibid. pp.52-57.
35. See the text of the Disengagement Plan at http://www.pmo.gov.il/PMOEng.
36. *Human Rights Watch*, "Israel: "Disengagement' will not end Gaza Occupation", October 29, 2004, available at http://www.hrw.org.
37. Op. cit., Hermann, 2006, p. 58.
38. Op. cit., Ben-Elizer, 2005.

11

Civil Society, Democratization and State in Turkey

Mujib Alam

Introduction

The status of civil society in a country can be assessed, by taking up the aspects such as the existence, extent and effectiveness of CSOs (Civil Society Organizations), NGOs (Non-governmental Organizations), and other voluntary associations/institutions, which operate—both quantitatively and qualitatively—outside and independent of the State and market forces or economy in that particular country. In the context of Turkey, civil society is relatively well placed if we take into account the above-mentioned dimensions and evaluate it in terms of the contemporary debates on the concept. A great many literatures concede that the civil society has taken root in the country, especially, after the establishment of the Third Republic in the early 1980s. [1] Though the status of civil society in Turkey is weak as per the standards of western European and other developed democratic countries, it is certainly better than many other West Asian [Middle Eastern] and Southern European countries. [2] In any case there has been a remarkable sign of expansion of civil society in Turkey in recent years. This improvement in the position of civil society in Turkey may be linked to the social, political and economic development coupled with democratization and democratic consolidation in the country. [3]

There are two dimensions to the study of civil society in Turkey. To begin with, one has to explain the status of civil society *per se*. In other words, one can explore and analyze whether civil society exists in Turkey, and what is its status vis-à-vis the state. One may also consider whether the mere existence of CSOs, NGOs, and other voluntary associations are sufficient to say that civil society exists in the country. Further, assuming that the civil society exists in Turkey, one has to scrutinize various aspects of contestation among different discourses within the existing space of civil society and their approaches in fulfilling their respective objectives. The second part deals with different civil society discourses that are based on diverse ideological perspectives. They touch different issues pertaining to the civil society space, which will be analyzed.

In this context, the present paper seeks to analyze the nature of civil society in Turkey juxtaposing it with the State in Turkey. We will also see to what extent the recent democratization has contributed to the development of civil society in the country and how the process has led to contestation among various discourses. While discussing various discourses and approaches related to civil society in the country, we will also attempt to explicate the diversity that exists in terms of strategies taken up by different discourses.

Civil Society in Turkey: A Historical Sketch

The state of civil society in the history of Turkish republic can be studied in two distinct periods: first, the period during mono-party system (1923-1946) and, second, the one starting with the transition to democratic politics (1946 onwards). For the purpose of our analysis the latter period may be further sub-divided into pre- and post-1980 *coup d'etat* periods so as to underline and understand the phenomena in the present-day context. For a clear understanding of the status of civil society in Turkey throughout these periods it is imperative here to outline a brief sketch about its absence/existence, its nature and its essence.

During most part of the one party rule of the Republican

People's Party (RPP), from 1923 to 1950, the civil society was generally non-existent in Turkey. [4] The Kemalist Turkey in order to carry forward its developmental and reformist goals discouraged any form of opposition which might originate in people's religion, traditions, culture or the power centres operating around these. The revolutionary ideology of the founders of the republic, the Kemalism, granted the Turkish state a great deal of control over civil society. The state, then operated by a secular and reformist centre, intended to act in opposition to the periphery, which was the base of the traditionalists and conservatives. With the adoption of the Law of *Takrir-i Sükun* (The Maintenance of the Tranquility) in early 1925, the state disbanded all associations in order to further consolidate the centre at the cost of the periphery. It is important to note that the strong state tradition, which was inherited from the days of the Ottoman Empire, favoured a strong centre vis-à-vis a week periphery throughout the Republican Party rule. The Republican elite had the perception that a strong state, through consolidation of power, is needed in order to preserve territorial integrity of the country, and to civilize the irrational masses of the periphery through modernization and Westernization. This was, in fact, the foremost impediment for the existence and sustenance of civil society in Turkey during the period starting with the establishment of the Republic till the mid-1940s.

With the transition to democratic politics and introduction of multi-party system in 1946 and especially after the coming of the Democrat Party (DP) to power in 1950 one can trace the appearance of western type of civil society in Turkey. The DP government's populist policies favouring the periphery, the deep economic and social transformation, and other factors led to the development of the periphery, which in turn, promoted political participation of the masses of the periphery and thereby demands of more civil and political rights from the state. [5] Moreover, the relaxed domestic political situation during the initial period of DP rule led to the surfacing of civil society institutions (CSIs) after the mid-1950s, such as associations, voluntary organizations, media, political parties, etc. The military intervention in 1960, however, came as an interruption, though for a brief period. With the introduction of the Constitution of 1961, which had comparatively liberal provisions as far as the freedom of associations are concerned, brought forth a favourable atmosphere for civil society in the country. In particular the 1960s and 70s saw the proliferation of civil society institutions and greater tolerance for freedom of thought, expression, association etc. However, during this period intense politicization took place among all segments of the society and eventually led to deep polarization along sharp left-right division in the country.

Though Turkey experienced its most civil years during the period of the Second Republic (1961-1980), the struggles between the extreme left and right groups, which later turned into relentless armed conflict, caused the 1971 military intervention and the 1980 military coup. After the 1980 coup, the military through its dominant clout in the National Security Council (NSC) remained in direct power for three years between 1980 and 1983, and later introduced a new Constitution (of 1982) and transferred power to the civilian government after 1983 parliamentary election. In fact, the military intervention in civilian affairs as well as the military dictated Constitution, adversely affected civil and political rights.

It is to note that in order to re-structure the political order during the military rule, the NSC disbanded all the existing political parties, curtailed civil and political rights of the individuals and groups, and a large number of people suspected of 'terrorism' and 'illegal political activities' were arrested between 1980-83 period. In these circumstances, the role of civil society in Turkey increased substantially, and after the coming of civilian government through 1983 election, the civil society began to expand. As a consequence of the policies of Prime Minister Turgut Ozal (the government of Motherland

Party) 'civilianization' and democratization process were accelerated. By the late 1980s a surge in civil society institutions and expansion of the civil society space in Turkey was witnessed. This process was further boosted by the demands of the citizens, affected by a host of factors including the massive democratic reforms undertaken by various governments in Ankara in order to fulfil the Copenhagen criteria for EU membership.

During the pre-1980 coup period debates on civil society revolved around freedom of association. However, towards the end of 1970s and especially after the return of civilian rule with the promulgation of the 1982 Constitution, the debate about the condition of civil society in Turkey became intensified, coinciding with the debate that emerged in the context of East European communist countries. Particularly since the mid-1980s the political discourse in Turkey revolved around two related aspects—the consolidation of democracy and the strengthening of civil society. [6] The debate this time was mainly concerning its nature, extent, expanse, and effervescence.

Before analyzing the above-mentioned aspects, it is imperative to look into theoretical debate concerning civil society and its linkages with state, democratization/democracy, and other aspects of state-society relations. In the following theoretical section state-civil society relations and relationship between civil society and democratization/democracy will be considered.

Civil Society, Democratization and State: Theoretical Debate

The concept of civil society has been used in the context of either state-society identification or state-society differentiation, or in the context of their complementarities. It has also been linked to the notion of citizenship and democracy. In the age of globalization the notion of civil society has also taken a new meaning particularly in terms of its expanse beyond the traditional border of state. A brief historical sketch of the development and transformation of the concept is desirable here.

The notion of civil society was used in the frame of state-society identification since the time of Aristotle and continued through the Middle Ages. Aristotle's concept of *koinonia politike* (a Greek term) or *societas civilis* (a Latin equivalent) meaning a 'political society', St. Augustine's *societas terresta* also meaning 'political society', and Thomas Aquinas's *ploitike communitas* implying 'society' were used interchangeably with the state, hence, denoting state-society identification. The contractual thinkers, namely, Thomas Hobbes, Jean Jacques Rousseau, John Locke considered civil society as a condition for changeover to the society with the state, and believed in soft-coexistence of the two. With Friedrich Hegel, however, the notion of state-civil society differentiation came into the debate in the political philosophy. Thomas Pain, Adam Ferguson and Alexis de Tocqeville viewed civil society as an alternative and anti-thesis of the state and opined that state power should be restricted in favour of the civil society. According to Marx the relation between the civil society (*bürgerlich gesellschaft*) and state is a dialectical relationship. Antonio Gramsci interprets state-civil society relations in terms hegemony.

In his work, Norberto Bobbio puts the opinions of these thinkers – from Aristotle to Gramsci – in three categories: *pre-state*, *anti-state*, and *post-state* conceptions. [7] In the context of changing notion of civil society and the expansion of meaning in contemporary times two more categories can be included: those as *non-state* and *trans-state* dimensions. [8] It is to underline here that the present discourse concerning civil society is debated from different ideological perspectives such as the liberals, conservatives, social democrats, and the post-Marxists. In our analysis, however, we will take up the view that the civil society is different from the political and economic societies, [9] and that it operates within and independent of state though sometimes its possible 'use' and 'abuse' cannot be overlooked altogether.

Civil society occupies a vital position in the process of social, economic and political transformations. Many political theorists hold the view that the civil society is the *sine qua non* of democracy. [10] The contemporary debate on the civil society was started in the late 1970s by those who advocated democracy in East European countries. With the disintegration of the Soviet system, the civil society debate gave way to the democratization processes in these countries. [11] Here, the notion of civil society was juxtaposed as a zero-sum opposition against a demonic state. The possible abuses of civil society either by the state or by some CSOs may work as impediment in the process of democratization.

However, according to some theorists one cannot essentially establish a positive correlation between democratization and civil society. As noted by A.R. Norton, 'Societies do not take two tablets of civil society at bedtime and wake up the next morning undergoing democratization'. [12] In any case whether or not civil society is in opposition to the state, we can see in the analysis below that the role of civil society in Turkey is immense in the democratization process in the country, and because of democratization the civil society has expanded substantially.

State, Democratization and Civil Society in Turkey

As mentioned above, Turkey in the 1930s inherited a strong state with bureaucratic tradition and a dominant centre as against a weak periphery from the Ottoman period. These factors, therefore, were major obstacles for the existence and emergence of civil society in the early Republican period. [13] However, with democratic transition, affected since the mid-1940s, one can find the development of civil society in Turkey with little aberrations due to military interventions in civilian affairs. Observers opine that the development of civil society in Turkey is contingent upon state tradition, which rests on bureaucracy, conception of secular principles, and the guarantee of gender equity and civil rights. To them, it is basically the Turkish state that prepares and facilitates ground for the existence of the civil society in the country, and without a strong state, the civil society could have degenerated into civil warfare over ethnicity, religion or class. [14] Some others consider the strong state tradition, military intervention and bureaucratic culture as some of the reasons that impede the full development of civic culture in Turkey. [15] However, since the late 1980s Turkey has been advancing towards democratic consolidation. The repercussion of this has been tremendous on the position of civil society in the country.

The recent democratization process leading to political transformation has been the result of both internal as well as external factors. [16] After the establishment of civilian rule in 1983 various governments endeavoured to civilianize the country's political system by introducing several constitutional and legal reforms. Particularly after the EU decision at Helsinki summit in 1999 to include Turkey as a candidate state, various governments at Ankara undertook several reforms according to the country's own adoption plan, *Ulusal Program* (National Programme). The present Constitution (the 1982 Constitution), which was prepared under undemocratic conditions and with the obvious influence of the military rule (1980-83), has been amended at least eight times (in 1987, 1993, 1995, twice in 1999, 2001, 2002 and 2004), and sometimes quite drastically. [17]

These developments, therefore, have obvious ramifications for civil society. The adoption of a new Law on Associations (October 2004) and Law on Foundations has essentially strengthened the legal framework for NGOs and CSOs and general development of civil society in Turkey. [18] A separate special unit within the Ministry of Interior, the Department of Associations, created since 2003, has been playing an important role in advancing reforms and enabling legislations for the benefit of civil society organizations.

Having its central office in the national capital city and local offices in all the 81 provinces, the department looks after registration and functioning of CSOs.

For evaluating the status of civil society in Turkey or any other country for that matter, we must take into account the aspects such as 'associability' and 'associational membership'. The extent to which the population internalizes these factors can provide a measure of the existence and quality of civil society in a particular country. [19] If we take into account the number of CSOs, NGOs and other associations that operate in Turkey as the indicators of the status of civil society in the country – though not very optimistic in comparison to many Western countries – their growth in recent years indicate an upward trend. In the past several years, the European Union in its selected country-specific Progress Report has commended Turkey's progress on civil society. [20]

So far as the numbers of CSOs are concerned, a newspaper quoting the Interior Ministry reported that there are 78,000 associations currently active in Turkey. [21] In an article published in 2000, Barbara Pusch mentions the number of CSOs in Turkey as 61,000, while another study by Binnaz Toprak a few years before places the number at 54,987. [22] By analyzing various studies, Kalaycioglu states that the number of officially registered voluntary associations is always higher than the active associations at a particular point of time. For example, he mentions that as of 1938, there were 205 officially registered voluntary associations, which rose to 2011 by end of the RPP (mono-party) rule in 1950. After the introduction of the multi-party system, the number rose to 11,000 by mid-1950s, 36,000 by mid-1960s, 38,000 by mid-1970s, 53,657 by 1981 (Turkey came under the military rule after the September 1980 *coup d'etat*), 112,000 by mid-90s, and 115,000 by the beginning of this century. [23] Hence, the number of active CSOs is much less than the registered ones according to the government figures. Kalaycioglu also mentions that despite the fact that the number of CSOs per person in Turkey have been more in comparison to many developed European countries (which suggests that the associability rate in Turkey are quite less), if one examines the overall trend of growth in the number CSOs in Turkey, the difference between Turkey and these post-industrial liberal democratic countries may indeed be narrowing. [24]

Civil society institutions in Turkey debate almost all crucial issues of contemporary relevance. Major thrust areas or issues of the CSIs, both in operation for a considerable period of time as well as recently formed ones, may be cited here. Among the civil society institutions, which occupy the traditional space of civil society, include confederations/organizations of labour unions and trade unions, such as Türk-İş, Hak-İş, DİSK, and KESK (the last one was formed recently by civil servants); organization representing businesspersons, such as Turkish Businessmen and Industrialists Association (TÜSIAD), Independent Industrialists' and Businessmen's Association (MÜSIAD), Genç İşadamları Derneği or Association of Young Businessmen, and Turkish Union of Chambers and Stock Exchanges (TÖBB), etc. [25] Besides these there are whole lot of private establishments linked to media – both print and electronic – including press, publishing house, radio, television, dotcoms, blogs, etc.

There has also been a surge of issue-based CSOs and NGOs in Turkey in recent years in concurrence with the expanded dimensions of contemporary civil society discourse elsewhere in the world. The major issues around which a significant number of CSOs/NGOs have grown are human rights, women/gender, environment, ethnicity and culture. Major organizations dealing with human rights issues are: (i) The İnsan Hakları Derneği (the Human Rights Association); (ii) The Türkiye İnsan Hakları Vakfı (the Turkish Human Rights Association); (iii) Mazlum-Der (Organization [of Human Rights and Solidarity] for Oppressed People). [26]

The women's organizations include: (a) The Kadın

Haklarını Koruma Derneği (the Association for the Protection of Women Rights); (b) The Türk Kadınlar Birliği (the Turkish Women's Union); (c) Mor Çatı Vakfı (the Purple Roof Foundation [for Women's Shelter]); (d) AK-DER or Ayrımcılığa Karşı Kadın Hareketi (Women Against Discrimination); (e) The Hanımlar Eğitim ve Kültür Vakfı (the Foundation for Women's Education and Culture), (f) ÖZGÜR-DER or Özgür Düşünce ve Eğitim Hakları Derneği (Association for the Freedom of Thought and Educational Rights), etc. The organizations involved with the issues concerning environment include: (i) Türkiye Çevre Sorunları Vakfı (the Turkish Environmental Problems Foundation); (ii) TEMA (the Turkish Foundation for Combating Soil Erosion, for Reforestation, and the Protection of Natural Habitats); (iii) Doğal Hayatı Koruma Derneği (the Association for the Protection of Wildlife); (iv) Yeşiller Partisi (the Green Party), etc. [27]

Other CSOs/NGOs that have been in existence since a longer period or have sprouted in recent past concern ideology, ethnicity, culture, religion/sect, etc. The organizations devoted to defending strict secularist policies and reforms of Ataturk include Atatürkçü Düsünce Derneği (the Association for Ataturkist Thought), Çağdaş Yasamı Destekleme Derneği (the Association for the Support of Modern Lifestyle), and Çağdaş Eğitim Vakfi (the Modern Education Foundation). The organizations and associations supportive of defending ethnic and cultural identities consist of a succession of political parties raising Kurdish issues in different forums, a number of large and small organizations that are not legally operative, including the legally short-lived Kürt Enstitüsü (the Kurdish Institute). There have also been several organizations formed in order to defend their religious beliefs and practices within the civil society space. The reappearance of the people of Islamic orientation and thinking, such as Nurcular, Fethullahçılar as well as the Alawites's have mounted demands for the protection of their identities and religious places (*cemevleri* or glass houses), leading to formation associations highlighting their concerns. [28]

The purpose of the above discussion is not to emphasize that the civil society situation in Turkey is very bright or optimistic. Rather, it is to emphasize that the recent democratization process as well as stability on state-society relations in Turkey has led to the strengthening of civil society in the last couple of decades, which in turn has paved the way for ideological debates among various discourses within the space of civil society. Hence in order to understand the nature of civil society in Turkey, it is important to take note of this aspect.

Civil Society Space in Turkey

In Turkey the civil society itself is highly fragmented in terms of discourses and strategies. Several large associations are better at rivalry with each other than mutual cooperation. However, they sometimes come to terms with the state in order to achieve their objectives. Some of the major associations like TÖBB, TÜSIAD, Türk-İş often benefit from their co-operation with the state, rather than aligning or cooperating with other associations to work as pressure group vis-à-vis the state. [29]

From the ideological point of view also there are sharp differences between various CSOs. Particularly, the debate within Turkey concerning secularism and secularization has a great impact on the civil society discourse. The social and economic change in the periphery due to democratization and political transformation that started since mid-1940s and the emergence and increased importance of the periphery in the political space has also led to alternative discourses within the civil society space. The influence of Islam—the religion of almost ninety-nine percent Turks—over the civil society can be clearly seen. The impact of so-called unofficial Islam, [30] manifested in movements such as the *Milli Görüş* movement (which emphasizes political Islam), Fethullah Gülen movement or the entire Nurcu movement, is reflected in the civil society space in Turkey. There has been an emergence of 'Islamic civil society' in the country in opposition to secularization of state policies. A study done on Istanbul indicates that there has been a substantial rise in the number of Islamic CSOs in the city, especially after the establishment of the civilian rule in 1983. [31] These CSOs are constructing an alternative discourse – a 'post-secular civil society', which is endogenous to Turkey. [32]

There have been steady rise of several organizations and forums, which project an alternative view in defiance of the strict official secular ideology and try to promote alternative discourses and strategies within the civil society space. For example, the formation of MÜSIAD, an organization of newly emergent businesspersons (with an Islamic bent of mind) in disagreement with the TÜSIAD which have been operating since past few decades. Similarly, the Mazlum-Der, AK-Der and Özgür-Der are few of the Islamic NGOs, which are taking up major issues such as human rights, women's rights, etc with different and an alternative perspective. [33]

It is argued that the inefficiency and corrupt practices associated with the political class in Turkey have led to the emergence of an alternative view of politics and a stern contestation within the civil society space has emerged. However, it is not to emphasize that these alternative views are detrimental to existence of the civil society itself in Turkey. [34] According to Ergun Ozbudun, 'The effect of the civil society over the political society does not involve an attempt to replace it but rather inform, observe, supervise as well as put pressure on it'. [35]

Conclusion

The status of civil society in contemporary Turkey is encouraging and it is increasingly acquiring significance in the political and social life of the people. There has been a steady expansion of civil society space in Turkey during the past few decades. The growth in numbers of CSOs and their advocacy of diverse issues are some of the important indicators of their vibrant nature. Civil society in Turkey is comparatively better developed than many of its neighbours in West Asia and southern Europe although it has to go a long way to match up to the standards of Western liberal democracies. Despite this, the condition of civil society in the country seems to be optimistic and the debate for further strengthening of civil society, both qualitatively and quantitatively, as well as the intra-civil society discourse, will certainly contribute to the expansion of the civil society space in the country. During the period of one party rule of the RPP, civil society was generally discouraged. However, since the beginning of the multi-party system in late 1940s civil society in its incipient form came into being, which took root in the country in the early 1980s after the establishment of the Third Republic. In fact, the transition to democracy since mid-1940s and the democratization process in recent years has significantly contributed to the strengthening of civil society in Turkey.

The civil society in Turkey cannot be said to be in completely opposition to the state. Many studies emphasize that the state in Turkey has been the facilitator for the growth and expansion of the civil society, though the possible use and abuse of civil society by the state cannot be denied. One can find several evidences when some of the large associations cooperate and come to terms with the state in order to achieve their objectives. Democratization and democratic consolidation in the country has paved the way for the emergence and functioning of CSOs with diverse discourses leading to severe contestation within the civil society space. The diversity of discourses among the various CSOs, NGOs, and other civil society institutions should be given due recognition in the dynamics of state-society relations in Turkey.

Notes

1. See, Nilüfer Göle, "Toward an Autonomization of Politics and Civil Society in Turkey", *in* Metin Heper and Ahmet Evin (eds), *Politics in the Third Republic* (Boulder, CO: Westview Press,

1994), pp. 213-222. Omer Caha in his article argues that liberal economic policies that Turkey undertook in the post-1980 period led to the emergence of a vibrant civil society. For detail, see, Omer Caha, "The Inevitable Coexistence of Civil Society and Liberalism: The Case of Turkey", *Journal of Economic and Social Research*, Vol. 3, No. 2 (2001, 2002 Preliminary Issue), pp. 35-50.

2. Some aspects relevant for the present study can be found in Fethi Acikel, "State Formation, Civil Society and Democratisation: Comparing the Turkish Experiences with Mediterranean and East European Cases", in Ayşe Güneş-Ayata, Ayça Ergün and Işil Çelimli (eds), *Black Sea Politics: Political Culture and Civil Society in an Unstable Region* (London & New York: I.B. Tauris, 2005), pp. 189-222.
3. E. Fuat Keyman and Ahmet Icduygu, "Globalisation, Civil Society and Citizenship in Turkey: Actors, Boundaries and Discourses", *Citizenship Studies*, Vol. 7, No. 2 (2003), pp. 219-234.
4. Binnaz Toprak, "Civil Society in Turkey", in Augustus Richard Norton (ed.), *Civil Society in the Middle East*, Vol. 2 (E.J. Brill: Leiden, 1996), p. 90. Quoting Robert Bianchi (*Interest Groups and Political Development in Turkey*, Princeton University, Princeton, 1984), Ergun Ozbudun asserts that there were few voluntary associations during the single-party era, but those were under strict control of the state. Ergun Ozbudun, *Contemporary Turkish Politics: Challenges to Democratic Consolidation* (Boulder, CO: Lynne Reinner, 2000), p.129.
5. Henry J. Barkey, "The Struggle of a "Strong" State", *Journal of International Affairs*, Vol. 54, No. 1 (Fall 2000), pp. 94-95.
6. Op. cit., Toprak, "Civil Society in Turkey", pp. 92-93.
7. Norberto Bobbio, *Democracy and Dictatorship* (Minneapolis: Polity Press, 1989).
8. B. Akşit *et al.*, "Türkiye ve Ortadoğu'da Sivil Toplum Tartışmaları: Sivil, 'Mivil', 'Tivil', Toplum," *Sivil Toplum*, Vol. 1, No. 3 (2003), pp. 38-39.
9. As Jean L. Cohen formulates: civil society is different from both political society and economic society. The political society encapsulates political organizations, political parties, and parliament; and the economic society is composed of the organizations of production, distribution, cooperatives, firms,

and institutions of collective bargaining such as unions, and councils. Jean L. Cohen, "Interpreting the Notion of Civil Society", *in* Michael Walzer (ed.), *Toward a Global Civil Society* (Berghahn Books: Providence, Oxford, 1998), p. 38.

10. See, Gordon White, "Civil Society, Democratisation and Development (I): Clearing the Analytical Ground", *Democratisation*, Vol. 1, No. 3 (Autumn 1994), pp. 375-90.
11. See, for example, Dorota I. Pietrzyk, "Democracy or Civil Society?" *Politics*, Vol. 23, No. 1 (2003), pp. 38-45.
12. Augustus Richard Norton (ed.), *Civil Society in the Middle East*, Vol. 2 (E.J. Brill, Leiden, 1996), "Introductory Chapter", p. 6.
13. Two of the renowned Turkish scholars, Serif Mardin and Metin Heper, have greatly emphasized on "centre-periphery" dichotomy and the "strong state" thesis respectively as their analytical and conceptual frameworks. For a comparative analysis on these lines, see Ali Riza Gungen and Safak Erten, "Approaches of Serif Mardin and Metin Heper on State and Civil Society in Turkey", *Journal of Historical Studies*, Vol. 3 (2005), pp. 1-14.
14. Op. cit., Toprak, "Civil Society in Turkey", p. 87.
15. Ersin Kalaycioğlu, "State and Civil Society in Turkey: Democracy, Development and Protest", in Amyn B. Sajoo (ed.), *Civil Society in the Muslim World: Contemporary Perspectives* (London: I.B. Tauris, 2002), pp. 250-51.
16. In order to conform to the *acquis communautaire* (the EU laws) as stipulated in the Copenhagen criteria during the last few years Turkey enforced various legal and constitutional reforms, basing certain guidelines what are popularly referred to as EU "harmonization laws". Since 2001 the Turkish Parliament, the Grand National Assembly (GNA), has passed at least eight such reform "packages" in order to harmonise the country's laws with those the EU *acquis*.
17. Of all the eight constitutional amendments, the most radical and comprehensive one was that of 2001 (which involved 34 articles), the 1995 amendment (15 articles), and the 2004 amendment (10 articles). Ergun Ozbudun and Serap Yazici, *Democratisation Reforms in Turkey, 1993-2004* (Istanbul: TESEV Publications, September 2004), p.13.
18. Filiz Bikmen, "Progress on Civil Society Legislation in Turkey", *International Journal of Not-for-Profit Law*, Vol. 7, No. 2

(February 2005), pp. 76-79. The TUSEV (Third Sector Foundation of Turkey) in conjunction with ICNL (International Centre for Not-for-Profit Law) provided inputs through their "Comparative Report on Association Law" to the review commissions, which consulted and accepted those while making recommendations to the TGNA.

19. Op. cit., Kalaycioglu, "State and Civil Society in Turkey", p. 252.
20. A brief analysis of one of the latest progress reports (2008) can be found at http://www.usak.org.tr/EN/makale.asp?id=773
21. *Today's Zaman*, online edition, 10 April 2008; http://www.todayszaman.com/tz-web/detaylar.do?load=detay&link=138546
22. Barbara Pusch, "Stepping into the Public Sphere: The Rise of Islamist and Religious-Conservative Women's Non-Governmental Organisations", in Stefanos Yerasimos *et al.* (eds), *Civil Society in the Grip of Nationalism: Studies on Political Culture in Contemporary Turkey* (Istanbul, 2000), p. 478; Op. cit., Toprak, "Civil Society in Turkey", p. 104.
23. Op. cit., Kalaycioglu, "State and Civil Society in Turkey", pp.252-53.
24. Ibid. p. 253.
25. M. Lutfullah Karaman and Bulent Aras, "The Crisis of Civil Society in Turkey", *Journal of Economic and Social Research*, Vol. 2, No. 2 (2000), p. 46.
26. While the HRA has been a fairly old organisation (formed way back after the transition to democratic system in mid-1940s), the Mazlum-Der was organised very recently.
27. Op. cit., Karaman and Aras, "The Crisis of Civil Society in Turkey", pp. 46-47.
28. Ibid. p. 47.
29. Op. cit., Kalaycioglu, "State and Civil Society in Turkey", pp. 257-58.
30. Ihsan Yilmaz has analysed the impact of Islam on contemporary Turkish state, law and civil society, and in his analysis he has used the term 'unofficial Islam' as against what he calls it a 'state Islam or Lausanian Islam'. Ihsan Yilmaz, "State, Law, Civil Society and Islam in Contemporary Turkey", *The Muslim World*, Vol. 95 (July 2005), p. 385.

31. A.N. Yucekok *et al.* (eds.), *Tanzimat'tan Gunumuze Istanbul'da STK'lar* (From Tanzimat to Today, NGOs in Istanbul) (Istanbul: Tarih Vakfi, 1998).
32. J. Keane, *Civil Society – Old Images and New Visions* (Polity Press, 1998), pp. 28-31.
33. For an interesting comparison and discussion of these three NGOs, see, Ayşe Kadıoğlu, "Civil Society, Islam and Democracy in Turkey: A Study of Three Islamic Non-Governmental Organisation", *The Muslim World*, Vol. 95 (January 2005), pp. 23-41.
34. Berna Turam, "The Politics of Engagement between Islam and the Secular State: Ambivalences of 'Civil Society'", *The British Journal of Sociology*, Vol. 55, Issue 2 (2004), pp. 277-78.
35. Quoted in op. cit., Kadıoğlu, "Civil Society, Islam and Democracy in Turkey", pp. 37-38.

12

Civil Society in the Gulf Monarchies

Shahid Jamal Ansari

'Civil Society' has become a term, which is now increasingly used to encompass social activity and societal organizations that directly or indirectly support, promote or struggle for democracy and democratization. It is not, however, clear what civil society means. Civil Society is said to refer to the space between the state and the individual. [1] There is an agreement in a broad sense that it comprises socio-political institutions, voluntary associations and a public sphere within which people can debate, act and engage with each other in order to deal with the state. [2] Civil Society is crucial for democracy because it is the space between the public and private spheres where civic action takes place. Organizations and individuals from within civil society can hold the state accountable, share their experiences, promote their interests and learn values of civility and trust. [3] As a rule, civil society organizations (CSOs) are voluntary, non-profit organizations; those who belong to such organizations join them out of free will and not as a result of coercion or compulsion. CSOs are a product of their environments and as such, they reflect the social and cultural dimensions of the settings in which they operate. [4]

Nature of Civil Society

The received wisdom from much of the literature on the West Asia is that civil society in the Arab world is at best at a nascent stage. Nowhere has this received wisdom been received more enthusiastically than in the study of the Gulf monarchies. Both the older literature, written from a dependency as well as modernization perspective and much of the more recent literature on the *rentier* state, conclude that independent groups are unimportant in the Gulf; that associational life is weak and that the public space between the nuclear family and the state is sparsely populated.

At the first glance, this appears to be true. As one writer observes about the Gulf states: At independence ... there were no trade unions, political parties, free presses or elected bodies in any of the shaykhdoms (except to a limited degree in Bahrayn) through which reformist inputs into the local decision making processes could be articulated with any hope of achieving success .... The legacy of the traditional system of rule by tribal chieftains, even since independence, continues to weigh against the establishment of such organizations or interest groups in the near future. [5]

To most writers, the historically important groups—the *traditional* groups—were bound to fade under the impact of modernization along with the Gulf monarchs. Until then, the monarchs' conservative traditionalism would naturally attract the support of these groups.

Those interest groups that do exist—the ruling families, other families of the ruling tribes, important non-ruling tribes, influential merchants, venerated religious lenders and selected representatives among the community of expatriate advisors—appear content with, and have positive interests in the survival of, shaykhly rule. [6]

Only the new middle class, an emerging group of liberal technocrats with a penchant for representative government could, most writers agreed, pose a threat to these monarchs, and that this 'small' threat could be forestalled with a judicious application of money and force. Even writers working from a dependency perspective arrive at more or less the same conclusion. Khaldoun al-Naqeeb, for example, writing from this perspective, places his hope, albeit guarded, in the human rights movement built around this new educated middle class. This movement, he hopes, will establish clearer boundaries between the state and society and secure autonomy for social institutions. [7]

The *rentier* state literature, like its predecessors, also-presents, albeit in a very different way, a view of civil society as fundamentally weak. As several writers have argued, oil revenues empower the state at the expense of society. [8] Oil revenues allow the state to undercut existing social groups and to pre-empt the formation of new ones. These revenues allow the state to lavishly provide resources—from jobs to housing to welfare—that other social groups once provided or would have come to provide in the absence of such wealthy states. Revenues also give state the power to weaken social groups by co-opting them collectively or by fragmenting them through selective co-optation of key members. Oil revenues allow the state to weaken civil society.

While this image of the Gulf is in some ways accurate, it is incomplete. The *rentier* literature helps us understand why societal pressures for change might be muted and why governments might be more able to contain even these muted pressures. It is certainly true that the Gulf monarchs have shown a considerable antipathy to organized groups, even groups with the most apparently apolitical intentions. They have gone to some lengths to prevent, pre-empt, or destroy a variety of social organizations. Nonetheless, despite their best efforts, incipient pressures from Islamist, human rights, tribal, technocratic and other groups have in fact appeared in the Gulf. Important, organized, and independent groups with interests that demand to be accommodated are alive in the Gulf actively petitioning the rulers. A variety of important groups have emerged or survived and have undergone transformation since independence and since oil.

Active political organizations, especially political parties, are banned in all the GCC countries, although political activities do find some expression in non-governmental organizations such as clubs, professional associations, women's societies, and philanthropic organizations. Voluntary organizations are embryonic, only having begun to take legal and administrative shape between the late 1950s and the early 1970s. However, soon after the First World War, the traditional aristocracy initiated the formation of associations for commercial elites.

In Bahrain (1919) and in Kuwait (1922), literary clubs began to appear. These clubs played a major role in introducing the political thoughts prevalent at that time in Egypt, Syria, and Iraq. The British authorities tried to shut down the clubs, for fear of political subversion to British colonial rule. However, in the late 1930s, a new generation of social groupings, including merchants, teachers, government employees, students, and oil workers, formed their own new clubs.

Religious associations have been better organized and more powerful dimensions of Gulf civil society. Usually less receptive to change, they have been highly influenced by specific traditional religious hierarchies, especially those aligned with the ruling elites. However, with the advent of modern political Islam, some of these associations began to be more visible and active. The Muslim Brotherhood activists, who had emigrated to escape Nasser's oppression in the 1960s and moved to the Gulf emirates, were politically dormant, due to the repression experienced in Egypt and the political sensitivities of the Gulf monarchies. Nevertheless, they came to permeate many professions during the oil boom, and it was around this core group that the majority of Sunni Muslim activists gravitated.

The first of these religious associations appeared in Bahrain in 1941 under the name of Nadi al-Talaba (Students' Club). It later became Nadi al-Islah (Reform Club), under the influence of Bahraini students who had been exposed to the Muslim Brotherhood while studying Islamic and common law in Egypt. Twenty-two years later, in 1963, the Jameiat al-Islah al-Ijtimie (Society of Social Reform) was established in Kuwait, and in 1984 the Jameiat al-Islah wa Altawjih al-Ijtimie

(Society for Reform and Social Instruction) was founded in the United Arab Emirates (UAE). These associations communicated and coordinated their activities throughout the Gulf and recruited in every Gulf state. The most notable Shia religious association was al Jameiat al-Thaqfah al-Ijtimaiyah (Society of Social Education). During this period, Shia religious associations were politically less active, focusing more on religious education. However, they became much more politicized and active in Kuwait during the Iranian Revolution.

Professional associations have not been viewed favourably by the states of the Gulf. Despite their exclusivity, their members' skills are a prerequisite for state maintenance, and foreign nationals performing such tasks were denied admission. These associations were formed in Kuwait in the 1960s, Bahrain in the 1970s, and the UAE in the 1980s. In the Gulf region, there were only about forty professional associations in the 1990s, sixteen in Kuwait, and ten each in Bahrain and the UAE. Labour unions were discouraged if not banned altogether.

Women's associations, which first appeared in Bahrain in 1955, were often social clubs and not politicized. Their early members were drawn mainly from the foreign community, predominantly the British colonial administration and the upper-class Bahrainis. However, by the early 1970s, these associations began to demand recognition and political rights for women. In the early 1960s, women's associations began to emerge in Kuwait, and by the mid-1970s a more activist, politically aware group from the upper classes established Nadi al-Fatat (Young Women's Club). This club represented the more educated young Kuwaitis returning from universities around the world, although they were religiously oriented and traditional. Only after the expulsion of Iraqi forces from Kuwait in 1991 did Kuwaiti women begin agitating for political equality, including the right to vote. In Saudi Arabia, women's associations did not begin forming until 1983. Drawn from the upper classes, they soon fell under the tutelage of the religious hierarchy of the Saudi state. In Oman and the UAE, women's groups did not appear until the early 1970s.

Saudi Arabia's special relationship with the other Gulf monarchies resulted in a Saudi hegemony in the region and the imposition of the Saudi-Wahhabi doctrine on religious thinking. Wahhabism does not tolerate other interpretations of Islam, such as Shiism and it considers the mere existence of Shias in the Arabian Peninsula a great challenge to their Puritan Salafi doctrine. Also, the Wahhabi doctrine completely rejects modern revolutionary political Islam, whether it is Shi'i or Sunni in orientation, and combats this throughout the Gulf. The religious establishment and the political leadership became partners in the Saudi state. A limited partnership emerged between the Saudi royal family and the Wahhabi leadership. Muhammad Ibn Abdul Wahhab enlarged the partnership to include the religious establishment, as represented by the leading ulama and the Saudi throne.

A marriage of convenience emerged and the Saudi king in the eyes of the ulama was seen as the enforcer of the Shariah; he was not meant to be a legislator. In this way the Shariah became the foundation and the king its defender. The king is the Imam who occupies the tip of the pyramid in the religious establishment. He is surrounded and watched by a phalanx of important ulama. In the Gulf, all the traditional Sunni Islamic movements are, in one way or another, allies of the Saudi establishment. Various associations have become an extension of the Wahhabi-Saudi establishment, basically because their overall political aims proved similar. Financial aid has flown from the Saudi state to these associations. Political support from the Gulf states, in addition to the protection by the Saudi state, has given these associations a free hand in society.

There are many CSOs which have sprung up in recent years. One estimate puts the number in about 900. These are active mainly in Kuwait and Bahrain. In Oman, too, many CSOs in professional fields have emerged. It is important to note that in Oman's past, non-governmental organizations were almost always women's associations. In the recent past, many professional and cultural associations have come into existence. CSOs exist in other GCC states also. However, the ability of such organizations to influence the *status quo* is limited due to many reasons, including their relative immaturity and their status within the dominant cultural and political context.

With the notable exception of Qatar, the GCC states are still governed by laws that are twenty to forty years old. Qatar issued a new law in May 2004 recognizing the right to establish professional associations and labour syndicates. The workers' union includes worker committees set up at the level or work organizations. [9] After Kuwait and Bahrain, Qatar is the third GCC State to allow such legislation.

Post 9/11 Scenario

As a consequence of the sustained war on terrorism and the international efforts to freeze possible terrorist assets, a number of ministerial decisions were issued in GCC states to regulate the activities of CSOs, particularly those operating in the field of charitable and humanitarian assistance, both domestically and internationally. To illustrate this, let us take the example of Saudi Arabia and Kuwait.

Saudi Arabia issued a number of resolutions banning individuals and groups to donate without securing an official permit as well as making it mandatory to disclose the source and the destination of funds.

In January 2004, four satellite offices of the Al-Haramain Charity Organization were included in a list of organizations and companies implicated in providing funds to terrorist groups. Saudi Crown Prince Abdullah bin Abdulaziz's statement (January 22, 2004) that four branch offices of Al-Haramain in Indonesia, Kenya, Tanzania and Pakistan provided financial and logistical support to al-Qaeda and other terrorist organizations was affirmed by US treasury. [10]

Following US pressure, Saudi authorities closed down the overseas [11] offices belonging to the organization and later froze its financial assets in the Kingdom. A new Saudi National Authority for Charity Work was established. It was decided that the Saudi authorities 'will determine and cut off the sources funding any terrorist organizations.' [12] In June 2004, as a result of US pressure, Shaikh Aqeel Al-Aqeel's bank assets were frozen and his financial transactions were terminated. [13]

In Kuwait, Foreign Minister Shaikh Al-Sabah openly stated that there are 'possible links between some charity associations and terrorist organizations.' Consequently, a set of decisions determining the rules and regulations governing fund-raising campaigns by strictly implementing the principle of transparency insofar as the sources and destinations of funds were concerned, was issued.

Recent Developments: Case of Kuwait and Bahrain

Even though existing legislation does grant some space for free movement and action for civil society organizations in some specific areas, it also provides the state with an arsenal of legal texts and stipulations that allow it to interfere in and impose regulations on the proceedings of CSOs. Some local authorities in the GCC states, sometimes prefer to ignore existing legislation that, when fully regarded, would severely incapacitate the CSOs. At other times, however, governments are forced to take a strong stance against CSOs clearly transgressing their boundaries.

Politics often tend to hamper the progress of many non-governmental organizations, particularly those of Kuwait and Bahrain. However, the presence of political associations in both Bahrain and Kuwait that enjoy a good margin of political freedom has rendered the relationship between CSOs and the state more dialectical in nature and has enhanced the dynamism of the political scene in both the countries. Consequently, though at times there have been tension between the CSOs and ruling regimes, yet they have contributed to a political vibrancy unmatched by any other GCC states. However, there have been strains between the political opposition and state authority resulting in violence which clearly shows the vulnerability of civil society vis-à-vis the state in Kuwait and to some extent in Bahrain.

The unstable security conditions prevailing in Iraq, security developments in Saudi Arabia, and wide Islamist presence in the National Assembly have helped Islamist groups impose their agenda on Kuwaiti society. Issues such as the US military presence in Kuwait, agenda of political reform given by the US, women's political participation, and the attitude towards terrorist acts in Iraq and other Arab countries, constitute the political aspects of the dispute between the Islamist movements and the state. The same issues stand at the core of the dispute between liberal groups and the government.

Tension between civil society and the state has also been noticed in Bahrain. In late December 2003, government banned the play entitled 'Abu Al-Aich' by Al-Wefaq under the pretext that the association did not secure a license from the Ministry of Information. Again, after a long-running tug-of-war, the association somehow managed to hold a conference in 2004. The socio-political picture in Bahrain appeared at times to have regressed only to be followed by periods of serenity. However, it should be noted that civil society has shown maturity, if not fully but partially in both Kuwait and Bahrain and to some extent in other GCC states.

Civil Society and Women

The position of women in the GCC states is not as black and white as it seems. A closer analysis reveals each of these states are striving in their own ways to provide 'the other half' of the population with better (rather than equal) opportunities. However, despite notable successes, each state has its own scale of progress and has a long way to go. The state-wise position of women is dealt with in the subsequent paragraphs.

Women's organizations existed in Bahrain as early as the 1950s. The first Bahraini women's group to emerge in 1953 was the special Society for Bahrain Women which eventually went on to become the Motherhood and Childcare Society. Another group established in 1955, the Nahdit Fatat Al Bahrain Society, continues to be prominent in promoting women's education. [14] Among the more active groups at present are the Bahrain Businesswomen Society (BBS) established in 2000, the Bahrain Women's Society (BWS), and the Mustaqbal Society. In the fifteen political societies in Bahrain, women held twenty-one board seats (or 16 per cent) as of 2005. [15]

The Bahrain Society Combating Domestic Violence also became an officially recognized organization in 2005. Within a month of setting up a hotline for abused women, the society received complaints from about 70 women, most of who alleged to have been physically abused by their husbands. The group aims to raise awareness about domestic violence, reduce physical, psychological and sexual abuse, and campaign for the formulation of laws for protecting women. [16]

There are currently 14 women's societies in Bahrain. The government supports these groups through the Ministry of Labour and Social Affairs which, in 1998, provided them with a fund of 74,000 dinars. [17] Attempts to establish the Bahrain Women's Union have been consistently blocked by the Labour Ministry, which insists that the name be altered to the 'Union of Women's Society,' a demand rejected by the activists. The members of the preparatory committee believe that changing the name to the government's liking would drastically modify the Union's entire purpose. They maintain that the government is merely trying to restrict the membership of the union to existing women's groups while, in fact, the group's intention is to extend membership to cover all of Bahrain's women. In 2004, the women activists filed a civil suit against the government [18] and after waiting for over a period of four years, permission was granted to set up the Union. The group has now christened itself the 'Bahrain Ladies Union (BLU). It has around 14 women's organizations and more than 1,000 members under its umbrella. [19]

Kuwaiti women have been strong defenders of their rights. After the rejection of the 1999 Emiri Decree in favour of women suffrage, female activists filed six court cases [20] against the Ministry of Interior, all of which they lost. Kuwaiti women are well-known for their aggressiveness in the region as depicted in 1961 when through a joint effort they managed to reverse the rule for women to veil or wear the 'abaya' at workplace. [21]

The government contributes towards the creation of women's organizations and there are about fifty-five such associations that are supported by the Ministry of Social Affairs and Labour. One the more important association is the Women's Right Committee that works in affiliation with the Kuwaiti Lawyer's Association. Other organizations involved in social and voluntary work include the Kuwaiti Federation of Women established in 1994 which is permitted by the government to represent Kuwaiti women internationally. [22] Though this group is said to have Islamist and Conservative women, they have participated equally in the fight for political empowerment. [23]

Among private groups, the Women's Affairs Committee and Kuwait's Union of Women are actively involved in promoting issues, especially those related to political postion of women. The concept of forming women's associations is not new in Kuwait, and both the Women's Cultural and Social Society (WCSS) and the Arab Women's Development Society (dissolved in 1980s) were the first organizations to be formed as early as in 1963, right after the enactment of the Constitution. [24] The WCSS is the most active organization and has lobbied hard for Kuwaiti women to gain political rights by conducting silent demonstrations outside the National Assembly [25] as well as by mobilizing liberal members of Parliament to lead discussions on women's issues. The

Kuwaiti women's movement, although active since 1962, only received wide support after the Gulf war, [26] when the Emir publically pledged to enhance the position of women. However, these women have had to wait until the Emir's pledge was finally executed in 2005. Women are not predominant in religious organizations, with the top positions assigned to men. In 1998, ninety-three percent of all board members of various associations were men, with only seven per cent of positions left to women. [27]

The Omani government is still to authorize the creation of a human rights organization in the country. Trade unions and industry-related associations are also banned. Around forty-two women's associations, granted approval by the government, exist. [28]

Qatar prohibits any private human rights group from operating in the country. The same is true for women's groups. [29] However, in 2002, the government established a National Human Rights Group with members from government and civil society that advises the state on matters related to human rights. As women are not allowed to form groups concerning their issues, they have chosen to take part in other forms of voluntary and charity work, including those conducted by organizations such as the Qatar Red Crescent Society. [30]

Apart from the General Women's Union, there are no other societies involved in women's work in the country. In 2006, the Ministry of Social Affairs announced the formation of the Emirates Human Rights Society to be based in Abu Dhabi which would have jurisdiction over the entire Emirate. The Society will cover all issues related to human rights, civil liberties, as well as matters that are socio economic and political in nature. [31]

The Kingdom bans the formation of associations although permission can be acquired to form professional associations. Any demonstration or gathering to discuss or pursue a political issue is also prohibited. Consent was given by King Abdullah in 2005 for the creation of a government human rights agency in accordance with the 'provisions of the Islamic Law'. [32] A year earlier, in 2004, permission was granted to set up the National Human Rights Associations and the National Society for Human Rights. Under the Family and Child Committee, as part of the Human Rights Associations, certain activities are devoted to the status of women.

Amidst restrictive policies and regulations women have, albeit silently, involved themselves in the struggle for change. In 2003, some fifty women gave a petition called 'In Defence of the Nation" [33] to the King, and sought reforms. Generally, women are not permitted to conduct public meetings on their own, and all other public meetings are required to be sex-segregated. Women can be a part of professional associations and, in recent times, are being selected to sit on the board of directors of such associations, such as the Saudi Journalist Association and the Saudi Engineers Council. [34]

If an overall analysis is to be made, then certain practices are indeed common in the GCC states. All six countries are constitutional monarchies which have only recently introduced partial democratic reforms. Policies concerning women are highly driven by the traditions and religious norms that are predominant in these societies. Some high-ranking leaders in these countries have chosen to be at the forefront of the struggle for women's empowerment. At the same time, there are considerable sections of the common population—including women themselves—who continue to embrace traditional ways of thought and exhibit resistance to change. This may be one reason why women belonging to the higher strata of society are among the first to challenge—and consequently gain from—these reforms.

Another prominent common hindrance is that the monarchical society is essentially gendered in nature, which means that in all the states the lineage is passed on only through the male descendants. If some sort of generalization is to be drawn, then broadly, it is that in all Gulf states women suffer the difficulties of various issues including divorce-related impasses, custody, the citizenship of children for those women married to non-nationals, and the impossibility of travelling abroad without the permission of a male guardian.

Although collectively, these countries might represent a united front, it will be unfair to group them under a single category. They appear to share a fair number of common dilemmas but each country has its own problems concerning the push for women's advancement. For instance, if comparisons were to be made among these six countries, then Bahrain seems to be seeing the most relevant progress as it is the only state pushing feverishly for alteration of the personal law. The Bahrain government, furthermore, grants basic liberties to women including the freedom to walk and drive unrestricted and the option not to wear the Islamic *hijab*. [35] Kuwait is home to the most active women's organizations in the region. Similarly, Oman appears to be relatively calm—but not stagnant by any means—with respect to women's activities as compared to its much active neighbour which is Qatar. Also, although in all states personal status cases are tried in the Shariah courts, the verdict in each state might be quite different. This emphasizes the point that though these states are in the same position at a more common level, individually each one is trying to promote the cause of women at their own pace, proving that any change can only arise from within.

And what about the question of whether or not pressure from the international community has had an impact on the campaigns for reforms? The states did not show explicit signs of any such pressure compelling them to take steps towards women's empowerment. During an assessment, no direct traces of foreign influence were found in the policies adopted by these states even as subtle hints were dropped such as in the case of Saudi Arabia. It can also be assumed that the leaderships of the states are being told confidentially at their level. This view is upheld by a group of people in Kuwait for instance. [36]

The GCC states in the past decade or so have realized the importance of pushing the so-called 'weaker' gender of their society forward, especially in the context of a labour market that is increasingly being localized to minimize dependence on foreign expatriates. If this objective is to be fulfilled, then they are left with no other choice but to rely on the other half of their population. Though leaders of these states have understood this fact, they are still playing it safe by promoting women to the supposed secure and protected working environments. Except for the UAE, the other states have only appointed women to ministries such as health, tourism, etc. Also, the maximum number of female employment in the government sector is mostly in the fields that are considered 'safe', such as education.

Overall, GCC women started slow because of the lack of formal education until the 1960s. As a consequence of this factor, a majority of the older generation women have lagged behind. Despite assurances from the GCC governments, class differences do exist in society. Women belonging to middle or merchant class families were the first to experience the freedoms previously denied. Due to limited educational opportunities in the country, the middle-class women grew faster in the employment arena as they managed to attend university abroad. [37] However, presently this situation has changed drastically and the number of women students at the university level in majority of the states exceeds that of the men; illiteracy rate among all classes of women has also decreased immensely.

Though the number of women achievers in these states is limited, the situation is nowhere near the grim and depressive picture that is commonly portrayed. Women are slowly taking every chance offered to them as depicted by the number of women involved in business ventures and the amount of capital held by them. Financially, the women of the GCC are not impoverished by any means and estimates show that businesswomen in the GCC owned between ten to twenty-nine per cent of the regions wealth [38] thus contradicting the assumption that women in the GCC are economically more backward than their counterparts in the rest of the world. Socially, each country seems to be at different grades of social freedoms. For instance, if Bahrain is compared to Saudi Arabia, the Kingdom will have to take some time before it can grant its women citizens the same status as their Bahraini counterparts. Yet Saudi Arabia is also not all that pessimistic. As far as political development is concerned, these states have recently adopted certain democratic practices and to be fair, have included women in these ventures. Though this opportunity has been presented to women, it has not led to the desired results because of a wide number of reasons shared equally by all these states. Some common ones include: traditional mindsets and chauvinistic attitudes prevalent in the society and the ironic presence of a section of women who fail to back their counterparts either due to ignorance or pressure exerted by their own family members.

Rulers like Shaikh Mohammed bin Rashid Al Maktoum of Dubai have realized the potential women hold in the promotion of their countries and have acknowledged this fact by saying, 'Arab women are half our community. Sometimes they are better than men. Perhaps in the past we lagged behind, but today she is growing to better heights in our society and is able to achieve goals within our communities. She will only grow.' [39] According to the Arab Human Development Report, 'despite laudable efforts (by the Arab countries) to promote the status of women, success remains limited. In general, women suffer inequality with men and are vulnerable to discrimination, both at law and practice.' [40] The governments of all the six GCC States are making an attempt to improvise the general perception of women in their states. As shown in this report, however, there are obstacles which must be tackled in time. Women of the Gulf have come a long way, and if provided with the right opportunities, would be able to go on to gain much further.

Conclusion

In general, civil society in the GCC states has shown good measures of development in some states, particularly, Bahrain and Kuwait. These two states remain on the top of the list not only in terms of the steadily increasing number of CSOs but also in terms of the strength of the relationship between CSOs and the existing political systems. In other GCC states some welcome changes are noticeable. For example, in Saudi Arabia, the most outstanding development during 2004 was the official constitution of a press association, even though the Saudi state retains the power to appoint one-third of its members. On the other hand, occasional strains are occurring between civil society and state. For example, in 2004, a number of CSOs were dissolved in Saudi Arabia (Al-Haramayan Charity Organization) and Bahrain (Centre of Human Rights). At times, the inner dynamics between state and CSOs reached at a point of near collapse (Islamists assertion in Kuwait). The women's issue in the context of CSOs, as discussed earlier, has shown much improvement. One should not forget that CSOs are moulded and defined by the social, cultural, economic and political milieu in which they exist.

Notes

1. M. Walzer., "The Civil Society Argument" in C. Mouffe (ed.), Dimensions of Radical Democracy: Pluralism, Citizenship and Community (London: Verso, 1992).
2. V. Perez Diaz, The Return of Civil Society: The Emergence of Democracy in Spain (London: Harvard University Press, 1993), p. 55.
3. Jean Grugel, Democratization: A Critical Introduction (New York: Palgrave McMillan, 2002), p. 93.
4. Baqer Al-Najjar, "Civil Society in the Arab World", paper presented at a symposium on the role of civil society in achieving reform in the Arab World, Alexandria, Alexandria. Library, June 2004.

5. John Duke Anthony, Arab States of the Lower Gulf: People, Politics, Petroleum (Washington: The Middle East Institute, 1975), p. 220
6. Ibid.
7. Khaldoun al-Naqeeb, Society and State in the Gulf and Arab Peninsula: A Different Perspective, (London, Rouledge, 1990). See my discussion of his work in "Authoritarianism and its adversaries in the Arab World", World Politics, Vol. 46 (January 1994), pp. 262-289.
8. Jill Crystal, Oil and Politics in the Gulf: Rulers and Merchants in Kuwait and Qatar (Cambridge: Cambridge University Press, 1995); Hazem Beblawi and Glacomo Luciani (eds.), The Rentier State (London: Croom Helm, 1987); H. Mahdavi, "The Pattern and Problems of Economic Development in Rentier States: the Case of Iran," in Michael Cook (ed.), Studies in the Economic History of the Middle East (London: Oxford University Press, 1970); Theda Skocpol, "Rentier State and Shia Islam in the Iranian Revolution." Theory and Society, Vol. 11 (1982); and Jacques Delacroix, "The Distributive State in the World System" Studies in Comparative International Development, Vol. 15 (1980).
9. Al-Sharq Al-Awsat, May 21, 2004.
10. Al-Sharq Al-Awsat, January 23, 2004.
11. Al-Sharq Al-Awsat, July 14 2004.
12. Al-Sharq Al-Awsat, June 30, 2004.
13. Ibid.
14. "Bahrain Brief", The Gulf Centre for Strategic Studies, Vol. 1 Issue 10 (November 2002).
15. "Women break ground in politics", Gulf News, December 20, 2005.
16. "Bahrain Breif", The Gulf Centre for Strategic Studies, Vol. 6 Issue 1 (January 2005).
17. "Bahrain Breif", The Gulf Centre for Strategic Studies, Vol. 1 (August 2000).
18. "Women's union sues Bahrain government", Gulf News, September 28, 2004.
19. "Group wins legal battle to set up women's body", Khaleej Times, March 7, 2006.
20. Haya Al- Mughni, "All roads lead to the franchise", The UNESCO Courier (March 2001).

21. Haya Al- Mughni, Women in Kuwait: The Politics of Gender (London: Saqi Books, 2001), p. 59.
22. State Report submitted to CEDAW, May 1, 2003.
23. Tetreault, Mary Ann, "Kuwait's Parliament considers women's political rights, again", Middle East Report Online, September 2, 2004.
24. Berkowitz, Peter, "An Oasis: Kuwaiti women make progress", National Review Online, March 3, 2004.
25. Tatreault, Mary Ann, 'Kuwait's Parliament considers women's political rights, again', Middle East Report Online, September 2, 2004.
26. Jennifer McElhinny, "Kuwaiti Reforms: Slow but Steady", Middle East Institute, June 27, 2005.
27. Op. cit., Al- Mughni, 2001, p. 39.
28. "Arab Political Systems: Baseline Information and Reforms – Oman", Carnegie Endowment for Peace and FRIDE, p. 11.
29. Ibid. p. 4.
30. "Qatari Women", available at the Ministry of Foreign Affairs website http://english.mofa.gov.qa/details.cfm?id=33.
31. "Emirates Rights society set up", Khaleej Times, February 22, 2006.
32. "Arab Political Systems: Baseline Information and Reforms – Saudi Arabia", Carnegie Endowment for Peace and FRIDE, p. 12.
33. "Can Saudi Arabia reform itself?" ICG Middle East Report, No. 28 (July 14, 2004).
34. "The improving position of women in Saudi Arabia", Gulf Centre for Strategic Studies (February 2006).
35. Darwish Adel, "Rebellion in Bahrain", Middle East Review of International Affairs, Vol. 3, No. 1 (March 1999), pp. 84-87.
36. Tetreault, Mary Ann, "Kuwait's Parliament considers women's political rights, again". Middle East Report Online, September 2, 2004.
37. Op. cit., Al- Mughni, 2001, p. 61.
38. "UAE businesswomen have Dh. 27.3b surplus to invest", Gulf News, 12 February 2006.
39. "Women in the UAE", Sheikh Mohammed bin Rashid Al Maktoum's website: http://www.sheikhmohammed.co.ae/vgn-exttemplating/v/index.jsp?vgnextoid=7d3c4c8631cb4110VgnVCM100000b0140a0aRCRD.

40. "Towards Freedom in the Arab World", Arab Human Development Report (2004), p. 10.

13

Civil Society: Pressures for Change in West Asia

Ishrat Aziz

The societies and political systems in West Asia have been increasingly beset with turmoil and challenges, ever since the creation of Israel in their midst in 1948 and the defeat of their armies, in the military encounters with Israel. Other events that have contributed to the pressures for change: are the defeat of the Arab armies in 1967; the 1979 revolution in Iran; Saddam's occupation of Kuwait in 1990 and the consequent 1991 Gulf War; 9/11 and the 2003 US attack and taking over of Iraq and the resultant quagmire in which US finds itself there today. But it is the continuing Palestinian tragedy that creates the most powerful pressure for change.

Yet another pressure for change comes from the inability of the leaderships of these countries, other than those blessed with oil and natural gas wealth, to improve the economic conditions of their people and provide them with a better life. In the GCC countries, natural resource based wealth, has brought sudden and unprecedented prosperity. But it has also resulted in the fastest population growth anywhere in the world, massive influx of expatriate population, education and contact with the outside world, all of them generating pressures for change. The biggest challenge that the GCC countries face is how to transform their natural resource wealth economies into diversified wealth producing economies for lasting prosperity and welfare of their people beyond the oil and natural gas era. It is an exceptionally daunting task, which has never been faced by any people under similar circumstances.

The basic thing that needs to be underlined is that pressures for change have been generated more by circumstances than initiatives on the part of the people or institutions. This is not because of lack of aspirations on the part of the people for democratic consultative governance and civil society, but because of absence of scope in the existing systems in these countries to pursue them. But things are changing and only a careful comparison with how things were five decades ago and how they are today will give an idea of the extent to which it has happened. As everywhere there is resistance to change from the beneficiaries of the status quo.

Civil Society: Definition and Scope

Civil Society deserves the term in the full sense of the word when it is active and participatory in promoting the interests of the people in diverse and specific areas.

In a rudimentary form, Civil Society has always been there. Activities of the Craft Guilds in the Mediaeval Age would definitely fall within the definition of Civil Society. Throughout history, religious institutions and endowed charities have fulfilled roles of what are civil society activities. Freedom, democratic governance, and the right to form associations to pursue legitimate goals peacefully, are basic for a healthy civil society. It is therefore hardly surprising that as the case for democratic governance has gained broader acceptance, the activities of civil society everywhere have expanded.

There is a symbiotic relationship between civil society and democratic governance. Freedom and democracy are essential for an effective civil society; but equally, an active civil society, following the rules of the game, can render invaluable service in strengthening the democratic political system and articulating people's aspirations and interests. An active civil society, where people are free to form associations, ensures that the voice of no group remains unheard or their genuine problems overlooked. Functioning civil society also ensures that interaction between the people and the government is continuous and not relegated into the background, only to be revived at election times. If people want their government to serve their interests better, an active civil society is essential. It can promote what is good in the government and check what is harmful, because it is part of human nature to abuse unchecked power. If eternal vigilance is the price of good self governance, then civil society has the duty to fulfill that role.

The London School of Economics Centre for Civil Society has given a definition of the term that is comprehensive and clear, and which should be kept in view as one examines the present state of civil society, democracy and state in West Asia: 'Civil Society refers to the area of un-coerced collective action around shared interests, purposes and values. In theory, its institutional forms are distinct from those of the state, family and market, though in practice, the boundaries between state, civil society, family and market are often complex, blurred and negotiated. Civil society commonly embraces a diversity of spaces, actors and institutional forums, varying in their degree of formality, autonomy and power. Civil societies are often populated by organizations such as registered charities, development non-governmental organizations, community groups, women's organizations, faith based organizations, professional associations, trade unions, self-help groups, social movements, business associations, coalitions and advocacy groups.' [1]

A robust civil society needs maximum freedom environment. Nothing except what violates similar rights of others or invites violence and conflict, or is clearly harmful for the interests of the people, should be excluded from the purview of the civil society activities. With the emergence of large states, having diverse populations covering extensive territories, the growing complexity of societies, huge urban population centers, the need of the government to be better aware of people's problems both vertically and horizontally, highly efficient and cost effective means of communication and dissemination of information have all led to increasing proliferation of civil society groups and diversification of their activities. Creating awareness as well as performing actual services, both fall within the scope of civil society activities.

An idea of the extremely variegated and ubiquitous nature of civil society institutions and their activities in a truly democratic polity can be had from the following illustrative, but by no means exhaustive list: non-governmental organizations (NGOs); non-profit organizations (NPOs); different interest groups; private voluntary organizations; activist groups; think tanks and policy influencing institutions; registered lobbies; faith based groups; charity foundations; support groups; women's groups; organizations for the protection of weaker sections of the society; groups for the promotion of rights of challenged people; gay rights; human rights; cultural groups; social centers and clubs; civic centers; community centers; cooperatives; trade unions; poverty awareness and removal groups; academic forums.

Some civil society groups develop trans-national links specially those active in economic and human right areas. Healthy functioning of civil society requires transparency and openness on the part of its institutions and organizations and non-interference on the part of the state. A detailed critique of civil society, democracy and state in individual West Asian countries would be beyond the scope of this article and the reader can go through the other articles in the present volume for this purpose. However, focus on a few broad trends will give an idea of the current overall position and the likely shape of things to come as far as civil society and democracy in West Asia are concerned.

First of all it needs reiteration that West Asia covers a large area and includes many countries with a very wide spectrum of situations. Hence uniform generalizations equally applicable to all of them are difficult to make and should be avoided. The uniqueness of each country should be kept in view and understood. However, one valid observation can be made: They all have freedom and democracy deficit with reference to the political, social, economic, cultural, intellectual and diplomatic challenges that they face and which they must successfully meet to break out of the catch-22 cycle they are in viz. absence of democratic governance as the major cause of the existing state of affairs and the existing state of affairs hindering the transition to effective consultative democratic governance.

At the same time it should be emphasized that this deficiency level differs from country to country—significantly more in some and less in some others. However an important distinction between the tribal monarchies of the Gulf and republican dictatorships of many of the West Asian countries may be noted. While both have unelected leaderships the Gulf regimes are not harsh like the republican dictatorships. The rulers of the Gulf countries have to, by and large, observe the basic tribal traditions which emphasize easing out and co-option rather than elimination of opponents. Like tribal chiefs these rulers also have to look after the welfare of their people. In both co-option and looking after the welfare of the people they have been greatly helped by the large oil revenues. There are pressures for change in West Asia as far as civil society and governance is concerned. Always there, these pressures have intensified since the beginning of 1990s and have further accelerated since 9-11 and the second Gulf War of 2003.

Pressures for Change: Internal and External

Necessity is always the mother of invention, and pressures for change arise from the inadequacy of the existing political dispensation in these countries to adequately cope with the internal and external challenges. Internally the existing political systems, whether in the Gulf or broader West Asia, have not fulfilled people's aspirations for participatory governance. Since 1950, in three countries of West Asia—Egypt, Iraq and Libya—hereditary monarchies fell but the hope that they would be replaced by elected leadership have not been realized more than five decades later. Monarchies became republics but the ideal of fully elected leadership has remained elusive. There have been changes of governments but not of governance. Unelected leaderships, without ballot box mandate, always face the problem of legitimacy. The issue was sought to be skirted by many regimes through a number of arguments and promises.

The fundamental underlying argument was that dealing with internal and external challenges required strong, stable leadership and that full participation by the people in the affairs of the government could come in due course. Criticism was also sought to be deflected by creating nominally democratic institutions which only rubber-stamped the leadership's decisions. The results of the elections, whenever and wherever they took place, were a foregone conclusion. With the passage of time, it is the inability of the political systems in these countries to meet the external and internal challenges that has taken the wind out of the sail of the arguments that transition to full democracy and an active civil society can await their resolution, and consequently pressures for change have now increased.

The resolution of the Arab-Israeli problem and the restoration of the rights of Palestinians were invariably made out to be the over-riding issue. Regime changes, through *coup d'etat*, were often justified on that ground with promises of more effective leadership on behalf of the Arab cause. But three disastrous wars and 60 years later the restoration of Palestinian rights, in much more diluted form now, looks if anything, more difficult despite the so-called strong leadership all these years.

Internally the reasoning was that economic progress and prosperity was much more important than the full fledged democracy. Often the argument was advanced that strong leadership was required to thwart attempts by former colonialist and imperialists to destabilize the state and the gains of the revolution. But promises of better standard of living for people remain unrealized. The Arab Human Development Reports of 2002 and 2003 paint a bleak picture of economic progress, of eradication of illiteracy, health care etc achieved in most of these countries According to these reports:

1. The combined GDP of the twenty-two Arab League Countries is less that of Spain.
2. Approximately forty per cent of the Adult Arab—sixty-five million people—is illiterate; two-thirds of which are women.
3. Over fifty million people will enter the labour force market by 2010 and 100 million will enter by 2020—a minimum of six million jobs need to be created each year to absorb these new entrants.
4. If the current unemployment rates persist, regional unemployment will reach twenty-five by 2010.
5. Only 1.6 percent of the population has access to the internet, a figure lower than that in other regions of the world, including sub-Saharan Africa.
6. Women occupy just 3.5 percent of parliamentary seats in Arab countries, compared with, for example, 8.5 percent in sub-Saharan Africa.
7. Fifty-one percent of the older Arab youths expressed a desire to emigrate to other countries, according to the 2002 AHDR, with European countries the favorite destination.
8. One third of the region lives on less than US$ 2 a day. To improve standards of living, economic growth in the region must move more than double from below 3 percent currently to at least 6 percent. [2]

Only the GCC countries, because of the geological serendipity and increased revenues from oil price hikes, in the 1970s and again more recently since 2001, have succeeded in giving their people a phenomenally high level of prosperity, education and health care in a very short time. But even in Gulf countries, transforming oil dependent *rentier* economies into diversified dynamic job-providing sustainable economies remains a formidable challenge that calls for a new approach.

Without effective regional economic cooperation, the small Gulf countries, despite high per capita income, cannot achieve modern, sustainable industrial economies individually. But only institution-based governance rather than the existing personality-centric rule can ensure political coordination and economic integration necessary to create a unified, viable market. The key to such a transformation is democracy, active civil society and creative partnership between the people and the leadership. Indeed multilateral institutions in West Asia have failed to grow in strength and cohesion because of political structures revolving around personalities rather than institutions.

There is one problem that is common to the entire region. Due to much higher than the world average rate of population growth, during the past 5 decades there is a huge youth population that must be provided with economic opportunities, a task difficult to accomplish without systemic changes. Since 1979, the year of the Iranian revolution and the entry of Soviet forces in Afghanistan, there have been developments that have increased pressures for change. Similarly the impact of Palestinian intifada that erupted in 1988 has brought the Arab-Israeli issue into sharp focus and affected the thinking of the people as to what changes must take place within their own societies so that they can del with this issue more effectively.

The Iranian revolution created a churning process in West Asia and strengthened the fundamentalist forces in the region because of their vanguard role, in the movement to overthrow the Shah. The 8-year Iraq-Iran War caused huge economic losses to the region greatly neutralizing the benefits of oil price hike and exposed the ineffectiveness of the regional leaderships and the institutions like the Arab League, the Organization of Islamic Conference to make any impact in resolving it. The war eventually ended through mutual exhaustion rather than regional diplomacy.

The Soviet military intervention in Afghanistan and the

consequent jihad removed checks on religious conservatism which metamorphosed into fundamentalism and terrorism. The victory of *mujahideen* against a super power in Afghanistan greatly enhanced their appeal amongst masses in these countries and they became a formidable challenge to the status quo in these states. The Gulf Wars of 1991 and 2003 have impacted the credibility of the existing political systems and institutions in these countries. The Iraqi occupation of Kuwait in August 1991 plunged the region in a major crisis and caused much soul-searching among the Arab countries. The GCC countries had financed Saddam's Iran War with their oil revenues in a big way and suddenly one of their members had been occupied and annexed by the Iraqi ruler. The Arab League proved totally ineffective and so did OIC in resolving the crisis. The Arab masses were treated to public display of Arab disunity with undiplomatic exchanges with Kuwaiti and Iraqi representatives at the Arab League meeting in Cairo convened to deal with the crisis. The people questioned the manner in which tens of billions of dollars were spent on the military and its costly hardware which could not resist Iraqi forces even for a day and a super power, had to be paid 75 billion dollars to clear Iraq out of Kuwait.

After the end of the war, the US and the UK managed to impose sanctions against Iraq avowedly to check Iraq's military capabilities for any more aggression and to disarm it of weapons of mass destruction. The unstated purpose however clearly was to emasculate Iraq and to remove Saddam from power. During the sanctions, which continued till the second Gulf War of 2003, the people of Iraq—men, women and children—suffered deprivation, lack of caloric nourishment and denial of medicines which caused hundreds of thousands of deaths especially amongst the children, while the Baathist regime remained very much in the saddle. The Arab masses watched with resentment but their leaders could do little.

Even more resentment-provoking was the 2003 Gulf War

imposed on Iraq by US and UK on the basis of doctored intelligence about Iraq's possession of chemical and biological weapons and allegedly an active program of nuclear weapons. What the people noticed was that as the duo of Bush and Blair, with their coalition of the willing trailing behind them, were taking decisions to attack Iraq, the Arab States were marginalized to the point of being ignored.

At the end of the war no weapons of mass destruction of any kind were found, nor any signs of an effective program for their manufacture. After the entry of the US forces in Baghdad, while the US army took to guarding the ministries of Interior and Petroleum, the Baghdad Museum with its priceless archaeological finds and artifacts and manuscripts, many of them thousands of years old were looted. In six years since the occupation of Iraq, hundreds of thousands of innocent Iraqis have been killed without the Arab leaders being able to do much relieve the misery of that country. The people of the Arab countries observe all this and feel strongly about it and think of how to overcome such humiliating situations.

Meanwhile the Palestinian problem seems nowhere near a just solution despite President George Bush's promise in 1990 to deal with the issue after ending Iraq's occupation of Kuwait and President George W. Bush's declaration in favor of a two-state solution in 2002, as he was trying to put together a coalition against Saddam. In fact with new ground realties like expansion of settlements, the construction of the fence, gobbling up large chunks of Palestinian territory, the obstacles to a just solution based on two-state concept only increase in their formidableness. The people also see the unending cycle of massive Israeli military action killing thousands of Palestinians in response to minor provocation by the people under occupation.

Again, the people find that their countries are ineffective in alleviating the misery of the Palestinians and giving them justice. On the other hand they also notice that it is organizations like Hamas and Hizbollah, variously characterized as extremists and terrorists, who stand up to Israeli military superiority, and offer credible resistance. Even those who do not agree with their outlook are impressed by their performance.

Impact of 9/11

Ever since 9-11, there has been much superficial analysis of the causes of extremism and terrorism. It is mainly attributed to religion, scriptures and theology to the exclusion of broader and more fundamental sources of economic injustices. Obviously nobody wants to open the Pandora's Box, of the true causes of terrorism but superficial analysis will only lead to ineffectual remedies. Following 9/11 declarations and discussions about the need for democratic consultative governance, as antidote to terrorism have increased dramatically. Here are two samples of Bush's rhetoric on the subject at its most intense:

For as long as whole regions of the world simmer in resentment and tyranny-prone to ideologies that feed hatred and excuse murder-violence will gather and multiply in destructive power, and across the most defended borders, and raise a mortal threat. There is only one force of history that can break the reign of hatred and resentment, and expose the pretensions of tyrants, and reward the hopes of the decent and tolerant, and that is the force of human freedom...So it is the policy of the United States to seek and support the growth of democratic movements and institutions in every nation and culture with the ultimate goal of ending tyranny in our world. [3]

To promote peace and stability in the broader Middle East the United States will work with our friends in the region to fight the common threat of terror, while we encourage a higher standard of freedom. Hopefully reform is already taking hold in an arc from Morocco to Jordon to Bahrain. The government of Saudi Arabia can demonstrate its leadership in the region by expanding the role of its people in determining their future.

And the great and proud nation of Egypt, which showed the way towards peace in the Middle East, can now show the way towards, democracy in the Middle East. [4]

Less florid in rhetoric but wide ranging in promises of change were statements on the Arab side. Here are two samples:

Lest anyone misconstrue, let me affirm here, with as strong a conviction as I can make, that the leadership in Saudi Arabia remain steadfast in their effort to push their programme for reform. For us reform is an absolute requisite for the advancement of the country and its people regardless where the opposition is coming from or where the external pressure is being applied. [5]

We assert our firm determination...[To] endeavour based on the Declaration on the process and modernization in the Arab World, to pursue reform and modernization in our countries, and to keep pace with the rapid world changes by consolidating the democratic practice, by enlarging participation in political and public life, by fostering the role of all components of the civil society, including NGOs, in conceiving of the guidelines of the society of tomorrow, by widening women's participation in the political, economic, social, cultural and fields and reinforcing their rights and status in society, and by pursuing the promotion of the family and the protection of Arab youth." [6]

It does not require genius for insight to see that the Tunis Declaration, while comprehensive in scope is short on directness and specificity. The phrases used are circumlocutory e.g. 'to pursue reforms', 'to keep pace with', 'consolidating the democratic practice', 'enlarging participation', 'fostering the role', 'widening women's participation', and so on. Even so one should welcome such promises and try to build on them. As for Bush's rhetoric Anthony H. Cordesman's remark in *Los Angeles Times* sums up the Arab masses' perception: 'The Bush Administration must accept that it is too unpopular to issue a US-led greater Middle East initiative. American call for democracy are viewed as hypocritical and tailored to creating regimes friendly to the US and Israel. Such an initiative will do more to undermine local reformers and label them as American tools to push reform forward.' [7]

A detailed critique of what has been done in pursuit of these and other similar declarations on both sides is beyond the scope of this article, which focuses on pressures for change rather than an evaluation of results achieved in the direction of Democracy and Civil Society in West Asia. One line would be 'not enough'. Few solid steps have been taken on the road to democracy, let alone introduction of a functioning democracy anywhere. Nobody expects democracy overnight, but meaningful steps can be taken without fear of instability or worse. Anything less is a sign of lack of faith in people, their intelligence, integrity and commonsense. At the same time it is too important a matter for cynical indifference. Those who are genuinely committed to democracy and civil society can use these declarations to pursue positive programmes for evolution towards consultative democratic governance. Mutual lack of confidence will only delay progress towards what is inevitable.

There is one issue, however that deserves to be dealt with in some detail, both because of its importance and because there is lack of honesty in dealing with it. This is the issue of whether democratic elections will bring Islamists and fundamentalists to power and if so what will be the consequences? The examples of Iran, Algeria and Gaza are given in this context. The issue deserves objective analysis and an honest answer. The first thing to keep in mind are the circumstances in these societies which resulted in the public support for fundamentalists, Islamists or extremists. [These are pejorative terms, and I do not agree with their implication, but quibbling over them will cloud the more important issues.]In Iran the fundamentalist followers of Ayatollah Khomeini, had stood up to Shah's tyranny, more than any other group, with sacrifice of lives and blood. In Algeria, again, it was Islamists who challenged the authoritarianism and corruption of the

Army and the FLN combine. Finally in Gaza, Hamas won, because in the eyes of the public, they had stood up to Israeli occupation, repression and violations of human rights, while the Palestinian National Authority was seen as corrupt and lacking in courage on behalf of Palestinian rights.

In all the three cases mentioned above the fundamentalists were seen as more forcefully challenging authoritarianism and injustice than others. In normal circumstances it is unlikely that they would have been elected. Wherever circumstances are normal fundamentalists do not motivate the public. There are few examples of fundamentalists of any hue getting traction in an honest functioning democracy where there is no national crisis. Even in Pakistan which falls short of a fully functional democracy benchmark, Islamic parties mostly got five to six per cent of the votes cast. Their political role often got amplified because of the dynamics of the political calculus of those wielding power in that country.

Aborting the public mandate of the Islamists in Algeria, and non-recognition of the electoral victory of Hamas in Gaza, has definitely harmed the cause of democracy in the entire region. In both places people voted those, who they felt, given the circumstances and available alternatives, were better choices, and not because of Islamic ideology per se. People wanted honest governance and they voted for Islamists hoping that clean Islamists might do a better than corrupt secularists.

The argument that allowing Islamists in Algeria, who do not believe in democracy, to assume power, would have led to the end of democracy and freedom in that country, as Islamists would have abolished, is stunning in its brazenness. It assumes guilt and gives no chance to prove innocence, and amounts to rescinding people's clear verdict on the basis of subjective assessment of intent. Such ill conceived if not male fide acts, drive people into the arms of extremists and damage the cause of democracy and make suspect the true intentions behind declarations about spreading democracy.

In Iran fundamentalists assumed effective power, after

outmaneuvering and eliminating their opponents, but Iran has had regular elections these past thirty years .It contradicts the argument that letting Islamists come to power through elections would mean 'one man one vote" a "one time" exercise. Iran may not have a perfect democracy, but its electoral process is far more credible than any other in that region. The Iranian leadership can do many things, but it will not abolish elections. The Iranian people will not accept it. Nor would have the people of Algeria, given the chance and necessary support. There better ways of dealing with recalcitrant fundamentalists who want to abolish democracy and elections than denying them people's legitimate mandate. Democracy can only be spread, if you believe in the people, their integrity and judgment and have faith in the strength of their aspirations for self-governance. Western apprehensions about fundamentalists taking over governments through elections and then jettisoning democracy and elections have into the hands of those Arab regimes, who do not want to take meaningful steps towards democracy and civil society. This, in no small measure is hindering the progress of democracy in the region.

There are other reasons also for the changing perceptions of the people of these countries about the nature of their problems and their solutions. In all west Asian societies, media and internet have significantly enhanced peoples' awareness of what is happening around them. This naturally leads to comparative thinking about the strength and weaknesses of various societies including their own. The role of Al Jazeera which reaches vast sections of the Arab population is a powerful influence on the youth in west Asia. Besides news and visuals about the Israeli military action against Palestinians not available elsewhere, it also brings into focus the state of affairs in the Arab societies.

In the case of Gulf countries, some additional points need to be emphasized. The oil prosperity has resulted in a large number of foreign educated youth, who travel extensively abroad and understand various issues well. They also know the political and social requirements of the globalizing world. In addition to foreign education and travel, the presence in the GCC countries of large Arab and non-Arab expatriates constituting probably twenty-five per cent to thirty per cent of their population, means constant interaction with the outside world. In percentage terms therefore there is more travel in and out of this area than anywhere else in the world and interaction is always thought provoking.

Again in the case of the Gulf countries, large oil price swings result in huge GDP fluctuations of twenty per cent or more, leading to large scale budgetary deficits and disruption of development plans. Such dislocations have a churning effect forcing many to think of how to achieve more diversified and stable economies and whether that also calls for review of existing systems and institutions, greater transparency and more openness in addressing issues. Consequently there is a lack of equilibrium between the aspirations of the people and the existing systems and mores in these countries. Unless the systems and mores evolve, to meet the expectations of the people, the growing friction between the two can become unmanageable.

Conclusion

The leadership in these countries is aware of the complicated nature of the problems but has not acted effectively enough so far, for a number of reasons. First is the opposition from those who are beneficiaries of the prevailing circumstances and are therefore opposed to change. Second, some at the leadership level believe that the present status quo can be maintained and therefore there is no need to hasten the pace of change. Apart from resistance to change, there is also absence of consensus on the direction that change should take. The liberals, drawing their inspiration from the west, would like modernization involving democratic governance, individual rights, individual freedom, change in the status of women etc. For many of them this is also compatible with essentials of Islamic thought. They are also agreeable to the change being measured.

The conservatives who have their own gradational levels want everything to be based on early Islamic system and values. However they are short on details about how these could be applied to a different and more complex world today. The extremists are uncompromising. They want complete change and want it immediately. But again like the conservatives they do not provide details of what they want in case of the existing system. They also call for reversion to original Islam, without detailed elaboration and specific ideas of how they will deal with the interlocked problems of modern diverse societies and globalizing economies.

The extremely difficult path to system change is complicated by the fact that while US calls for change in west Asia it wants the new dispensation to be in consonance with its policies and interests in the region. People's right to elect their leadership ends where US interests begin. Experience points in the direction of active civil society and democracy as essential for all round and sustained progress of societies—economic, social, political, intellectual and moral. While democracy and civil society have a symbiotic relationship, the former is the first gear that sets the process in motion. Without the foundations of democracy and individual freedom, civil society cannot attain full-bloodied robustness.

There is a lot of talk of civil society in West Asia and the Gulf countries. Change is in the air but not on the ground. Civil Society institutions and organizations have been created but often they are structures without inner vigor and vitality. The form is there but the substance is inadequate and excessive government control and guidance stunts their growth. Without real democratic governance creating a symbiotic partnership between the people and the leadership and an active Civil Society, long term sustainable solutions to the problems, whether internal or external, faced by the countries in West

Asia, as indeed elsewhere, cannot be effectively worked out.

Notes

1. "What is civil society?" Definition by the Centre for Civil Society, London School of Economics, available at http://www.lse.ac.uk/collections/CCS/what_is_civil_society.htm (1 March 2004).
2. Talmiz Ahmed, *Reform in the Arab World* (New Delhi: India Research Press, 2005), pp. 99-100.
3. "President Bush's Inaugural Address, January20, 2005", ibid., 2005, p. III.
4. Ibid., p. III-IV.
5. "Tunis Declaration", Arab Summit, May 22-23, 2004, ibid., pp. III.
6. Ibid., pp. 118-9.
7. *L.A. Times*, May 26, 2004, quoted in ibid., p. IV.

References

Akhtarul Wasey and Farhat Ehsas, *Education, Literature and Islam - Writings by Mohammed Mujeeb* (New Delhi: Shipra Publications, 2008).

Anthony H. Cordesman, *Saudi Arabia enters the 21st Century - Political, Foreign Policy, Economic and Energy Dimensions* (Santa Barbara, CA: Greenwood Publishers, 2003).

David Menashri, *Post Revolutionary Politics in Iran - Religion, Society and Power* (London: Frank Cass, 2001).

Europa Yearbook on Middle East (2008).

Fatima Mernissi, *Beyond the Veil* (Bloomington, Indiana: Indiana University Press, 1987).

Fatima Mernissi, *Islam and Democracy* (Cambridge, MA: Basic Books, 2002).

Hamid Ansari, *Travelling Through Conflict: Essays on the Politics of West Asia* (New Delhi: Dorling Kindersley, 2008).

Ian Richard Netton (ed.), *Islamic Philosophy and Theology - Critical Concepts in Islamic Thought*, Vol. I (London and New York: Routledge, Tailor and Francis Group, 2007).

Madawi Al Rashid (ed.), *Kingdom without Borders: Saudi Arabia's Political, Religious and Media Frontiers* (New Delhi: Foundation Books, 2008).

Mehran Kamrava (ed.), *The New Voices of Islam* (London: I.B. Tauris, 2006).

N.S. Sisodia and Ashok K. Behuria (eds.), *West Asia in Turmoil: Implications for Global Security* (New Delhi: Academic Foundation, 2007).

Olivier Roy, *Secularism confronts Islam* (New York: Columbia University Press, 2007).

R. M .Abhyankar (ed.), *West Asia and the Region: Defining India's Role* (New Delhi: Academic Foundation, 2008).

Sima Baidya, *Dissent in the Land of Arab* (New Delhi: Academic Excellence, 2007).

Talmiz Ahmed, *Reform in the Arab World, External Influences and Regional Debates* (New Delhi: India Research Press, 2005).

Will Durant, *The Age of Faith - A History of Medieval Civilization - Christan, Islamic and Judaic - from Constantine to Dante* (New York: Simon and Schuster, 1950).

World Fact Book.

Zoya Hasan (ed.), *Democracy in Muslim Societies - the Asian Experience* (New Delhi: Sage Publications, 2007).

Index